HET DAGHET OVERAL

Prelude to Independence
SKEEN'S 115 DAYS

BY
BRIGADIER A. SKEEN O.B.E., M.P., p.s.c.,
Rhodesian High Commissioner in London
July–November 1965
With a foreword by
THE HON. IAN SMITH M.P.
Prime Minister of Rhodesia

NASIONALE BOEKHANDEL
1966

Nasionale Boekhandel Bpk Cape Town
Regional Offices
Bloemfontein Port Elizabeth
Johannesburg

National Commercial Printers
Elsies River

Contents

Foreword

Much has already been said and written about the reasons for the Declaration of Rhodesian Independence on the 11th November, 1965, and today arguments and feelings 'for' and 'against' are running high. However, I am sure that before long the ground will be cut away completely from those who make the stand that our action was either wrong or premature.

I am confident that what we did that November morning was the only way in which a Christian civilisation could be preserved and given the climate to flourish on a continent rapidly regressing to its nineteenth century title of "Darkest Africa".

History will record the justice of my claim.

Meantime my old friend, Andrew Skeen, has written his version of the events immediately preceding and following the Declaration and I think that he has successfully captured, albeit on a very wide canvas, something of the drama and the agony of those days.

I commend this book to all those who wish to know more about this significant period in Rhodesian history.

I. DOUGLAS SMITH

Salisbury
23rd February, 1966

Introduction

On 11th November 1965, at 11 a.m. London time, the Rhodesian Government declared its independence of the British Parliament in Westminster, whilst retaining its loyalty to the person of the Monarch and the Queen of Rhodesia.

At the time of writing the full implications of this small nation's taking this action have not become fully apparent, but nevertheless it is a turning point in history.

Twice in the history of the world pressures from the East sought to overwhelm Western culture and civilisation, and on both occasions came within an inch of success. In both cases this Eastern tide was halted and ultimately turned back by a few determined and resolute people.

The first time was when the Greek states halted the Persian hordes at Thermopylae, and finally defeated them at Marathon and Salamis. The second time was when the Turks were defeated in the sea battle of Lepanto in 1571, and finally routed at Vienna in 1683.

These struggles were fought with conventional armies and navies, and the weapons and fighting techniques of the age were employed.

In the twentieth century the forces of the East, which now again seek to overwhelm the Western world, are fighting with subtler weapons, such as the ideology of Communism, the various methods of transmitting information and by exploiting world organisations originally dedicated to the cause of peace. All this is now known as the technique of the cold war. The ultimate weapon as of old, but now kept in reserve, is war, and this will only be used when the will of the West is broken, its strategic positions compromised or lost, and its powers of resistance and co-ordination broken.

This process had gone a long way by the summer of 1965 when it received its first serious check in Rhodesia. This small progressive country is situated in a key part of Africa and forms a bastion to the Republic of South Africa.

South Africa's wealth, geographical position on the sea lanes of the world and isolation from the Eurasian land mass make it the link between the two main centres of Western civilisation in the Atlantic and Pacific.

With South Africa secure to the West, for the third time in history an Eastern invasion of the West can be halted and turned back.

It was my privilege to represent Rhodesia in London as High Commissioner during the crucial period when the fate of Rhodesia hung in the balance. This book tells of the events which led up to the moment when Rhodesia assumed the role of champion of Western civilisation. It is for history to judge what will be the long-term results of this momentous decision.

1. Review of the Past

As the title and sub-title of this book indicate, this narrative only gives the history of events immediately prior to Rhodesia's assumption of independence as seen through the eyes of the Rhodesian High Commissioner in London. It covers the short period from July to December 1965, of which I, as that High Commissioner, spent exactly 115 days in England.

In order to appreciate fully what led up to the climax on 11th November 1965, it is necessary to sketch briefly the background of the events as seen through my eyes. This book is not an autobiography, but it is necessary to relate the story through the experiences of individuals during this period.

Rhodesia towards the end of the 19th century was a virtual wilderness. It was inhabited by certain Bantu tribes who had entered the country from the north about 800 years previously. Before that time it had been the home of the Bushmen, long since driven out by these successive waves of intruders, whose memory is preserved solely in the numerous rock paintings throughout the country.

It is estimated that on the arrival of the European only 400,000 Bantu lived in what is now called Rhodesia, south of the Zambezi. Of these the Matabele, the dominant tribe, had entered the country from the south under half a century earlier.

By the end of 1965 their numbers had swelled to about 3,500,000 of whom 2,600,000 were under the age of 21. This was in itself a tribute to the Europeans who had imposed the rule of law and by creating health and welfare services had provided the conditions for this spectacular increase in the Bantu population. Warfare, disease and want had kept the country in a depopulated state until the advent of the European.

These Europeans, unlike those in other African and Asian lands under British rule, had made this country their only home and today many of them are third and fourth generation Rhodesians, and newcomers as they arrived had taken root in a similar fashion. Like Canadians, Americans, Australians and New Zealanders, the Rhodesians had come to regard their country as their own, and when they talked of home, it was of Rhodesia they spoke, not of Britain, as did some colonial expatriates who worked and traded in other African countries.

The Europeans and the Bantu were at first both alien to the high plateau of Central Africa. Both races were in fact "settlers" in this country, and both had an equal right to its occupation – as much legal right of occupation as the successive waves of Celtic and Saxon invaders had to the British Isles, or the European migrants to the New World. The significant difference was that in the case of Rhodesia the stronger and later arrivals had not expelled or exterminated those who had come before.

To achieve harmonious coexistence these two entirely different races had to make adjustments which required time and freedom from outside interference. This was granted, and lasted till the years immediately following World War II.

At this date the country was a self-governing colony, but with ultimate control over its affairs vested in the British Government. It had its own Parliament, elected on a franchise open to all races but limited by educational and property qualifications. These qualifications were not stringent, and any citizen of a European country could easily have qualified.

Over half the country had been set aside for the Bantu population under the Land Apportionment Act, and into this area Europeans were not allowed, except under permit and supervision. On the other hand the Bantu were free to move into and work in the other areas not set aside for their sole occupation. Large areas of this section were Crown Lands, and these were from time to time opened up for purchase by all races.

The machinery and legislation thus existed for a harmonious development of the country, one that was fair to all races and safeguarded the less sophisticated from exploitation.

Unlike England of the 18th century, the peasant population could not be driven from their homes by enclosures, or forced into urban industrial employment by the loss of their ancestral lands. Like England of that period, a limited but expanding franchise existed. This had taken England several hundred years to evolve. In Rhodesia it was proceeding at a much faster rate, without agitation or political upheavals.

2

In 1946 and the years immediately following Rhodesia experienced a big influx of people, mainly from Britain. Most of these were anxious to make new lives away from the ministrations of the new Welfare State that was arising in their home country.

I had married in early 1939, and Honor and I had decided, even then, that we would emigrate to Rhodesia as soon as it was possible for me to retire from the British Army. We anticipated doing this in about ten years' time. However, the war intervened, our married life was interrupted by the exigencies of the service and we were not able to be together for any length of time till it was over. During 1946 I was at the War Office, and the discomforts and frustrations of life in England determined us to put our plans into effect much earlier than we had anticipated.

I was forty years old in 1947, and had completed twenty-one years' service as a regular soldier. I was thus entitled to a pension of sorts. I sent in my papers and we prepared to leave for Rhodesia. Passages were almost impossible to get, so we bought an army lorry and motored overland and through Africa.

With us we took our small son, then aged four, and our immediate family, fired by our example, followed by sea later in the year. This consisted of my wife's sister and her husband, a brother officer in my regiment, and my mother-in-law who wished to live near her two daughters. My own mother, then in her 70's, followed soon after accompanied by her widowed niece, my cousin, and her son aged nine. The whole family, with children, numbered in all ten souls, whose ages ranged from seventy-one to two.

By early 1948 we had bought property and built houses, largely with our own hands, on the Vumba near Umtali.

This process was not unique. Whole families were arriving and settling throughout the length and breadth of Rhodesia. They had cut all ties with Britain and were becoming Rhodesians. The valley in which we had bought land, virtually empty in 1947, was by 1950 filled with a dozen family units similar to our own.

Meanwhile a new phenomenon was manifesting itself, known as the cold war. The effects were soon felt in Africa, and the old colonial powers aided and abetted by America sought to enlist the continent on their side. This was to be done by granting early independence to a host of small and non-viable colonial territories, totally incapable of governing themselves by any modern civilised standard. These independent states should have been motivated by feelings of gratitude to their masters to side with the West in its struggle against Communism. The fact, which should have been obvious to all, was that they would play one side off against the other, and ultimately through corrupt and inefficient management of their affairs fall a prey to Communist infiltration. Central Africa was reduced to such a state of affairs by becoming a pawn in the cold war.

The first move in this game was to federate the three central African territories of Southern and Northern Rhodesia and Nyasaland, through an undefined and vague political principle known as partnership. This would undoubtedly lead to immature and early African rule and the speedy elimination of the minority European population, but it would also absolve Britain of the odium of being a colonial power.

Federation was therefore a real threat to Rhodesia, and all that had been achieved in its economic and political development over the past seventy years. Few people in Rhodesia realised what Federation implied for the future of the country. The well-publicised economic benefits blinded them to the political trap that was concealed within its new constitution.

Honor and I, along with about one-third of the electorate, fought against the idea of a Federation and voted in the referendum against it. With my knowledge of the British Government's intentions, gained through my services in Whitehall and elsewhere, I was deeply suspicious of the good faith of the British Government towards the Europeans in Africa. This suspicion proved to be well founded. The story of the Federation and its break-up is well known, and was revealed in Sir Roy Welensky's book.

It needed Mr. Harold Macmillan's famous wind of change speech and events in Kenya, Tanganyika and Ghana to open people's eyes to what was in store. The fiasco in the Belgian Congo and the resultant exodus of Europeans through Rhodesia finally convinced them that unless they called a halt to the precipitate rush to early African rule their days in Southern Rhodesia were numbered.

With the advent of Federation there had been a regrouping of political parties in Rhodesia.

Sir Godfrey Huggins's United Party, which had ruled Rhodesia for so long, had advocated acceptance of the Federation at the referendum of 1953. All those who supported this idea now grouped them-

4

selves under his leadership and that of his successor, Sir Roy Welensky, in a party known as the United Federal Party. Its Southern Rhodesian territorial counterpart became the United Rhodesia Party which, under Mr. Garfield Todd's leadership, incorporated all the leftist elements in the country and became less conservative than its senior counterpart under Sir Roy Welensky.

In opposition, at first, was the Confederate Party, to which I belonged. This right wing party suffered eclipse at the first elections after Federation was accepted by the electorate. In its place rose the Dominion Party which operated under the same name in the Federal sphere. This party had more success and obtained a few seats in the Federal and Territorial Houses of Assembly.

The United Rhodesian Party under Mr. Todd began to move too far to the left for the supporters of Sir Roy Welensky, and it soon repudiated his leadership in favour of Sir Edgar Whitehead, a former Minister in Sir Godfrey Huggins's old territorial United Party, and changed its name to the United Federal Party, becoming the territorial division of that party with the same principles and policies.

At the next territorial election in 1958 Mr. Todd's supporters were completely eliminated and the Dominion Party gained sufficient support to become a serious threat to Sir Edgar Whitehead's territorial United Federal Party. In an effort to save the Federation this party under Sir Edgar Whitehead moved further to the left and produced the 1961 Constitution. This was put to the electorate by referendum and was accepted by an overwhelming vote, but this was due to a misunderstanding that it would grant Southern Rhodesia its complete independence from Britain should the Federation break up.

When it became apparent to the voters that they had been misled on this point, there was a revulsion against the United Federal Party, and in the December 1962 elections the Rhodesian Front won the election. The Rhodesian Front had been created out of the Dominion Party. It also included many bodies that had been formed to save Rhodesia from those policies that might lead to the fate that had befallen Kenya and Northern Rhodesia. Many old supporters of Sir Godfrey Huggins and Sir Edgar Whitehead had also seen where their party was leading them, and had joined the Rhodesian Front.

As a member of the defunct Confederate Party and its successor the Dominion Party I was also a member of the Rhodesian Front. I had become the chairman of the Manicaland division of the party and was also chairman of the constituency in which I lived, and Honor and I threw ourselves into the task of organising a strong party in our area.

Events in Northern Rhodesia and Nyasaland, where the UFP had compromised itself out of existence, together with the repudiation of the Federation by these two countries, brought more and more supporters to the Rhodesian Front. Soon from the 40 odd members of the Dominion Party in Manicaland the number of Front members increased to 1,600.

The report of the Monckton Commission[1] and the acquiescence of the British Government in the dissolution of the Federation finally opened the eyes of Rhodesians to the bad faith of the British Government. They now saw for the first time that the British Government intended to appease African Nationalism at all costs, firstly to hold together their multi-racial commonwealth, and secondly to keep in the good graces of the United Nations and America. They were to be a pawn in the cold war, and whatever concessions they might make to African advancement and ultimate majority rule, it would never be enough. Their rule of advancement by merit, regardless of race and colour, would operate far too slowly for British intentions, and so the Federation was formally dissolved on 31st December 1963, and Rhodesia was on her own.

Nyasaland, now called Malawi, and Northern Rhodesia, now termed Zambia, were promised their independence in 1964, each after only a year's trial of self-government.

Southern Rhodesia, now Rhodesia, self-governing for 40 years and by far the most viable and developed country, was to be denied hers, albeit that its electorate had been given to understand that the 1961 Constitution was designed for its independence.

Negotiations for Rhodesia's independence started as soon as the Federation had been dissolved. These made little headway owing to the procrastinations of the British Government.

During one of his visits to London in the latter part of 1964, the Rhodesian Prime Minister, Mr. Ian Smith, was given to understand that if the people of Rhodesia wanted independence and demonstrated this, it would be granted. A referendum of all voters was held

1. The Monckton Commission was set up by the British Government to report on the future of the Federation. It reported in October 1960.

and 90 percent voted in favour. To ascertain the wishes of those Africans without a vote, their leaders were consulted at an indaba of over 600 chiefs and headmen. They were unanimous in demanding independence on the 1961 Constitution.

A general election in England occurred at this moment, which brought the Labour Party under Mr. Wilson to power, but the results of the referendum and indaba were completely ignored by the incoming Government.

It was becoming obvious that the British Government was determined not to grant Rhodesia independence unless majority rule could be guaranteed in the very near future, and this would be hedged about with restrictions that would make independence a mockery whilst the Europeans were still in control.

At this time the opposition party under Sir Edgar Whitehead, once known as the UFP, but now known as the Rhodesia National Party, held 27 out of the 65 seats in the Assembly. They had lost two seats in October 1964 through by-elections, reducing their original strength of 29. At one of these by-elections Sir Roy Welensky had stood at Arundel and had been heavily defeated by the Rhodesian Front candidate. This was a sign of how completely the electorate was disenchanted with the policy of appeasement and co-operation with British designs that had been the aim of the old United Federal Party.

In April 1965 it was decided to hold a general election to demonstrate the solidarity of the Rhodesian people behind the Rhodesian Front's stand for independence. At this election the Front won all 50 seats on the A roll[2] and obtained well over 80 per cent of the votes.

With a united and determined people behind him, Mr. Ian Smith could now negotiate and press for our long-delayed independence from a position of great strength. He had the vast majority of the European and African people behind him, and this had been demonstrated for all the world to see.

Since 1952 I had struggled with Honor's help for such a situation to arise, always hoping that the people of Rhodesia would come to

2. Of the Legislative Assembly of 65 members, 50 are elected to represent constituencies by the more highly qualified voters on the "A" Roll, whilst 15, representing electoral districts, are elected by the voters with lower qualifications on the "B" Roll. For further particulars see page 199.

7

recognise that the long-term policies of the British politicians were designed towards the extinction of their influence in Rhodesia, and their ultimate expulsion. Otherwise we had taken no prominent part in public affairs, though it is true we had some influence in the Rhodesian Front in our own part of the country and were working hard in gathering support for the party.

I was a member of several statutory boards and local government committees, and in such small ways we were doing what we could to further the interests of our country.

But in May 1965, unknown to us and waiting round the corner, was a far greater opportunity for us to serve our country.

2. They send a Soldier

On Monday, 31st May, there was an Executive meeting of the Rhodesian Front in Salisbury, which sat at 9.30 a.m. and continued till lunchtime.

I had intended to stay overnight at my son's flat because the afternoon would be occupied by an industrial dispute at which I had been appointed a mediator.

I got up very early that morning and motored up to Salisbury, arriving at the conference room at party headquarters with a few minutes to spare. I was chatting to a group of friends at the door when the Minister of External Affairs, Cliff Dupont, drew me aside and asked if I was free to have lunch with him at the Salisbury Club.

During the tea interval two other Ministers spoke to me, and from their questions I began to wonder what was in the air. It had been a matter of speculation in the Press as to whom the post of High Commissioner in London, shortly to become vacant on the return of Evan Campbell to Rhodesia, would be offered. I began to wonder if the choice had been made and I was being approached to accept it.

Now one of the reasons why I had retired from the Army was to escape from Whitehall, and neither my wife nor I was particularly anxious to leave our home and the wonderful climate of our Vumba farm for the fogs of London. During the discussions of the Executive that followed, I must confess, my attention wandered, for I knew that I had to make an important decision if Cliff Dupont should ask me to be Rhodesia's next High Commissioner.

In view of the fact that the next six months would be crucial for my country, and my knowledge that the Rhodesian Front was more than anxious that the High Commissioner in London should be a man who was in tune with its thinking, I realised that whatever the personal inconvenience, it would be my duty to accept the post if offered, should the other names submitted not fit this bill.

There were three other factors which would influence my decision. The first was that I had no connections in business circles or the City of London which might prejudice my judgment when and if I

9

took up the appointment. Secondly, I had many friends and acquaintances in Britain who, with the passage of time, had risen to influential positions in the Services and in politics. Moreover, I was no stranger to London and Whitehall.

As well as anyone in Rhodesia, and better than most, I knew the psychology of the British public, and the pressures, prejudices and long-term aims which influenced the thinking of the British politician. After all, I had been born, brought up and educated, and had worked within the Establishment before I became a Rhodesian. I would go to London with few illusions, unbrainwashable, and immune to the many subtle pressures that Britain can exert to her advantage on the visiting diplomat and statesman.

Lastly, should the appointment be of as short duration as I thought likely, and as it proved to be, there would be no desire on my part to prolong it by advising my Government, against my country's interest, with councils of delay in negotiation. The Executive meeting ended and Cliff drove me to the club, and a wink and a smile from my friend Jack Musset, Minister for Local Government, confirmed my suspicions. We had a preliminary drink at the club bar, where mine was a ginger ale, for alcohol had given me up a couple of years previously when my friend Lt.-Col. John Wolf's home-brewed beer had nauseated me with it for ever. In passing, this indeed was an invaluable asset to a diplomat.

After the fish course had been eaten and removed, Cliff Dupont asked me the hundred-dollar question. Would I accept the appointment as High Commissioner in London? He said he would give me a couple of days to consider and consult my wife. I asked if he had any other suitable candidates in mind, in which case I would withdraw. He mentioned a few names that had emanated from certain quarters and I was somewhat shocked at these and made my decision quickly. I replied, "In that case I will take the job and bear the wrath of Honor if she disagrees." An excellent lunch over, we parted with an arrangement that I should see the Prime Minister at his house that evening.

I then attended the industrial council meeting over which I was presiding and was happy to get a great measure of agreement between the opposing parties. This seemed a good augury for the diplomatic life ahead of me.

That evening I visited Ian Smith at his house, where I confirmed my acceptance of the appointment and went back to my son's flat.

My name of course had to be submitted to the British Government for approval, and until it was made public the matter was secret. However, my immediate family had to know in confidence and having told my son, all that remained was to inform my wife when I returned home next day.

She was quite flabbergasted when I told her, but after calling for a stiff drink, she took it very well and womanlike became reconciled to being uprooted from her home when she realised that she would have to buy a large and suitable wardrobe for her new life. Apart from the numerous domestic details that had to be settled in a short time, this congenial task occupied much of her time ahead.

My own Rhodesian wardrobe was somewhat sketchy, but I overcame this by the simple expedient of enumerating the number and types of suits and accessories which seem to be necessary for a diplomat, not forgetting that most un-Rhodesian article of headware – a bowler hat – and then sending the list to my old London tailor, asking him to have them made and ready for me on my arrival in London. Fortunately my measurements had not altered an inch in the past eighteen years, and the only problem was the bill, which was a shock.

My appointment was announced about ten days later, and caused considerable astonishment in some circles, which had regarded the High Commissionership as a peculiar prerogative of theirs, but times had changed since the days of the Huggins Bureau. The Press was remarkably reticent, though it uttered dark hints of political appointments, and these were taken up by the opposition party in Parliament who referred to me with sinister undertones as "a man of war".

I then began a five-week period of intensive briefing and tours round the country, in a programme arranged by the efficient Protocol section of External Affairs. This started at 8 a.m. each day and finished sometimes at midnight. It was so closely dovetailed that on one occasion I discovered that the time allotted to move from one visit to another could only be covered by a pigeon and window entrance in ninth floor offices.

The moment that my appointment was announced, the Government Information Department got through to me with a warning not to talk to the Press until I had been suitably briefed and groomed for this ordeal. I was touched by this anxious solicitude, but they need not have worried. Through long and bitter experience I had become very wary of the Press who had never liked my uncompromising opposition to the political view they cherished and propagated on all and every occasion.

My wife and I were photographed in studio and home by that most able and distinguished photographer, Basil Shackleton, and were suitably flattered by the results, though the Press seemed reluctant to use these works of art and pestered us with requests for flash bulb snaps in unsuitable lights and backgrounds. Most of these we were fortunately able to evade by presentation of the official photographs, few of which they ever used.

I then had the ordeal of appearing in a mock press conference with full radio and T.V. coverage, and about fifty journalists were invited to do their worst upon me as a helpless victim. The result was then analysed and criticised ruthlessly, but I was soothed by the assurance that never in real life would I have to cope with anything so difficult. Actually it was quite fun, but I was not so pleased when I saw the end result of myself on the screen, a sight which destroyed quite a few fond illusions that I harboured about my appearance.

Then I was loosed upon the Press without supervision and passed, I hope, without discredit the Monday night RTV Profile programme. This was quite painless and as the studio arc lamps provided a warm glow in sharp contrast to the bitter July night outside, I was sorry when it was over. Scheduled for twenty minutes it stretched for over forty-five, and I was asked far more awkward questions in my homeland than ever fell to my lot in London. There were several other press interviews with which I dealt with discretion and care, carefully sidestepping questions about my, to press pens, discreditable political past.

On one occasion when John Gaunt, the designate diplomat to the Republic of South Africa, and I were guests at a municipal function, two journalists who had been hot on our heels for some days managed to gate-crash the party and reported our remarks in reply to a toast. There was nothing startling about these, but a sharp reprimand reached us from Salisbury which caused me some surprise, though possibly not to John.

The offending remark attributed to me was that I hoped to gain public sympathy for our case in Britain by representing ourselves as underdogs which are always in favour with the British public. Then through this sympathy I would exert pressure on the politicians to meet us. It was precisely this approach, among others, that I adopted in London, and events have proved that it was the right one and is bearing fruit.

I was subjected to a final press and T.V. conference on the morning of our departure, but it was a tame affair with only a few desultory questions. The assembled journalists, few in number, were obviously preoccupied and in a hurry to get away. The reason for this was the imminent arrival at Salisbury airport of Mr. Cledwyn Hughes, the Minister of State for Commonwealth Relations, and Mr. Bottomley's No. 2. He was arriving from Britain to continue discussions with our Government and was a far tastier dish than a departing High Commissioner who was becoming an adept at passing platitudes.

I noted this fact for further reference and made use of it in the months ahead. Crisis and headline news follow one another with unfailing regularity in London, and when news unfavourable to Rhodesia reached London I did my utmost to time its release to match these occasions so that it drew only a small paragraph on the back pages.

We had decided that there was not enough time to close our house and store our furniture. So we left it open, keeping on our indoor and outdoor staff. My son undertook to come down from his job in the High Court in Salisbury and keep an eye on the place, and this he was able to do most Sundays.

The decision proved to be a wise one, because when we returned we were able to walk in as though we had left it a few hours previously for a day's shopping in Umtali. Moreover, at the back of our minds we felt that it might not be long before we would need our house again, and in a hurry.

Honor and I had resigned from the various offices we held in the Rhodesian Front party on my appointment, the chief of which was the post of Divisional Chairman in Manicaland. During our last week-end at home, the members of the Division had arranged a farewell party for us. This was a most enjoyable function, but at the same time Honor and I were depressed at parting from so many of our good friends and fellow workers. I was called upon to make a parting speech, and in this I jokingly remarked that it was upon Manicaland that I had cut my diplomatic teeth, and that in comparison the diplomatic task ahead would be child's play for, tough though the British politicians might prove to be, under no circumstances could they be as tough as my colleagues in the party.

Though spoken in jest, this remark was no less than the truth.

So, after eighteen years of a peaceful undisturbed existence, my wife and I were back to the old life of a soldier – packing and moving at short notice, and not knowing what the next day might hold.

On the evening of Wednesday, 21st July 1965, Honor, Julia, our nine year old daughter, and I flew off to London by BOAC, VC10, after being seen off by our son and a large number of friends at Salisbury airport.

"Off", as the Rhodesian, and in particular the British Press described it, "to the toughest diplomatic post in London" and to fight as *The Times* described it, "Rhodesia's last battle for Independence".

How right they were.

3. Arrival in London

Modern jet air travel is one of the wonders of the age. Honor, who had never flown before, concealed the anxiety natural on such occasions with admirable aplomb, while to Julia the whole idea of air travel was a most exciting novelty, till sleep overtook her. Sleep and the chance to do so is one of the problems in these luxury vehicles of the air. Drinks, snacks and bon-bons were thrust upon us in never-ending succession, and then after the Nairobi halt in the middle of the night, a magnificent meal was placed in front of us. Eventually we were able to lie back and sleep, and in a remarkably short time we had reached Rome, where we were able to wash and prepare ourselves for the arrival in London a couple of hours later. In all, only a twelve hour journey from Rhodesia to England, but sufficient in the eyes of the left wing liberal, to transform one from a monstrous oppressor of our fellow humans to an average decent individual and vice versa. This was a fallacy which I was able to correct to some extent during my short time in London.

It was a fine day for England and considerably warmer than the July weather of Salisbury. I quickly discarded my waistcoat before descending from the aircraft and meeting Norman and Peggy Heathcote, my Deputy and his wife, who had held the fort since Evan Campbell's departure. The Assistant Chief of Protocol for Commonwealth Relations was also there to present his Government's greetings, and after a short press interview in which I hypocritically expressed my delight at being back in England after eighteen years, we drove off in RHO 1, the ancient Princess car of the High Commission, with the Rhodesian flag flying from the bonnet.

London appeared much the same as we drove from London airport to the Strand, and we saw no appreciable difference in 18 years though we were surprised to see that London appeared emptier than we remembered. This was accounted for by the fact that in 1946 it was filled with foreign troops in transit, and large parts had been heavily bombed and the inhabitants had crowded into the more fortunate areas.

15

Until we had succeeded in renting a flat or house, arrangements had been made to accommodate us in a hotel. I had chosen the Savoy for two reasons. Firstly it was close to Rhodesia House and secondly it was the place my wife and I had chosen for our brief honeymoon, just before war broke out, and had used during the short periods of leave I had when back from overseas service.

Before leaving Rhodesia we had had several engagements booked, and first of these was an invitation by an old friend to the Gentleman at Arms reception at St. James Palace on the evening of our arrival. We hurriedly unpacked and aired our diplomatic garments, and after lunch I walked over to Rhodesia House to meet some of the staff and inspect my office.

Of all the diplomatic missions in London Rhodesia House in the Strand has possibly the best but noisiest site. Accessible to would-be tourists and immigrants, close to the City and the contacts it affords, it has everything but space. Ever since it was occupied by the Rhodesian High Commission in the period between the wars, it has seen an expansion of staff and an increase in its work. With about 120 employees of whom about 40 were Rhodesians, it is in effect a minor Government in which are represented nearly all the Government Departments from Rhodesia. There were plans afoot to increase the representation of three of these in Rhodesia House – Immigration, Information and Commerce and Industry. This was leading to a crisis in accommodation, which was being met at the time of my arrival by the acquisition of the 5th floor of the Civil Service Stores next door, and the later possibility of taking over part of the 4th floor of that shop. In addition there was a very large unused basement, crammed with junk, which I had plans to put to good use for information and industrial and commercial exhibits. Apart from that, the whole building needed redecoration and from the security angle, reorganisation.

Consideration of these matters was to preoccupy my time to a certain extent, and planning went ahead. I later requested a Ministerial Mission to go into the reorganisation of Rhodesia House and this duly arrived under circumstances that gave rise to press speculation.

After this first short visit to Rhodesia House on the Thursday afternoon of my arrival, my wife and I had to make hurried arrangements for a baby sitter for Julia, a word which she indignantly repu-

16

diated in favour of keeper, one which satisfied her pride but seemed even more invidious to my mind. We duly departed in style from the Savoy courtyard in the beflagged and magnificent vehicle whose outward splendour failed to match its engine, and I remarked to my wife that it was indeed a change from the battered half tonner, loaded with baconers, in which we were accustomed to journey to Umtali.

We met many old friends in the diplomatic and official world at the reception and found them very pleased to see us, and sympathetic to Rhodesia's cause. On entering the reception room and joining the throng I was struck by the similarity in dress and bearing and particularly age of the guests, in comparison with scenes I had witnessed when accompanying my father to similar functions in my youth. At that time with the normal arrogance of youth I had thought the company inexpressibly ancient, but now I realised with a shock that I too was one of those whom I had viewed with awe and pity over thirty years before. This was a feeling I was to experience many times in the days ahead when I remet my contemporaries after eighteen years' absence from England, and glimpses of myself on T.V. and in press photographs did nothing to dispel it.

The following day and on Saturday I was free to meet and address my staff, some of whom had not been back in Rhodesia since Federal days. I put them in the picture as to feeling in Rhodesia over current events and reviewed the political changes that had taken place. Finances permitting, it is essential that members of the staff on a mission overseas should be able to return home at least once during their term of duty, for rebriefing as I described it, or as one of my staff put it in jest, for brain-washing. This latter task now fell to me, and I carried it out on all possible occasions.

My first task was to call on the Secretary of State, Mr. Bottomley, and present my letter of accreditation, and then to sign my name in Her Majesty's book at Buckingham Palace. Unlike other diplomats, in fact alone amongst the throngs of them in London, I did not have to present myself in person before her. This was due to the fact that my country was not fully independent and although the Mission was listed in the Diplomatic List, yet it was not included in the seniority appendix at the end of that book. Ambassadors and High Commissioners came high up in the General Table of Precedence, immediately after The Lord Privy Seal, but the Rhodesian High Commissioner came about thirty places lower, below the Vice-Chamberlain of the Household, and above eldest sons of Viscounts.

Thus in many subtle ways Rhodesia was shown to be a minor in the diplomatic world. Yet, surprisingly, I was accorded the high sounding title of an Excellency.

Meanwhile a flood of invitations to receptions, banquets and lunches came in, and here we seemed to have been granted full recognition. I might have been wrong and misjudged my hosts, but I wondered if curiosity had overcome protocol in some border-line cases. We were already the cause of intense speculation and this was to increase as the weeks passed.

I was due to present my letter of accreditation to the Secretary of State for Commonwealth Relations at 3 p.m. on Friday, 24th July. In the morning Sir Arthur Snelling of the Commonwealth Relations Office came to Rhodesia House to pay me a courtesy visit. He had been to Rhodesia with Lord Gardiner and Mr. Bottomley earlier in the year and we discussed our respective climates, my previous service with the Colonial Office in the early thirties, and I asked after various colleagues of his who were juniors in those far-off days. We did not discuss the Rhodesian situation.

Shortly before 3 p.m. I donned my bowler, took my umbrella and sallied forth with Denzil Bradley, my personal assistant and nephew of a fellow councillor of mine in the Umtali-Odzi Road Council. Apart from a very few city men my headgear and garb of the London of my day had disappeared. It was still the mufti uniform of the Army in London, but the main throng of tycoons and politicians seemed to go hatless. As a result I could always spot a fellow soldier, either active or retired, a mile off, and the only place one could find a bowler hat in quantity was in the hat racks of the service clubs.

Dress, even in the diplomatic world, was very informal, a dark lounge suit being the only garb necessary for the numerous evening receptions. Only at very formal dinners did one wear tails, and a dinner jacket met the occasion at most times. My expensive morning dress was reserved for religious ceremonies.

The House of Commons is a gloomy labyrinth of passages and staircases, equipped with old-fashioned lifts. I was greeted by one of Mr. Bottomley's secretaries at the entrance of a side portal in one of the courtyards, where I was at once photographed. I was then led

18

to the Secretary of State's small office off one of these passages. I was warmly greeted by him and two or three of his officials, where again we were photographed together, with cheerful smiles on our faces.

This was my first meeting with Mr. Bottomley, a trade unionist and railway official. I became very fond of him as I got to know him and at one time in our discussions on Rhodesia I was bold enough to tell him that if he had emigrated to Rhodesia after the war and joined our railways, by now he would probably be a member of the Rhodesian Front Bench. If the remark embarrassed him, he did not show it, and he was obviously too polite to deny it. Our first interview lasted half an hour, and I did my best to explain the position of my country, disabuse him of the fact that we were reactionary white settlers, and explained that we were people like himself living 6,000 miles away under different conditions. I enlarged on our Industrial Conciliation Act and its machinery, a subject I knew he would be interested in as a trade unionist, and suggested that Britain's industrial relations, even at that moment plagued by an unofficial strike, might well profit by its study.

I also enlarged on the role of our chiefs in tribal life, but here I encountered a certain amount of prejudice, not surprising in view of the Socialist dislike of anything smacking of hereditary privilege. In all my time in London this was a subject on which I did my best to enlighten public opinion and while I may have made some impression it was hard work. Europeans tend to equate African chieftainship with a feudal nobility, and regard it as outdated and pernicious.

It is very difficult for anyone who does not know Africa to realise that the African does not only differ in pigmentation from the European, but also in his spiritual and thought processes. This is at the root of most of the misunderstandings about race in the modern world.

The interview over, we parted on the most cordial terms, and I later discovered through diplomatic channels that I was personally acceptable, and not the extremist that they had expected Rhodesia to send to London at this juncture.

Later that afternoon I collected my clothes from Saville Row and much to the relief of my tailor found that they fitted perfectly, though I had noticed as a precaution they had left ample silk backing to my numerous waistcoats. Properly equipped and with credentials ac-

19

cepted, I was now ready to enter the diplomatic world, whilst my wife was already loose in the shops completing her wardrobe.

Rhodesia House did not normally work at full pressure on Saturday mornings and those officials who lived in the country or suburbs were not expected to turn up. Commuting is a tiresome and time-wasting business, and it was hardly worth the journey into town. Those who lived in Central London appeared however and cleared up their desks for Monday. As the tempo of our crisis increased I managed to reverse this rule, and in the latter days we worked all day on Saturday and sometimes on Sunday as well.

This weekend saw the Conservative Party crisis over its leadership, and Mr. Cledwyn Hughes – the Minister of State for Commonwealth Relations – was in Rhodesia, so perfect peace reigned at Rhodesia House. I had always regretted that even when living in London I had never been to see the Tower of London, Westminster Abbey or St. Paul's Cathedral. My small daughter was anxious to sample all these delights as well as the museums and places of interest, so on Sunday we sallied forth to the Tower by underground. Alas, it was closed to the public much to her annoyance, though she saw it later, especially the headman's block, axe, and place of execution. I was not particularly disturbed at not being able to go inside. We wandered round the walls and with a military eye I examined weaknesses in its defences, not through any desire to lay siege to the fortress, but from a sense of prudence in case I should be incarcerated there as a traitor, should our independence negotiations fail. In that case I would see plenty of the interior.

With a worthy desire to preserve my country's finances and win the regard of John Wrathall, the Minister of Finance, I had arranged to move to the Hyde Park Hotel, equally comfortable but less expensive, and this we did on the Monday. It was also closer to the areas in which my wife was going house hunting and the park was handy to amuse Julia.

Before I left Rhodesia an invitation to lunch with an old friend Dick Hull, now Field-Marshal Sir Richard Hull, Chief of the Defence Staff in succession to Lord Mountbatten, had reached me. We had travelled out in a troopship together to India in 1932 and during the war he had commanded an armoured force which formed part of the 78th Division in Tunisia of which I had been the GSO 1. The last time we had met was in the early hours of a November morning in my farm billet when I had generously presented him with the one and only unlooted egg for miles around for breakfast and which my batman had reserved for me. Those who have existed on compo rations will appreciate the generosity of this gesture, and on the Monday I was to receive his hospitality in return. This was one of the pleasures in a diplomatic post which was not exactly a bed of roses, namely meeting up again with old service friends. Mr. Denis Healey, the Minister of War, Sir David Luce, the first Sea Lord, and their wives were the other guests.

Then next day we were the guests at Lords of the Chairman of the MCC to watch the South Africa-England Test and Colin Bland, the Rhodesian, put up a magnificent display of fielding. Never much of a performer at the game myself and soured by hours of compulsory watching at Wellington, I felt that our complimentary tickets were wasted. The following day's tickets I gave to one of my staff who was a fan and he took the day off to watch it. He was delighted and I was able to get down to some work.

There seems to be a general misapprehension that a diplomat's life is one long round of functions and entertainments. This is probably quite true for the representative of a country whose international problems are few and whose trade links are well established.

The social diplomatic life of the Rhodesian High Commissioner, at least so I found it, was a sparetime occupation, to be fitted in after the office closed or during the lunch breaks. My wife liked it, as was natural, but to me it was irksome except on those occasions when the function served some definite purpose by which our image was improved, or good propaganda could be made by our appearance. Generally the functions which fell into this category were those at which I had been invited to speak.

On Tuesday, 27th July, occurred the first functions at which I was able to put my country's case and views on independence. We had been invited as the Guests of Honour at the reception given at Marlborough House by the Commonwealth Secretary of State, the usual honour accorded to a High Commissioner taking up his post in London. Here Lord Taylor was acting as host for Mr. Bottomley who was detained in the Commons. At this time the small majority held by Labour was imposing a great strain on both sides of the House, and political hostesses were bitterly complaining that their

21

dinners were spoilt and getting cold owing to the delayed and compulsory absence of their guests and often the host.

I was engaged in conversation by Mr. Duncan Sandys, the then shadow Commonwealth Secretary, and Lord Taylor for the Government. Both impressed on me that the terms offered by the Labour Government were far more generous than the Conservatives could ever have offered, on the assumption that the Conservatives would back any solution that Labour offered but not the other way round. There was truth in this, but when I confessed complete ignorance of these terms, they were astounded. I asked what they were, and was told that a blocking third was required in our Assembly, the Land Apportionment Act must be greatly liberalised and discrimination, whatever that meant, must go.

I replied that I had gleaned all this from the Press, but that I and my Government had never seen it in writing from either party. In fact, what had transpired during Mr. Bottomley's visit in February was the presentation of a vague set of five principles, and Mr. Hughes's visit at that moment to Rhodesia was an effort to translate these into something concrete.

When Sandys left to return to the House, I had an idea he considered I was either a very dim-witted and ill-briefed envoy, or close-mouthed and discreet. I hope the latter. Lord Taylor was charming, but I felt he was remote from the problem. In fact, he vacated his post in Commonwealth Relations shortly afterwards.

Immediately after this reception we drove to Major Patrick Wall's charming house in Cheyne Walk on the Embankment, where we had been invited to dinner. Amongst the guests were three M.P.s who were interested in Rhodesian affairs and Dr. Carel de Wet, the South African Ambassador, whom I was meeting for the first time. He is a most able diplomat who is serving his country well, and we became as close friends as was possible in the short time I was in London. Both he and his wife were overwhelmingly kind to us during our stay in London.

After the ladies had left, I was closely questioned on the political situation in Rhodesia and was able to tell them that we were determined to obtain our independence on our 1961 Constitution come what may, but were genuinely agreeable to meet the British Government with such concessions as would not lead to the ruin of Rhodesia. I heard later that they were impressed, even shocked, at the

The Hon. Ian Douglas Smith, Prime Minister of Rhodesia. (Photo: Basil Shackleton. Permission: Rhodesian Ministry of Information)

Brigadier Andrew Skeen with his family at their home in the Vumba, near Umtali. (Photo: Basil Shackleton. Permission: Rhodesian Ministry of Information)

firmness of my Government's attitude as expressed by myself.

It was obvious to me on my arrival in London that the British politicians and officials, even those sympathetic to our cause, had not realised the depth of disillusionment that existed at that moment in Rhodesia regarding British intentions. Nor had they realised that the Rhodesian Front had ceased to be a political party and had become a national movement, of which Mr. Smith was not only the leader but its incarnation.

We had witnessed the process of handing over power rapidly to immature and often vicious demagogues in the African countries to the north of us – a process by which constitution after constitution was agreed upon and then discarded to the fetish of majority rule, regardless of whether such majority rule was in the interests of the majority itself. The time had come to make a stand against this, and this stand was what I was intended to demonstrate in London.

This change in feeling in my country was not fully understood in Whitehall. One of the main reasons for this was the information that was reaching the Commonwealth Relations Office through its High Commissioner in Salisbury. The diplomatic world is a small one and consequently a diplomat, if he is not careful, can have his views coloured by a small section of the population of the country to which he is accredited. This is especially true if this section and the country's Press are at variance with the views of the Government and belong to that class of the people who have social contacts in the diplomatic world.

I venture to suggest that if the High Commissioner in Salisbury had extended his contacts beyond the small group of politicians belonging to a discredited political party, church circles and expatriate business interests, and had moved amongst the people more, he could have given more accurate information to his Government. I had confirmation of this in a conversation with a retired member of his staff who had not made this mistake and who had himself moved in a different milieu.

I took steps to determine the type of visitor from Rhodesia who sought contacts with the Commonwealth Relations Office in London, and found that these were the same types of persons who had close contacts with the High Commission in Salisbury, and who therefore were reinforcing the official reports.

To this fact I attribute much of Mr. Bottomley's troubles at a later stage, and also the British Government's difficulty in understanding the situation and modifying its attitude. There seemed to be little awareness of the tremendous support for Mr. Smith in Rhodesia. The fallacy that Mr. Smith was being driven by a small group or junta in his party could have been eradicated to the benefit of the negotiations which followed. To correct false information reaching London from Salisbury was one of my main tasks in the months ahead, but it took a long time for the penny to drop.

I was most impressed by the personality and character of Major Patrick Wall, the Conservative M.P. for Haltemprice. He belonged to that section of the Conservative Party to which I would have belonged if I had remained in Britain. He possesses the utmost integrity and great courage in pressing within and without his party for those principles which distinguish the Conservatives from the Socialist Liberals. At that moment it was a losing battle, and was jeopardising his future with his party. But these are short-term trends and I am convinced that the Rhodesian issue amongst others, and the change I had already sensed amongst the British people towards the United Nations and Afro-Asians would shortly operate on Conservative Party thinking, and bring him and his devoted colleagues into positions of commanding influence again. For fourteen years, I myself have battled against odds which seemed overwhelming, confident that the day would come when the mass of the people would awake to the dangers that faced them, and that day had come.

I was to see much of him later, and his sympathy and advice were a great help to me. Rhodesia owes much to the unselfish efforts of Patrick Wall.

My engagement book was rapidly filling up, I was getting into the saddle and my initial introduction to London was over.

4. The Situation in London

Before I left Rhodesia I had talks with all the Ministers and Parliamentary Under Secretaries, many of whom had representatives of their respective departments in Rhodesia House. I had only one brief interview with Cliff Dupont, the Minister for External Affairs, before he was unfortunately taken ill and had to fly for treatment to Cape Town and I had not seen the Prime Minister, Ian Smith, since I had seen him at his house to accept the appointment of High Commissioner.

The day before I left Salisbury I was due to see him in his office in the Legislative Assembly Building. I had expected to be given a lengthy briefing on the task ahead of me, but this was not to be the case. He informed me that an arrangement had been made for the Commonwealth Relations Office in London to inform me of the verbal conversations he was and would be having with the British High Commissioner in Salisbury. Thus I would be kept in touch with the independence negotiations as they proceeded, for nothing was being put formally in writing at this stage. The famous five principles which had been formulated by the British Government were at this time not known to me, but I enquired how far the Rhodesian Government were at this time prepared to go to meet the British requirements.

The P.M. informed me that there was the possibility of a blocking quarter in the "B" Roll. That is two more seats and that it was felt these should be held by representatives of the chiefs. Moreover an increase in the numbers eligible to vote on the "B" Roll could be possible.

This was in line with my own thinking at that time, and I regarded this as a face-saving compromise for the British Government, should they be in earnest about giving us a negotiated independence. I already had my doubts about this, but was determined to keep an open mind till I had seen what the attitude was in London.

The negotiations at that time were being handled by the two Governments direct, and the Rhodesian High Commissioner was not to be brought into it. The arrangements by which I was to be informed of progress by the Commonwealth Relations Office instead of direct by my Government appeared strange to me, and would put me in a very difficult position in London, knowing as I did, the manner in which the officials in Whitehall operated. However, I said nothing and bided my time till this arrangement displayed its obvious dangers, when I reacted, as will be shown in a later chapter.

I regarded the scanty nature of my briefing on these vital negotiations as a compliment to myself, and used my intimate knowledge of the Government and Party thinking to fill in the gaps, and let me play the situation by ear, till such time as absence and distance would put me out of touch.

I had one other formal letter of instruction handed to me as I boarded the aircraft. The salient points were as follows:

1. To cultivate amongst the British Government and people the maximum sympathy and goodwill towards the Government and people of Rhodesia.

2. To present the aims and objects of Government policy in the most favourable light, having regard to the political traditions of the British people.

3. To promote the foregoing objectives in other Commonwealth and Foreign Diplomatic circles accessible to me in London.

4. To report on the main trends of Government, Opposition and public opinion affecting Rhodesia, or the plural societies in Africa generally.

These were explicit instructions, and my main efforts were now to be directed towards them.

Contrary to the opinions of British politicians, who regard themselves as above public opinion once elected and furthermore as leaders and moulders of public opinion – not followers – I held the view that every politician in a party system of government had to hold his ear to the ground. In general the British public are more concerned with their bread and butter existence, but occasionally issues arise which spark off an emotional reaction which all politicians fear. This is especially so when the parties are evenly matched and there are many marginal seats. Such a situation existed in Britain at this time.

If I could succeed in the first two objects in this directive, and the necessary conditions could be fostered to light this dormant spark, who knows what pressures could be exerted on the politicians to meet us in negotiations, or if these failed, dampen or nullify the sanctions with which we had been threatened. This appeared to me my most important task and one which should take precedence over all the others. The problem was how to achieve it.

Cornelius Tacitus in his history of Rome relates that the Senator Gaius Cassius speaking for a motion in the Senate, discoursed as follows: "I have many times, Conscript Fathers, been present in this House when novel measures have been called for, but have remained silent, because I desired not by constant clamour to destroy such influence as I possess, but to preserve it unimpaired should my counsels ever be urgently needed."

I proposed to act on this sound principle because the British people have learned to disregard the man who is always in the headlines and unconsciously to dissociate themselves from his views. This is a lesson that leftist bodies and the coloured propagandists have not yet learnt. The more embittered and shrill their outbursts against Rhodesia became, the more public opinion swung towards us. I was happy to let them do my work for us on T.V., Radio and through public demonstrations, though these latter were few in number. The extraordinary appearance of the persons who took part in the demonstrations was enough to cause a revulsion in decent, ordinary people, and I soon found out that a commercial organisation called "Rent a crowd" used to provide these lay-abouts as demonstrators to any organisation, from ban-the-bombers to anti-blood sports.

So I avoided being reported in the Press, except on those occasions that suited my country's cause, and caused disunity amongst our avowed enemies. At the same time I made myself as charming as possible to leading journalists and treated them to long off-the-record discussions on our problems, in which I gave them facts of which they were unaware. I think I was able to detect in some of the journals a more accurate and not unsympathetic reporting as these interviews progressed.

There is little doubt that at the time of my arrival a broad sympathy with Rhodesia was becoming evident throughout the mass of the ordinary people, though their ignorance of conditions in Rhodesia was abysmal. To reinforce this sympathy with facts that they could support on moral and ethical grounds, we distributed literature and latterly spent many thousands of pounds on advertisements in the leading newspapers.

The franchise was explained and the position of our chiefs clarified, whilst facts on population were published and the progress of African education and welfare was made known. Rhodesia House windows on the busy Strand pavement were utilised with a series of displays which attracted much attention. It is interesting to note that one of the first acts of the British Government on our assumption of independence was an order to have these displays covered up – a tribute to their effectiveness. So, to the limit of our small staff and the paucity of the means at our disposal, we prepared the fuel for the spark, which later we were able to ignite when our Prime Minister came over to London in October.

Public relations, or propaganda as it used to be called, has become an art and a science, a fact by which many astute individuals have amassed fortunes. We could not afford to employ one of the great public relations firms, but had to make use of our own staff and later a group of patriotic individuals from Rhodesia who came over to help us. The Information staff in Rhodesia House, on whom fell the gigantic task of educating the British public on Rhodesia, was very small, with only one officer, Mr. Dimond, acting as a lecturer and public relations officer, who could travel outside London to spread the gospel. I had plans to get over more staff from Rhodesia to help him in his work and assist him in his other role of looking after the throngs of visitors to Rhodesia House and keeping them happy. Unfortunately, apart from the voluntary and temporary team that came over in late October, these reinforcements never materialised.

However, I was most fortunate in being able to get Alan Izod, the Director of Information in Rhodesia, to come over soon after I arrived, and act as my Information Adviser in the period between his existing appointment and his prospective promotion to the Immigration and Tourist Department in December. On him fell the task of co-ordinating and directing our public relations, and the vital organisation necessary to present our Prime Minister to the British public on his arrival in London. To him, Mr. Read, and his assistants in the Information Department of Rhodesia House go the credit for such success as we had with the British man in the street. Jack Brenden, whom I knew in Umtali as District Commissioner, had obtained a secondment to the Information Department and he arrived by sea during the last hectic three weeks in order to take over from Alan Izod, and he was a most welcome reinforcement. Of his resources more presently.

I have mentioned the pitfalls a diplomat may encounter by limiting his contacts to the political, diplomatic and business worlds. Whilst individuals who move in these circles undoubtedly wield great influence, their views are always coloured by financial, political and personal considerations, and such support as they could give our cause would be hampered by these considerations. This is not to say that I neglected my contacts with the City of London, but I was fortunate in that my predecessor, Evan Campbell, had made extensive inroads into this world so that it was well aware of Rhodesia's problems. I also made a great number of calls on the Ambassadors and High Commissioners in London and was received most cordially, even by those whose countries had expressed hostility to Rhodesia. I was able to call on twenty-seven mission heads of whom seven returned my call before I left. Well over a hundred missions are accredited in London and the protocol of calling and returning calls takes up to a year to complete. Diplomats' wives call formally on one another and my wife had some amusing experiences in this respect with regard to wives of diplomats representing what are now politely called emergent nations.

During the last few days of July I was able to call on Mr. Cledwyn Hughes on his return from Rhodesia. We chatted amicably on any subject not connected with Rhodesia and I was struck by the musical intonation of his Welsh accent which nostalgically took me back to pre-war days when I was a Brigade Major to a Welsh Brigade in Newport, Monmouthshire. I spoke thus inconsequently of deliberate intent to see if he would refer to the talks he had had with Rhodesian Ministers and so put me in the picture in accordance with the arrangement made between the two Governments.

Nothing was passed on, as I had expected, but I had a pretty shrewd idea of what must have happened. It confirmed the suspicions I had already formed that this agreement was unlikely to be carried out from the British end.

It is the happy if somewhat naïve practice for diplomats of various ranks from ambassador down to give and receive luncheons with their opposite numbers in the diplomatic world and with the officials of the host government, and then to report snippets from the conversation back to their respective governments as "gleaning". Unless the diplomats are incredibly indiscreet, or the conversations are carried out after many convivial bottles, one may be sure that these indiscretions are skilfully or clumsily leaked for the benefit of the recipient. In this negative way they are useful, and some minor diplomats spend hours after good lunches concocting literary and witty despatches filled with these trifles for the amusement of their seniors.

To write a witty and well-turned phrase is often the surest avenue of promotion in the service. Wives also play their part in this comedy, and possibly provide a better way for gaining information if the lady concerned is noted for indiscretion. Here again a diplomat of ingenuity with a frivolous wife may be sure of passing misleading information to the correct quarter. Honor was amused sometimes by the crude attempts that were made in her presence to gain information, but for her part was carefully briefed as to what she should say and leave unsaid, not that she required such briefing after her experience of politics in Rhodesia.

Personally I left the gleaning to my juniors and such information as I had to pass to my Government was sent in manuscript and highly secret form direct by bag to the Prime Minister or to the Minister of External Affairs, marked Strictly Personal. Curious historians will therefore find nothing of this nature in the files of the Rhodesian Ministry of External Affairs.

The United Kingdom Parliament went into recess in the first few days of August, not to reassemble till the end of October. There was an immediate exodus of politicians and diplomats from London, and a number of civil servants began to take their holidays.

It would not begin to fill up again till the end of September. We decided to give our first big reception towards the end of that month and set our personal staff to issue invitations. To the list already existing in the office I added a number of names, including my own and my wife's personal friends. I had hoped to see a number of these and we had received numerous invitations to visit them at weekends in the country. This seemed a very good opportunity to get them all together as well as a chance for them to see one another again, for unlike Rhodesia, travel is a difficulty in England, small though the country is in comparison. Furthermore with all the domestic difficulties that plague the housewife in England, visiting friends entails considerable planning. Surprisingly many of our friends had not managed to see one another for years, but had kept in touch only through letters and verbal messages.

Indeed, during our short stay in London we were not able to make contact with them all. This, on our return to Rhodesia, was one of our few regrets. Generally speaking all these personal friends were very much on the side of Rhodesia. Many would have liked to emigrate, but family ties and habits had made it impossible. However, we are hoping that some may still break away and join us in Rhodesia.

Although Britain seemed prosperous, money could not make up for so many of the inconveniences of life there today. It was terribly expensive, domestic help was obtained with difficulty, the climate, though it was reasonably kind to us that autumn, impossible; but the worst was the crowds of people. One could never get away into the open spaces and when one could these too were swarming with people. This fact more than anything else made Rhodesia seem so attractive to us, and nightly we gave thanks for having such a homeland, and it strengthened our utter determination to preserve it.

Britain has a habit of enfolding its foreign diplomats. Some of those I met had already become more English than the English, had bought homes in England and almost dug roots in the country. This of course can be detrimental to the country they represent.

If I were a Foreign Minister I would always choose my diplomats from those who intensely disliked the capital to which they were accredited. Paradoxical though this may seem, it is the only way to get devoted and accurate advice.

Courts in medieval times were well aware of this. The Spanish Ambassador to the Court of James IV of Scotland, Don Pedro de Ayala was recalled to Spain by Ferdinand and Isabella because "he loved Scotland too well", and there were other instances.

As far as my wife and I were concerned, this certainly applied, though of course in our case it was somewhat different. We had no need to become anglicised to know the people. We knew them well, and followed their thought processes with the detachment of an 18 years' absence.

Paragraph 4 of my directive read as follows: "To report on the main trends of opinion affecting Rhodesia, or the plural society in Africa generally."

Here I gradually began to discern a new trend of thinking amongst the British men and women in the street. They had been originally taught to think of, to use a euphemism, the less developed peoples of the world and in Africa especially as ill-treated underdogs. A decade of watching these underdogs disporting themselves within their midst and on the international scene had produced a certain amount of disillusion. After all, it is not pleasant to be taxed to the hilt and find one's hard-earned money going into the pockets of corrupt politicians and wasted on useless amenities one cannot enjoy oneself. Nor is it pleasant to provide this money and have ungracious insults hurled in exchange, and finally after handing over millions to some newly emergent state, to be called mean because it is not enough.

Closer home, one does not like to see one's neighbourhood turned into a bedlam of noise, smells and dirt, or expose one's child to the dangers of nameless alien perversities. Furthermore, when one justly complains, one does not take kindly to being turned upon by a junta of liberal fanatics and called unchristian and intolerant.

During the past years the public in general and particularly what used to be called the working classes have come to feel that they themselves are becoming the underdogs in a world turned upside down by the United Nations and the Afro-Asian group that now dominates it. This created an undercurrent of unconscious sympathy for Rhodesia which was daily strengthened by the arrogant demands and shrill complaints of Afro-Asian dictators.

I noted this feeling and did my utmost to further it to the best of my ability through those contacts I was able to make whilst pointing out by contrast the dignified and civilised behaviour of my countrymen who made no demands on the British, managed our own affairs efficiently and had never turned to the British taxpayer for a penny. By the personal behaviour, dress and demeanour of my wife, myself and my staff we tried to impress this point on our contacts.

Rhodesia was civilised, Rhodesia was dignified and Rhodesia was different. This may appear to be priggish and holier than thou, but it was effective and we maintained this attitude to the very last. The numerous letters we received after our expulsion from London told us that it had been appreciated.

5. Diplomatic Camouflage

Rhodesian affairs became back page news in August. It was during this month that Britain became engaged in the battle for the pound sterling.

There were also several industrial disputes boiling up in the docks and in the motor industry. Mr. Harold Wilson, holidaying in the Scilly Isles, had many preoccupations to disturb him on the domestic front, and the Secretary of State for Commonwealth Relations was preparing to depart for a tour of West Africa. It was only from this quarter where the West African states tried to keep the pot boiling with shrill indignant voices, that Rhodesia came into the news.

The Rhodesian Front Congress in Salisbury was due to be held on 7th August, and a certain amount of Press interest was concentrated on this event. It was the erroneous view, fed by false information, that Mr. Smith would be assailed on all sides by vociferous extremists in his party who were urging him to action. A wistful note of wishful thinking crept into press comments, that this would throw Mr. Smith into alliance with Sir Roy Welensky, "moderate" elements would then rally to this coalition and the "extremists" would retire defeated into their backveld fortresses.

Anxious journalists came to me for confirmation of this theory and I had great pleasure in informing them that there were no extremists or moderates in the party or the country, but that all were Rhodesians and all had the utmost confidence in their Prime Minister whose thinking and theirs were in complete accord. As regards Sir Roy Welensky, I added that so discredited had he become with the electorate that the surest way Mr. Smith could lose votes was for this retired statesman to come out in his support, and that this did not apply to a section of the people but to the whole.

I predicted that the congress would be a triumph for Mr. Smith and indicate the wholehearted support he held throughout the country, except for a small unrepresentative minority. They departed abashed and disappointed, and soon my predictions proved true.

All along this myth seemed to have coloured the thinking of people in authority. It was imagined that Mr. Smith was the prisoner of irreconcilable elements in the country and manipulated by a junta of wealthy tobacco farmers. The truth that he was in essence the incarnation of his party and Rhodesia as a whole, and that he spoke for us all and had our absolute confidence, took me a long time to impress on these people.

Wishful thinking, an occupational disease of the British politician, might have had a great deal to do with this, but it was reinforced by the very indifferent information that was reaching Whitehall from its contacts in Rhodesia.

The Press of course constantly harped on this theme, but then the Press, both Rhodesian and British, has an infinite capacity for self-delusion. The pity was that it also deluded its readers.

Honor and I, now living in the Hyde Park Hotel, had to find a house or flat to live in. Furthermore we had the almost impossible task of staffing it. To wash up, cook, make beds and clean a house at the best of times is a task that most women find a full-time occupation. A diplomat's wife has to be ready at short notice to be immaculately turned out and take her place as her country's representative on the distaff side at as many as seven social functions in one day. To perform both tasks is beyond any woman's capacity. With the added distraction of the care of a small and lively child it is an impossibility.

During the period of Federation the High Commissioner had a large and well-furnished house provided by the Government, and into this we would normally have stepped and possibly taken over the staff as well. This is the normal procedure for diplomats. But the Rhodesian High Commission had lost this mansion to the Zambian Government when the assets of the Federation had been distributed amongst its former members. Evan Campbell had suffered the same liability, and his rented flat was no longer available.

After intensive house-hunting, with a careful eye on my Government's exchequer, we finally settled on a small house in Markham Square, Chelsea. It was the usual tall, narrow-terraced house that one finds in this part of London, and had as our chauffeur snobbishly remarked "a good address". My personal staff also had lodgings in this neighbourhood which was an advantage.

I thought the rooms were cramped and rather inconvenient, with a small cubby-hole for a dining-room, which ruled out any thought of lavish dinner parties in the house. In fact, the ground square footage of the place could have fitted into half the drawing-room of our house in Rhodesia. Nevertheless, to save further weeks of search we took it on a two years' lease subject to the usual diplomatic clauses for surrender. My wife deserved credit from her fellow Rhodesian taxpayers by getting £10 a week knocked off the rent by bringing her own silver and ornaments from Rhodesia.

We took up residence on Saturday, 14th August, and occupied it for exactly three months. But we still had no staff, and spent our first three days with the forgotten tasks of washing-up and making beds – a chore we had last done before we left England in January 1947. We were not amused.

Employment agencies having failed, we put up a small notice in a newsagent and on the Wednesday an elderly lady presented herself as a cleaner. She demanded 5/- an hour for a four hour day, Mondays to Fridays, which still left us two days a week to experience the full domestic horrors of English life.

Mrs. Mopp, as I called her, was regarded as an exception to most of her calling insofar as she was graciously prepared to make beds, in addition to a little gentle dusting and hoovering. Once or twice she actually operated the Colson washing machine. But alas, one Monday morning, having been paid the previous Friday, she failed to turn up. As we had never learned where she lived, and she had come without the blessing of an agency, we were unable to contact her. Perhaps she had been run over by a bus or found she had to pay income tax, I don't know, but personally I suspected that the 95 stairs in the house had been too much for her. My wife, never fond of stairs herself, supported this theory. She then experienced a three weeks long purgatory.

Julia, our nine-year-old daughter, whose future school in Cornwall was closed for the holidays, was only a nominal help. We had acquired a television set to which the child was glued at all hours, and so we had to write off her assistance as bed-maker and dish-dryer while this infernal contraption was on the air.

We had the active sympathy of all our friends, but we were on the point of abandoning the house and going into a hotel, when a miracle occurred. A young Italian woman came into the employment agency at the exact moment when my wife was sending it a last agonised appeal. The husband was a waiter in a night club, and in order to

35

get her child into a crèche Franca was anxious to get a job which lasted more than four hours a day. Unlike most people we were prepared to take her on for as long hours as she liked and so she came to us hot-foot.

She was the proverbial treasure and though she cost us £9 a week for a 30 hour week, she was prepared, even anxious to do everything, including laundry, which with laundry bills being what they were, made her worth a dozen Mrs. Mopps. Our troubles were over, and the cooking of breakfasts became a trifle of inconvenience. All our other meals we took out at one or two excellent little Chelsea restaurants when we were not entertaining or being entertained. She was in tears when we had to leave finally, and if ever we have to return to London, it is to Franca, her husband and mother-in-law, a cook, that we shall turn for a domestic staff.

The catering and hotel world in England is almost entirely dependent on Italians, Spaniards and Maltese for its staff, and first-class workers they are.

We had evolved an elaborate ritual for early morning tea in this house of 95 steps. All the requisites were brought up several flights of stairs from the basement before we went to bed, and in the early morning it was my duty to fill and heat the electric kettle in the bedroom and make tea. When we had guests, I used to fill a cup, place a lump of sugar in the saucer and take this rather sordid offering down to our visitor in his bedroom.

Ian McLean, the Minister for Labour and Health, stayed with us a few days, and I remarked to him that seldom in the history of diplomacy could an Excellency in his pyjamas have woken and presented the early morning tea to an Honourable. When Andrew Dunlop, Deputy Minister for Roads, spent a couple of nights with us, Julia was back from school and she eagerly demanded the honour of this task, and as her nickname was "The Duchess", protocol was still observed in this matter.

Our domestic troubles having been solved, our next task was to further Julia's interrupted education. Foster Melliors, a small boarding and day school for young girls at Bude, Cornwall, was chosen by my wife. It was owned and run by Miss Zambra, the aunt of our immediate neighbours on the Vumba and we had met Miss Zambra when she and her brother had been out on a visit to Rhodesia a year of two before. Apart from the day scholars there were seven boarders.

36

It was at the seaside and in a part of England where the climate was less severe for a child used to a warmer climate. She was to have a short, happy but somewhat interrupted schooling there.

I had been invited by the Imperial Tobacco Company to visit their Bristol factory at the end of September. This date coincided with the school opening and so we set forth by car on the Sunday morning accompanied by Miss Wendy Lee, my secretary-stenographer. She had been working late hours under pressure of her cypher duties and we felt this break from London would rest her.

The drive down to Cornwall was broken by a detour to Camberley and Fleet, where Honor saw her old home at Dogmersfield and its attached cottage where we had last lived in England. The area had not changed much but we had no feeling of nostalgia for our old surroundings, and proceeded on our way west with the happy feeling that we had chosen rightly in emigrating to Rhodesia when we did.

After depositing Julia at her school, we drove next day to Bristol and had an interesting afternoon at the Wills factory. I also had a confidential discussion with Mr. Partridge, the Chairman of the Company, on certain aspects of the independence issue as it might affect the tobacco industry. I told him the views of my Government on this matter which were of great concern to his firm.

We were presented with samples of the firm's products which were much appreciated, so much so that Wendy Lee, a non-smoker, took to small cigars with enjoyment, an addiction that caused her leg to be pulled considerably by her colleagues.

Our return journey took us through Broadway in the Cotswolds, and here we spent a night at the Lygon Arms. I revisited my old home, now a hotel, where the proprietor gave us drinks in the bar, now part of the old dining room. In return I told him something of the history of the house, and showed him the place at the foot of the stairs where a ghost in the shape of a little old lady was said to appear out of the wall of the sixteenth century part of the building which had dated from Tudor times. My father had seen this apparition on two occasions and my mother on one.

My wife spent a morning in the numerous antique shops where 20 years previously she had bought many bits of furniture and china. She was gratified to learn that these had now appreciated up to three times what she had paid for them. Though tempted she did not add to her collection.

This was the one and only time I was able to get out of London while I was in England, though Honor paid two other short visits to Cornwall and one down to Kent to see her aunts.

A great number of my old friends and those of my father came to see me during August, and I lunched with them in various service clubs. Through them and several Members of Parliament and the Lords, who knew my predecessor and were kind enough to ask me to lunch, I was able to gauge opinion on Rhodesia and wider issues.

August was the month when armed with bowler, umbrella and regimental tie, a protective camouflage for the colonial I now had become, I was able to assess public opinion, bring people in England in touch with the change of Rhodesian opinion, and in a limited way prepare opinion for the negotiations that lay ahead.

Sometimes I had as many as twelve visitors to Rhodesia House in a day.

There had been complaints, some justified and others not, that Rhodesians visiting London had not received sufficient attention from Rhodesia House. A number of these complaints had been passed to me by members of our legislative assembly as well as others and I did my best to investigate them. Many were unfounded, some were justified, so I gave orders to the reception staff that I was, subject to my being available on the premises, always ready to see anyone who wished to speak to me. As a result I had a number of visitors who would not normally have been seen by a diplomat. Apart from dealing with their problems, I found these people very useful as a contact with feeling in Rhodesia, and how it had developed during my absence. I made a particular point of asking those who had just arrived to see me, and also those on the point of departing home. The latter I briefed on the situation in London as I saw it with instructions to put the people at home in the picture. Many of these visitors were able to tell me what the man in the street, especially in Britain at large, outside London, was thinking.

Every visitor to a foreign country is an embryo diplomat, and full use of them should be made in furthering one's country's aims. I would recommend that every diplomat should interview as many such people as possible and not confine his contacts to the V.I.P.s.

It was to further this aim that I had asked for an additional Public Relations Officer, with the sole duty of meeting people in our reception lounge and giving personal attention to their problems. I had made plans to increase the reception space in Rhodesia House by utilising the large basement. In this I had intended putting industrial exhibits and material to publicise our local authorities, enterprises and corporations. All this would have come under this additional member of my staff.

Unfortunately the mission was closed down before I was able to get this done, but should Rhodesia House reopen, this will have to be one of the first improvements to its facilities.

At weekends and during unoccupied evening hours Honor and I, incognito and more informally dressed, moved among the ordinary people in the street, in the shops and elsewhere and did what we could to enlighten people on Rhodesia and discover what they thought. We were immensely encouraged by what we heard.

People were becoming aware of Rhodesia, for the Press was memtioning us daily, and the public were eager for news and opinions. At any other time the message would not have got across, and so we took full advantage of our situation.

During my predecessor's term of office and through his efforts and those of the Parliamentary Under-Secretary for Information an organisation called the Friends of Rhodesia had been formed. A body of this nature, officially unconnected with the embassy or the Government, is an invaluable asset in presenting a country's case to the public.

Unfortunately the Friends of Rhodesia for various reasons had never got off the ground. This was largely due to lack of funds, but also to the mistake, to my mind, of getting involved in the political issues of our claim to independence. Once a body such as this becomes involved in an internal political dialogue, strains and stresses are set up within its membership, and it inevitably attracts people of strong and extreme views, which is often detrimental to an increased membership.

Just before my arrival the Friends of Rhodesia virtually broke up and its place was taken by the Anglo-Rhodesian Society. I met the new committee soon after I had arrived and advised them to direct their efforts to purely factual information, sympathetic to our cause and to dispel ignorance about our internal affairs amongst the public. I was also able to put them financially on their feet and from time to time get them additional funds, till such time as they were able to exist on their own resources. I then fed them on information, and got them to work closely with our Information Section at Rhodesia House who were instructed to give them all the help they could.

On 9th September, they held their inaugural dinner at the Savoy, which was very well attended, and which I addressed, giving them a brief lead on what I felt their new task should be. The society slowly began building up its membership, which increased rapidly after our Prime Minister's visit to London. To all those who wrote to Rhodesia House expressing their sympathy with our country, an answer was sent recommending them to join the Anglo-Rhodesian Society and the donations which many people sent us, I passed to the treasurer of the Society, Mr. Lardner Burke, son of our Minister of Justice, who was working in London at the time.

The society began forming branches in the provinces which, apart from working on their own, later were to provide platforms for our lecturers and speakers. It is to this society that we mainly look to help our cause now that Rhodesia House is closed down. Rhodesians owe a debt of gratitude to this unselfish body of men and women who have worked, and are working, so hard for us in Britain.

The lull in our affairs which occurred in August and early September was now coming to an end. The Rhodesian Government had inherited the right, under the Federal Entrustments, to appoint diplomatic representatives to foreign countries, and was only required to notify the British Foreign Office in advance of the intention, but permission was not mandatory.

The Commonwealth and Foreign Offices maintained, quite wrongly in our view, that these entrustments required re-negotiation now that the Federation had been dissolved. We had, however, a written note by the previous Commonwealth Secretary that confirmed our view that we had inherited the right under the Federal Entrustments.

Such an occasion had arisen in Lisbon where we intended with the agreement of the Portuguese Government to appoint an envoy. The British Government maintained that he should be part of the British Ambassador's staff in that capital. We maintained that he had the right of separation.

Here was a new point of discord between our two Governments, and the incumbent Mr. Harry Reedman was on the high seas and on the point of arriving at Southhampton, for a fortnight's leave in England, prior to proceeding to Lisbon. The diplomatic pot was now beginning to boil.

6. Rogue Diplomat

Mr. Bottomley, the Commonwealth Secretary of State, had by now completed his tour of the West African States.

At our first meeting I had enlarged upon the sensationalism of the Press and informed him that it was not my intention to make statements which might be misconstrued and misreported or even distorted and thus embarrass the negotiations between our respective governments. I knew he was in silent agreement with me over this matter, for he himself must have felt some embarrassment over alleged statements uttered in Lusaka some time previously, and which had excused the behaviour of the African Nationalists in Rhodesia.

We therefore had an unspoken but well-understood pact on this subject and one which I had scrupulously observed. However, certain statements emanated from Lagos, mostly as replies to questions on the use of force against Rhodesia.

As a result of this an article appeared in *The Times* by the defence correspondent of that journal, and this stated that Britain had a military plan for intervention in Rhodesia under certain circumstances. It created quite a stir and brought forth an instant denial from Mr. Healey, the British Defence Minister, and several questions from Conservative members of Parliament, who also got through to me on the telephone.

Having been a staff officer in the British Army, I was well aware that such a plan must exist in the files of the Director of Plans in the War Office. In fact, if no such plan had existed and I had been the CIGS, I would have severely reprimanded the Director of Plans. There are plans for every conceivable political situation and many that are inconceivable, and there must undoubtedly be one for Rhodesia. This would be a contingency plan, in the event of any *de facto* government of the country calling for aid to restore law and order and deal with a situation it could not control itself. This would be irrespective of whatever government held power at that time, in Britain as well as Rhodesia.

I felt that Mr. Bottomley had been caught unawares or misreported and contented myself, when approached by the Press for comment, by saying that Rhodesians could and would defend themselves against aggression from any quarter.

As it happened, the Rhodesian Army and Air Force Chiefs of Staff were in England attending the autumn Services Conferences, and I had arranged a luncheon in their honour at the Savoy to which I had invited their opposite numbers in the British Services. This was an enjoyable and purely social occasion, devoid of any political undertones, which had been arranged some weeks before. We had a good laugh among ourselves at the fuss the Press was making over this affair, but otherwise did not refer to it.

I was amused to see the subject was again referred to in a front page column next day, and carefully inserted in a paragraph below was a news item which read that the Rhodesian High Commissioner had given a lunch to the service chiefs of the two countries at the Savoy. So does the Press operate by insinuations, which may give a totally false and sinister impression on the public mind.

At our next encounter Mr. Bottomley did not refer to his alleged remarks in Nigeria, nor did I. The *status quo* was restored.

The subject of Rhodesia's diplomatic representation in Lisbon now took up the headlines for nearly three weeks. Harry Reedman, who had been a Cabinet Minister in Ian Smith's government, had been selected to represent Rhodesia in Portugal and a dispute arose between the two governments over this appointment. The British view was that a Rhodesian diplomat must operate within the British embassy, as was the case in Washington, and could not set up shop on his own. There was precedent for a Consul-General and this might be acceptable to the British, but such an individual would not have access to Portuguese Ministers, and in view of the importance of close relations between Portugal and Rhodesia it was essential that an independent and high ranking diplomat from Rhodesia should be stationed in Lisbon.

The Portuguese Government was willing to accept Harry Reedman as an independent diplomat, the British had been informed according to the requirements of the Federal Entrustments, and he had already set sail to take up his appointment in Lisbon.

A triangular battle developed between London, Lisbon and Salisbury over the question of his recognition. As far as we were concerned the Rhodesians stood firmly on the entrustments, and I was instructed to see Mr. Bottomley and inform him of our intention, which by these entrustments was all that was required of us. I refused to be drawn into any discussion over the entrustments, stating that we now intended announcing Mr. Reedman's appointment within the next week.

Intense diplomatic activity followed. The Americans appeared to be actively supporting the British and even NATO was brought into the matter, with a view to bringing pressure on the Portuguese Government. The Press received a brief on the entrustments and the Rhodesian view on this disputed affair. Meanwhile Harry Reedman arrived in London for a fortnight's leave before going to Lisbon.

It was now accepted that Harry Reedman would establish himself in Lisbon in an independent capacity. The issue was one of title and status, and this would cause considerable embarrassment in diplomatic circles in Lisbon. The main object was access to Portuguese Ministers, and this was to be achieved, for the Portuguese authorities handled this delicate business with great skill and, I think, with a certain amount of amusement. It is certain that they got back a little of their own over Goa and the let-down on that issue by their oldest allies.

The day before Reedman's arrival I received a signal from Salisbury which laid down our policy in this matter. It ran as follows: "Minister instructs that Reedman is not to see United Kingdom Ministers or officials regarding Lisbon appointment, and that he is not to discuss it with the Press. Minister also instructs that whilst you are obviously open to receipt of messages in this regard from the British Government, you are to make no pronouncement on the Government's stand."

As the Press hounds were swarming round Rhodesia House and it was thought that a statement on our position to certain responsible journalists might assist our case in London, we asked Salisbury if we might put the correct legal position again to the public.

To this request a signalled reply was received: "Minister of External Affairs states that all policies and information in this matter must remain centralised in Salisbury. No interviews must be given. It is highly probable that a full statement will be made this week."

In this delicate matter which also concerned the Portuguese Government, this was a wise decision. We in Rhodesia House were ignorant of what communications had passed between Lisbon and

Salisbury, and anything we said from our London end might queer the pitch.

I heaved a sigh of relief when I received this signal and informed the Press to expect news from Rhodesia. From then on, apart from the interview I had been told to have with Mr. Bottomley and to which I have referred, my task was to keep Harry under wraps till he left England. Unknown to the Press he then departed on holiday to his family in England.

While he was away the almost dormant issue of our independence flared up. Discussions had been going on between the British and Rhodesian Governments through the High Commissioner in Salisbury. I was supposed to be kept in the picture by the Commonwealth Relations Office in London, but as I had suspected nothing was passed on. The excuse was that these talks were purely verbal and there was nothing formal to pass on to me. However, on 11th September a signal was received by me which referred to a previous signal from the Secretary of State to our Prime Minister, which I was instructed to deliver. I had no idea to what this previous signal referred because the CRO had never sent me a copy.

This was exactly the occasion I required to make my protest and to demand to be put fully in the picture as to what had been going on. The message I had to deliver to Mr. Bottomley reached me on Saturday afternoon, 11th September. It ran as follows:

1. Thank you for your message of the 7th September.

2. Considerable time has elapsed since Mr. Hughes's visit, which was itself preceded by the visit of you and Lord Gardiner. As you know these occasions have been preceded by other visits in both directions, and discussions with the British Government extending over a long period of time. The real value of personal contact in the course of negotiations is largely nullified if the issues raised, and the proposals resulting from the discussions, receive no definite response from the British Government. I share your disappointment at the lack of progress, but I can only point out the reason, which is that the British Government has still not replied to the proposals put forward by my Government at the time of Mr. Hughes's departure from Rhodesia, on the 27th July.

3. I have repeatedly over (past) weeks, without success, pressed your High Commissioner for a reply, and I regret to say the impres-

sion is gaining ground that your Government has no intention of granting independence to Rhodesia. This impression is deepened when, to the delays in reaching agreement over independence, is added the reaction of your Government to the appointment of Mr. Reedman to Lisbon. Your expressions of anxiety to see – we quote – a successful conclusion – unquote – do little to counteract this.

4. My Government regards the matter of Rhodesia's independence as one of extreme urgency. While I expressed my willingness to meet with you again, it was in anticipation of an early and effective response to our proposals which Mr. Hughes carried back to England.

5. In these circumstances, consider that the next step is for your Government to let me have a definite reply as to whether these proposals are acceptable to yourselves or not. End.

Denzil Bradley called for me with the signal, and we went to Rhodesia House to have it typed out. We then arranged through Mr. Bottomley's Secretary to deliver it to his home at Woodford Green. We motored out via the City and arrived about 4.30 p.m. Having half an hour to spare we parked near the common, which included such pastoral scenes as grazing cows and a golf course, and then in due course went to Mr. Bottomley's house, a small unpretentious villa in a row of semi-detached houses.

Here I was greeted warmly by Mr. Bottomley where I delivered the message. Smiling broadly he informed me that he was intending to visit Rhodesia between 13–14th October and had arranged this with my Prime Minister two days previously. I concealed my astonishment, and obliquely asked what had transpired since Mr. Hughes's visit, hoping that I was not betraying my ignorance.

He informed me fully about the five principles that his Government had put to Mr. Smith and said he was now awaiting concrete suggestions by our Government as to how these were to be implemented. These five principles were:

The principle and intention of unimpeded progress to majority rule, already enshrined in the 1961 Constitution, would have to be guaranteed and maintained.

There would have to be guarantees against retrogressive amendment of the Constitution.

There would have to be immediate improvement in the political status of the African population.

There would have to be progress towards ending racial discrimination.

The British Government would need to be satisfied that any basis proposed for independence was acceptable to the people of Rhodesia as a whole.

I then suggested it might save time and be better all round if the British Government were more specific and themselves suggested the practical means by which these should be implemented. "No," replied Mr. Bottomley, that was for our Government to do, and then the suggestions would be examined by the British Government.

In fact, it was the old expedient of horse trading, a technique as old as man, by which one got one's opponent to name his price, and then with this advantage commenced bargaining. The end of such a dialogue had been illustrated time and again in the constitutions which had been framed in Kenya and Northern Rhodesia. Our previous governments had been naïve enough to fall for this one, but times had changed considerably since those unenlightened days.

I elaborated on the 1961 Constitution and informed Mr. Bottomley that in my view all these principles were already enshrined in it, and that it had already been accepted in accordance with the last principle as far back as 1962.

I was informed that this was 1965, not 1962, and world opinion and times had changed.

It was at this moment that I realised that our hopes of gaining independence under the constitution were slim, however far back we bent to meet the British Government. At the same time I was aware, not for the first time, that delay in negotiation was a principle of British tactics, and if the negotiations could be delayed till the unpleasant dish could be passed to another party, or to the Commonwealth as a whole in the following year, so much the better.

The topic turned to the Indian-Pakistan war, then well under way and another headache for the long-suffering Secretary of State for Commonwealth Relations. Over a glass of orange juice I spoke of both these countries as I had been born in India and my father in Lahore where the fighting was taking place, and I knew the sub-continent well.

46

Denzil Bradley and I took our leave at 6 p.m. after a very pleasant hour with the Secretary of State in his home, and I apologised for disturbing him during a Saturday afternoon. Later I discovered that during this visit I had dropped my tobacco pouch somewhere in the village of Woodford Green, as a memento of this visit. It was filled with Rhodesian tobacco which will presumably now be a rarity in England.

We returned hot-foot to Rhodesia House where I sent off the following signal:

From High Commissioner to Prime Minister. Your message delivered to Bottomley 5 p.m. Saturday at his home. He informed me that he was going to Salisbury from 13th to 14th October for agreed discussion with you. Understand arranged 2 days previously but I not repeat not informed.

I took this opportunity to hear what had previously transpired and could only presume your message designed extract written proposals or agenda. Asked if these would be forthcoming before visit Bottomley hedged.

Present loose arrangements keep me in picture obviously not working. C.R.O. adept taking advantage this rather nebulous channel which could lead to dangerous wire crossing to our disadvantage. Forced to rely on quick wit and political acumen to keep end up. Report follows bag.

Followed up at once by this letter:

"I am afraid you are incorrect in assuming I would have received a copy of Mr. Wilson's letter from the Commonwealth Relations Office. The British Government rarely, if ever, sends a copy to Rhodesia House of communications that have been addressed to your Office and this present instance is just another example of the unsatisfactory nature of a system which relies upon my being kept in the picture by the British rather than by my own Government.

" I shall be grateful if urgent consideration may please be given to taking steps at your end to overcome the disadvantageous position in which I am placed."

I knew it would bring a reaction, and I was not wrong. Our cypher-machine became red-hot during the following week as signal after signal poured in with the information that the CRO had neglected

47

to give me. Then the diplomatic bags arrived with more detail and at last I was fully briefed up to the minute.

It was towards the latter end of this week that Harry Reedman arrived back in London, and during the few days before his departure I arranged for him to meet Mr. Villas Boaz, the Portuguese Chargé d'Affaires, who was acting as Head of Mission while Mr. Rocheta, the Ambassador, was on leave in Portugal. Through him we kept in touch with the situation at the Lisbon end and I briefed Harry on our affairs in London and the progress of negotiations which would help him in Lisbon.

One of my problems was to get him out of London without the Press swarming round him. He had already decided to take a leaf out of Mr. Bottomley's book, who when he encountered the press men at Salisbury airport the previous February blandly remarked on the lovely weather. The day of Harry's departure was fortunately fine and such a remark would be apt. I accompanied him to London airport, and had made arrangements with Villas Boaz to hurry him up to the Portuguese airline office, waiting till the plane was about to depart and smuggle him aboard.

I began to think that Harry had other ideas. On arrival at the airport we were met by Villas Boaz, and the manager of the Portuguese airline, but Harry had also arranged for two of his friends to see him off. Our plan went wrong at once for Harry insisted on chatting at the car to his friends. I hurriedly dispatched it with its tell-tale flag to the car park, and urged him into the building. The place was swarming with camera-men on the look-out, but they were unable to identify their prey. Read, our Information Secretary, suddenly spotted the bold initials on Harry's brief-case, and we swiftly turned them inwards towards his legs, but it was too late, they had identified him. So we hurried through various lounges, past barriers and the queues waiting there, managed to dodge most of the journalists, and only a snap or two were taken. There was one final exit lounge beyond which his plane was waiting but this was thronged with camera-men. We could go no further with him so we said our good-byes, and watched him blithely march on. Suddenly Read nudged me and pointed. The brief-case was once more reversed and the initials H.R. were plain to see. How this had happened I do not know, but my responsibilities were over and I could do no more. The cameras popped and our rogue diplomat was swallowed in a mass of press men.

48

I later learned that the aircraft was filled with hopeful correspondents who were on the way to Lisbon to report the fun on arrival. I eagerly and anxiously scanned the evening papers and next day's editions, and was relieved to see that Harry had commented on the weather and nothing else as arranged. We were also treated to a fine series of photographs of him, in and out of his car, seated in the aircraft with a magazine and so forth. Unlike myself he was obviously photogenic and moreover a politician, and so I forgave him.

What happened in Lisbon was another story.

But from now the limelight was to be turned on Rhodesia House. We were watched like hawks, and it took all my ingenuity to avoid the Press and the ubiquitous camera.

7. The Public Approach

The Rhodesian Government had managed, in the spirit of the Federal entrustments, to get some sort of diplomatic representation in Portugal and from now on tried with the quiet and sympathetic aid of the Portuguese Government to have the *de facto* recognition turned into a *de jure* one.

To achieve this required a "softy softy catchee monkey" approach, or a constant nibble in tiny bites at the apple. Unfortunately small incidents and a Portuguese radio broadcast by our new envoy, all blown up by the British Press, kept the matter in the headlines for the next week or so and caused me a few headaches in London. The Commonwealth Relations Office, with an eye on the forthcoming negotiations which pressure from Salisbury made impossible to be delayed, was anxious to drop the matter, but the Foreign Office was not to be kept quiet so easily.

These press reports and interviews did nothing to mollify them, but fortunately the situation became very quiet from the Lisbon end, and reports came to me that Harry Reedman had got his diplomatic privileges and the CD plates on his car. His title, the main bone of contention, became the Rhodesian Agent, or Envoy in Lisbon, or something equally nebulous and the full story of this fascinating diplomatic incursion will, I hope, be told by Harry Reedman in a book which will cover many more days than my 115 and may possibly stretch to the 4,000 of a previous epic in Rhodesia's historical bibliography.

During the latter days of the Federation the Federal Government had launched a massive and costly publicity campaign through "Voice and Vision" which caused an influential body of people to become interested in Central Africa and the ex-colonies in general. They deplored the break-up of the Federation, and in particular the collapse of the multi-racial experiment it contained. How many of them realised that this latter concept was a non-starter at this period of history and African advancement, I don't know. With all the goodwill in the world by the European in Africa it could never work at this stage. The African politicians were too avid for power, a power they would never share, and should they wish to share it for practical reasons of economics and administration, the pressures from their ignorant one-man-one-vote followers would be too great for them. If they resisted, the one-man-one-vote system itself would sweep them from power in favour of less educated demagogues.

Even if a man strong enough to resist these pressures could be found, the Afro-Asian states and the United Nations would turn their hostile attentions to him. The examples of Tshombe and the Congo were plain for all to see. Even Dr. Banda, who was endeavouring to resist such pressures, had to resort to undemocratic methods to maintain his position and fight a slow battle of resistance in which the position of the European in the multi-racial society would become impossible.

We in Rhodesia had realised this from what we had seen happening to the north of us, and were determined to control the rate of African political advancement to power till time and education had made it a safe possibility. Moreover we wished to have the power to retard it, should that advancement outstrip the capability of the African to govern wisely and fairly.

No arbitrary time limit, so desired by the British politician, could be put on this empiric and realistic approach to the problem. We could not say five, ten, fifty or a thousand years. It could not be forced, it had to develop in accordance with the character and nature of the African and his hitherto unproved qualities of democratic behaviour. After all, it had taken England five centuries to develop from autocratic monarchy to universal franchise and this had not been completed till recent times and within the lifetime of most of us. Even Switzerland, that democratic model, has yet not enfranchised the female half of its population.

Those who supported the British point of view were not in touch with reality. To these people I tried to put across the view that their ideals could only be maintained if the people of Rhodesia were given independence, and the freedom to solve their own internal racial problems during an indefinite period of time. I put out the analogy of the young couple where mother-in-law was still installed in the house. As long as she remained there, they could never make the adjustments necessary for a successful partnership.

In other words, we had to be allowed to settle matters without outside advice and interference, and be trusted to do this fairly. After all, we were the same kind of people as they were, but we were on the spot and had to live in the country, and it was therefore in our interest to evolve some system of racial harmony that in the end would satisfy their ideals.

The realists amongst them soon adjusted themselves to this idea, and even resigned themselves to the possibility of our taking matters into our own hands as the best means of achieving our mutual aims. The others however were concerned at the effect this action would have on the Afro-Asian members of the Commonwealth, and the possibility that this Commonwealth would break up.

I put the view that the Commonwealth was in dire need of a shake-up, and those many new nations who were not obviously subscribing to the ideals of the Commonwealth were better out of it. Many shied away from the idea of such an upheaval, some through fear of economic loss to Britain and others through fear of a new alignment of African states to the Communist world. This of course was happening anyhow, particularly in Ghana and the East African states, and it would continue whatever appeasements were made.

It was the old story of Munich again, and with far less cause. What some people in Britain never realised, was that the African always gravitates to the stronger. The best way of retaining the African states to Britain's cause was a strong approach and a sharp reprimand. The crack of the whip was what they understood best and in the long run appreciated. This was the way to retain them in the Commonwealth, not by constant appeasement and turning a blind eye to their shortcomings.

To my mind the Rhodesian issue could be used for this purpose. We had to be given our independence, their outcries to be ignored, and they had to be told bluntly to mind their own business.

Unfortunately the days of Palmerston were long past and it seemed that neither party in Britain had the courage to take this action. I was convinced that such an approach to these new Commonwealth nations would be greatly appreciated by the bulk of the British nation, who were now getting thoroughly tired of being pushed around by these client states.

Honor and I had last observed the British political scene at close quarters in 1946, and were now able to assess it on the spot. We came to the conclusion that the British people were frustrated and apathetic about politics in general. There seemed to be no real leadership in either political party since the days of Churchill and Eden. The Conservatives had adopted a policy of "Me too", and both parties were following the line of least resistance in foreign and domestic affairs. Harold Wilson's apparent success seemed due to the fact that he represented some show of strength, even if wrongly directed, and he gave at least an impression of determination. If a really strong Conservative leader emerged, one who was prepared to take a firm line on foreign and Commonwealth affairs, as well as on the domestic front, and was able to reassert Britain's independent role in world affairs without equivocation and hesitation, then, we thought, the British people would respond wholeheartedly to such a lead. Lacking such a lead, there seemed to be no alternative to a Labour Government under Mr. Wilson.

The publicity campaign launched by the Federal Government had however made little impact on the man in the street to whom the whole concept of a multi-racial Central African Federation was of academic interest only. A much more personal approach to the general public was needed and we aimed at a sense of personal, even emotional identity with Rhodesia. In this we were greatly helped by the liberals and the Afro-Asians who, by overstating their case in the numerous well-attended "teach-ins" at universities and T.V. sessions, did much to turn public opinion in our favour.

We published advertisements in the papers, and by dignified and reasoned statements through such channels as were available to us, together with articles by journalists favourable to us, we did much to enlighten public opinion and provide material and arguments. A general appreciation of our aims and ideals became noticeable throughout Britain, and the tremendous publicity which attended the arrival of the Rhodesian Prime Minister, and his appearance and demeanour on T.V., did much to foster our cause with the general public.

It was also brought home to the British public that the Rhodesians, in relation to their numbers, had done as much to help the Allied cause during the Second World War as any other part of the Commonwealth, and considerably more than the newer nations of the Commonwealth. Three windows of Rhodesia House were latterly filled with photographs of our cabinet members and their war records. I personally represented my country at the various memorial ceremonies, laying my country's wreath, and these occasions were widely publicised on T.V. and in the Press.

There still remained two important sections of the British public – the businessmen and the politicians – whose self-interest had to be geared to our cause. Both sections regarded our insistence on early independence as an irritating nuisance.

The business world wanted nothing to interfere with their profits for at least the next five years. They were all for maintaining the *status quo,* even if at the end of that time an African nationalist government were in power in Rhodesia, with which they could make their terms. They were naturally unconcerned with the Rhodesians who were wholly committed to Rhodesia and whose future was dependent on responsible government.

The only way to enlist the help of hard-headed businessmen was to tell them frankly that we would not let matters drift to suit them or anyone else. We would negotiate to the bitter end, hoping that the British Government would come to an agreement, and hoping that the businessmen would lend their influence to this end. When the question of our assuming our independence inevitably cropped up, and they intimated the effects it would have on their trade relations with us, the reply was given that we were aware of all the repercussions and had weighed them up very thoroughly, but would still go ahead as we considered this was firstly to our long-term benefit, and secondly to theirs. In such a case they should put pressure on the British Government to play down the sanctions in the interests of British business, or failing that, take steps to bypass them.

For good measure I added that British industrial and commercial interests were not paramount in our scheme of things, and that other nations were only too eager to step into their shoes and would remain there. They were well aware that this was so, and were politely told about our determination so that they could assess the situation and take such action as they thought necessary for the future.

The politicians were preoccupied with retaining their power or wresting it from the other party. Neither party wanted to be accessory to breaking up the Commonwealth as it existed or offending the United States and United Nations. The only lever which could shift them was public opinion, through the votes of the electorate at the next election.

At this time the Labour Government had a majority of two in the

54

The Hon. Ian Douglas Smith, Prime
Minister

The Hon. W. J. Harper, Minister of
Internal Affairs and Public Service

The Hon. D. W. Lardner-Burke, Minister of Justice and Law and Order

The Hon. J. J. Wrathall, Minister of
Finance and Posts

The Rhodesian Ministerial Delegation. (Photos: Basil Shackleton. Permission:
Rhodesian Ministry of Information)

The Hon. P. K. van der Byl, Minister of Information

The Hon. I. F. McLean, Minister of Labour, Social Welfare and Health

(Photos: Basil Shackleton. Permission: Rhodesian Ministry of Information)

House of Commons, in which over Rhodesia, they were sustained by the Liberal vote. Even so, with 55 marginal seats in which a comparatively few votes might unseat the ruling party, sympathy for Rhodesia was a political factor that neither party could ignore. The key therefore, in negotiations, and in the latter event of a declaration of independence by Rhodesia with the consequent application of sanctions by Britain, lay with the man in the street and his vote. This fact must have troubled many a politician. The difficulty was to translate this anxiety into concrete action.

This could only be done by constituents, sympathetic to Rhodesia, writing to their M.P.s, giving their views, and by friends of ours exerting such influence as they had in the parties. Many letters were published, especially in the provincial papers, and must have influenced the politicians.

The British electorate probably has very little idea how their politicians' minds work, or to what depths they can sink. Both before and, as it turned out, after 11th November subtle suggestions were put to the Rhodesians, not only in London but also in Rhodesia and as far afield as its other diplomatic missions, by British politicians or their emissaries. The suggestions were verbal, of course, never in writing and all "off the record".

They intimated: "Look, you chaps, be sensible. We all want to settle this independence issue. Why not accept our conditions and a new constitution, get your independence and soon afterwards tear the thing up? No one will bother you. After all, everyone is doing it now. Look at Ghana."

Our reply to this was straightforward. We did not act that way. Our word was our bond. If we gave an undertaking we carried it out to the bitter end. Maybe this was an old-fashioned way to act, but we had been brought up on the old British values. Maybe we had been too long in Africa and were out of touch with British political thought, but we were not prepared to change.

Moreover we had to live in Rhodesia, and to act in this dishonourable manner would not foster harmony between the races. We had always behaved with justice and fairness towards our African people, and this they knew and understood. They admired honesty, and responded to it.

The politicians smiled pityingly at our naivety. "These colonials, you know – so out of date and unworldly! "

Our distrust of the British politician was increased by this cynical solution to the problem, and we began to suspect a trap behind this approach. If we had lowered ourselves to act in this way, what guarantee had we that they would not have then turned upon us in holy and righteous wrath, denounced our bad faith and with the justified backing of public opinion moved in to destroy us. After all, true to custom, this suggestion had not been given in writing. The reader may judge how disillusioned the Rhodesians had become with years of double-talk and this sort of chicanery.

Our publicity campaign was strengthened by a team of prominent Rhodesians who were sent for a period of three weeks. It consisted of Mr. John Strong, a surgeon; Mr. Wickus de Kock, a farmer; Mr. Jeremy Field, a farmer; Mr. Ian Tunmer; a mayor; Mr. R. Henwood, a company director; Mr. Charles Allen, an advocate.

The leader of this team, Mr. C. G. Tracey, had great experience of this type of publicity work. He was the founder and moving spirit behind the Rhodesian Promotion Council which had been active in interesting visiting overseas businessmen in investing in Rhodesia, and he had moved about in the States, Britain and the Continent on behalf of this council. He had as a result a great number of invaluable contacts. A man of tremendous energy, drive and imagination, he arrived while the Prime Minister and his team were in England, and during the week before the arrival of his lecturers was able with the help of Mr. Dimond, our PRO, and the Information Section under Alan Izod, to prepare platforms and engagements throughout Britain for the next three weeks.

This team, which covered a wide field of interests and talents, spent a very busy time touring the country and contacting business organisations. They gave TV and Press interviews, and held meetings in the country sponsored by the Anglo-Rhodesian Society, the Rotarians and other bodies. Neither my staff nor I were able at this time to leave London, but this team was able to cover ground which would have taken Rhodesia House several months to deal with.

For ten days during their stay in England I was absent in Rhodesia for consultation with the Rhodesian Government, while Mr. Wilson and his colleagues were in Salisbury. During this period, apart from lecturing round the country, some members of the team were in close contact with business interests, and here they reinforced the views I had put before these people. From the findings of this tour they compiled a valuable report for the Rhodesian Government, and in this report one fact became very clear:

When Rhodesia House opens again in London, either as a High Commission or an Embassy, the staff should include a private individual with business or financial experience with the rank of Minister, under the High Commissioner or Ambassador. Heading the trade section of the Embassy, he should have the sole task of developing the external trade of our country. Most missions in London have a diplomat of this high rank who is charged with this task and he is listed in the Diplomatic List as Minister in charge of Commercial Affairs. This diplomat has access by virtue of his rank to the board-rooms of all important concerns, and can deal on equal diplomatic terms with his opposite numbers in the missions of other countries represented in London. Our overseas trade and investment would benefit enormously through such an appointment.

During the period of October and early November Rhodesia House was filled with Ministers, top civil servants and others. Office accommodation was somehow improvised for them, and our earlier routine thrown out of gear. The place was a hive of activity and there was never a dull moment. By 6th November Tracey's team, the last of the visitors, had departed with a vitally important task well done, and we were alone again. With the approaching crisis upon us, we indeed felt out on a limb and very lonely.

However, we had done all we could to put the Rhodesian case to the British public. From now on it became a holding action till interest faded and new issues occupied the British scene. The public were becoming bored with our affairs, and for one whole day Rhodesia appeared briefly on back pages, a thing that had not happened for weeks. Then on 11th November we jumped back into the headlines and became the centre of interest again, but by now it was an interest that was far better informed than it had been four months before.

To that extent our efforts had been successful and our time and the comparatively little money we had spent, not been wasted.

8. Preliminary Moves

From the urgent signals and letters from Salisbury, which now kept me informed of the negotiations between our Prime Minister and the British Government, it appeared that nothing so far had been put in writing, though notes of the conversations had been made by the respective parties. No formal minutes of these meetings had been taken or agreed.

Ideas had been exchanged and something had vaguely emerged. Working on the five principles enunciated during Mr. Bottomley's visit to Rhodesia in February, it seemed that there was a possibility of a House of Chiefs being formed, which could meet the necessity of a blocking third. This was an idea I had myself touched upon in a private letter to the Prime Minister of Rhodesia during August. There had been talk of an increase in the franchise for the B roll with the elimination of the cross vote.* The British Government seemed to be determined that the first move in this horse trading game should come from the Rhodesians, and that they should be the first to put their ideas on paper.

This process could go on for ever, until the Rhodesians had been worn down and confidence in their Government dissipated.

About this time urgent warnings reached me from influential

---

*The "B" Roll voters vote not only for one of the 15 electoral district candidates but also have a vote for the "A" Roll candidate in the constituency contained in their electoral district. But here their votes count for 25% of the number of "A" Roll votes cast in that constituency, and are accordingly devalued if the number cast exceeds one quarter of the "A" Roll votes cast. If the number of "B" Roll votes cast is less than 25% of the "A" Roll votes cast, their vote is accordingly a full vote.

Likewise the "A" Roll voters cast a vote for one of the electoral district candidates for the electoral district which contains their constituency. Likewise their vote counts for only 25% of the "B" Roll votes for the electoral district candidate, and is devalued accordingly.

In practice, during the last two elections under the system, very few "B" Roll voters have turned out to vote. In all cases less than the "A" Roll votes were cast and so they have had a full vote in practice. But the "A" Roll voters have in consequence had their votes devalued very considerably when voting for the electoral district candidate.

friends that unless we were able to meet the British Government requirements, the whole process of negotiation would be dragged on till the next Commonwealth Premier's Conference in June or July, 1966.

A Commonwealth Secretariat was already being set up in London, and at this conference Britain's predominant place in its councils would be abdicated. The Afro-Asians who would have a predominant vote in this miniature United Nations, would demand early action on Rhodesia, and concerted Commonwealth pressure would be exerted on Rhodesia with the object of bringing the African nationalists to power. Britain, even if she had the will, would not have the desire or power to resist these pressures, because these states would threaten withdrawal from the Commonwealth unless action was taken to bend the Rhodesian Government to their will.

At the last Commonwealth Conference Britain had been pledged to speed up African rule in Rhodesia. She would be expected to produce results at the next. But the pledge implied that the present constitution did not provide for sufficient development or speed. To meet the pledge Britain would have to change that Constitution. The British Government was bound by convention not to interfere in Rhodesia's internal affairs, but it had also stated publicly that, in this situation, Commonwealth interests had to be paramount. Amidst the cynicism of modern politics Rhodesians could be excused for their belief that the convention would not long be a protection.

Nor would the changes be merely a matter of degree, for Britain was committed to the Commonwealth line, laid down by the predominance of Afro-Asian members, who were racially united in their denial of any racial bias. That line was majority rule for Rhodesia now. The British Government disagreed with this line, but by its own admission of Commonwealth commitment, it was no longer a free agent. To Rhodesians the implications were obvious.

Thus we in Rhodesia would be faced with sanctions, force and embargoes, and this at a time when our tobacco was being sold and payments being made for it.

Furthermore by that time the many distractions that afflicted the Americans and British, such as Vietnam and the Malaysian confrontation together with the Indian-Pakistan war, might have been dealt with and Britain could turn her undivided attention upon us. In addition, the shelving of the British responsibility for Rhodesia to the Commonwealth would provide a perfect alibi to both parties in Britain and clear them with their electorate if any action was taken against us.

I checked these warnings from various sources, and came to the conclusion that they were genuine and that real danger faced Rhodesia if these negotiations were allowed to drag on to the following year. The fact that we took our stand on our existing 1961 Constitution, and that the onus rested on the Commonwealth taking matters into its own hands, would avail us little, legally or morally, when such

"... but you – you're just an Enemy of the Queen!" (From the "Daily Express", October 2, 1965. Permission: London Express Service)

concerted pressure was brought to bear on us at such an unfavourable time.

Moreover, it was possible that a general election would occur in early 1966, and one or other of the two parties would be in power with a clear majority for five years and unresponsive to public opinion as a result. This was a major factor which influenced the need for an immediate solution.

There seemed to be a marked disinclination on the part of the Labour Party to tackle the problem. There it lay on the political plate with other unsavoury items to be digested, a bit of gristle to be eaten last if possible, each party hoping that it would fall to the lot of the other to devour it and possibly choke itself to electoral death as a result.

So the matter had to be settled before Christmas 1965. The Rhodesian public was getting restive, confidence in the Government's firm resolution was beginning to wane. Investment and development were suffering, and all the time the bogy of emigration, halted and reversed since 1963, was in the minds of responsible Rhodesians.

Bottomley had suggested that he pay another visit to Rhodesia on 13th October, as indicated in his message to the Rhodesian Prime Minister dated 13th September 1965.

"I have received the message which you asked your High Commissioner to deliver to me on the 11th September. I have also had from our own High Commissioner in Salisbury a full report of your long conversation with him on the same day, which you described to him as more important than the message itself. I am treating it accordingly.

"I frankly do not understand your request for a definite reply to the proposals put forward by your Government at the time of Mr. Hughes's departure from Rhodesia. There were no concrete proposals put forward by either side during Mr. Hughes's personal conversations with yourself. There was further exploration of possible ways whereby effect might be given to the major points of principle on which the British Government would need to be satisfied before granting independence to Rhodesia. You commented in your final talk with Mr. Hughes that there was still a wide gap between us, but it was agreed that the possibilities should be further examined.

"We have been giving thought to all this and I now want to discuss the whole problem with you. I cannot help being greatly concerned over the apparent hardening of your views, as you have now put them to our High Commissioner, on all essential aspects of any settlement, as compared with the prospects of a negotiated solution which seemed to be opened up by the talks which you and I had in February. Nevertheless, I have proposed a visit to Salisbury and you have agreed, and I am sure this is the right step. I think you will agree it would hardly be responsible to come to vital decisions on which the whole future of Rhodesia depends by long-range correspondence."

It seemed that this would only drag on to a further inconclusive result. If he came to some sort of decision, it would still have to be argued and ratified by the British Prime Minister and his Cabinet.

Accordingly Mr. Smith decided to come to London for talks, and intimated that these were to be the final ones. The bluff had been called by the Rhodesians at long last – the chips were down. A decision one way or another would be made within a month or so.

Anxious persons approached me – almost wringing their hands – and told me how worried they were about Rhodesia, for they understood the implications of this confrontation. I blandly replied that we Rhodesians were not worried; on the contrary, those of us of British extraction were exceedingly worried about Britain. What was wrong with the nation of 1940? Couldn't they stand up to these new insolvent nations who made such a noise; why were they so worried, who had never worried in the dark years of the war? Word got round and came back to us that everyone in Britain was worried about Rhodesia's future with the exception of Rhodesia House and Rhodesians in England. I hoped it would create the correct impression for the talks which lay ahead.

On 16th September I had received a message to deliver personally to Mr. Bottomley which was a reply to his letter to the Rhodesian Prime Minister on 13th September.

"From the Hon. I. D. Smith, Prime Minister of Rhodesia to the Rt. Hon. Arthur Bottomley, O.B.E., M.P., Secretary of State for Commonwealth Relations.

"1. Thank you for your message of the 13th September. I had been expecting to receive some definite and concrete opinions from the British Government on how they viewed my ideas put to Mr. Hughes when he was out here. In particular, the concept of a Senate was raised and quite definite views were put forward to your Legal Adviser, Sir William Dale. I had hoped that I would have received by now comments from the British Government on these suggestions.

"2. The purpose of my talk with your High Commissioner on Saturday was to introduce a further element into our negotiations, namely, that if we cannot come to terms with the British Government for our Independence within the Commonwealth, we would be quite prepared to accept Independence outside the Commonwealth. I had been hoping to have received the views of the British Government on this suggestion also, and I regret that these have not been forthcoming.

"3. To judge from your message, the British Government apparently intends to do nothing more until you arrive here for further discussions. I regret that this will not be satisfactory to us because I must make it clear that if you do visit us for discussions those discussions must reach final decisions on our position. I would hope, therefore, that you will be enabled to come out with concrete proposals to present to us and that we will be able to reach final decisions.

"4. No good purpose would be served by your coming to Salisbury for further exploratory talks or general discussions without a mandate. While I agree that vital decisions on the future of Rhodesia should not depend on long-range correspondence, I am sure you will agree equally that they cannot be allowed to be deferred much longer. The hardening of our views here in Rhodesia is not merely apparent; it is very real and serious. So long as the delay in reaching a decision persists the gap between our respective Governments will continue to widen. Six months have elapsed since Lord Gardiner and you visited us; two months have passed since Mr. Cledwyn Hughes arrived here. Our planting season, which affects our all-important agricultural industry, is upon us, and before planting, our farmers expect and are entitled to a decision on our Independence. I have been given no adequate reason as to why there should be any further delay over this question so vital to our future. In view of this, as I have already suggested to your High Commissioner, I believe that you should make your trip here as soon as possible, and at the latest before the end of this month."

The following is an account of the interview that followed, as reported by the Political Counsellor of our mission:

"I accompanied the High Commissioner to the Commonwealth Relations Office at 5 p.m. on Thursday afternoon, 16th September 1965 when Brigadier Skeen kept an appointment with the Secretary of State. Mr. Bottomley had with him Mr. K. J. Neale, Head of the Rhodesia Department, and Mr. O. Forster, his Principal Private Secretary.

"The High Commissioner handed Mr. Bottomley our Prime Minister's reply to the message that Mr. Smith had received from the Secretary of State on the 13th September. After giving Mr. Bottomley time to read this, the High Commissioner said it appeared to him that two main points emerged. Firstly, Mr. Bottomley should do all he could to put forward his visit to Rhodesia and secondly, firm proposals should be set down in writing and forwarded to Mr. Smith in order that consideration might be given to these in advance and that there should be a firm basis upon which discussions could take place in Salisbury.

"The Secretary of State said that, in regard to the first point, he was just about to ask Mr. Johnston to assure our Prime Minister that if at all possible, he would leave for Salisbury earlier than the 12th October. It was only fair to add, however, that with the best will in the world he doubted whether this could be done in view of the serious situation in Kashmir which, if China intervened, could escalate into war on a global scale. There was also the Labour Party Conference at the end of the month – he was just as much a politician as Mr. Smith was and for much the same reasons he would not wish to be absent from the Conference.

"Regarding the second point, Mr. Bottomley disagreed with the High Commissioner. He considered that if anything was to be committed to writing, it should be Mr. Smith's reasons why he no longer felt able to negotiate on the basis of the five principles discussed between our Prime Minister and the Secretary of State last February. Unless these were accepted as the basis upon which discussions should proceed, there would be little point in expressing definite and concrete opinions.

"The High Commissioner explained that since last February, as indicated in the Prime Minister's message, there had been a harden-

64

ing of views in Rhodesia. There was a feeling that matters were being allowed to drift and doubt was becoming widespread as to whether the British Government really wanted to find a solution to the problem of Rhodesia's demand for independence. The Secretary of State found it difficult to believe that public opinion should have moved that much further to the right and considered that our Prime Minister was in a strong position to influence considerably the direction of opinion amongst the Rhodesian electorate.

"In response to the High Commissioner's request, the Secretary of State then outlined the principles that had been discussed last February as follows:

(i) There should be a 'blocking third' or some similar parliamentary safeguard to protect the interests of black Rhodesians.

(ii) Positive steps should be taken to promote rapid African advancement.

(iii) Steps should be taken to abolish racial discrimination.

(iv) The grant of independence conditional on these should command the broad acceptance of the majority of the people of Rhodesia.

(v) There must be no retrogression in any of these directions after the grant of independence.

"The Secretary of State said that whilst these were the British Government's minimum requirements, they were receptive to views from our Government as to how these principles might be put into practice and would not take up a rigid attitude over the time-table for implementing this programme.

"In regard to the first point, Brigadier Skeen pointed out that a 'blocking third' or even a 'blocking quarter' could be achieved in a variety of ways. It would be helpful to have the considered views of the Secretary of State's advisers on this aspect – hence the Prime Minister's reference to the concept of a Senate.

"Concerning the second, this too was a complicated question that required a great deal of thought and opinions should be expressed in order that the two Governments might reach accord as to the nature and extent of what should be done over and above what was being done already in this direction.

"The third point was so nebulous that the High Commissioner felt a statement of intent by his Government should suffice. The Secretary of State disagreed and cited the Land Apportionment

65

Act as an example of discriminatory legislation. Mr. Bottomley added that whilst most governments' intentions were good, in this instance the British Government would have to have something closer to a guarantee than an intention. Brigadier Skeen said he did not wish to argue the merits or demerits of the Land Apportionment Act which was designed to protect the African. He would only point out, however, that the original Act had been amended on many occasions and modified considerably over the years and that this gradual process was continuing. It was declared Government policy to establish multi-racial areas and the delay in translating this policy into practice was largely due to the reluctance of the two racial groups to take up residence in such areas. There was virtually no racial discrimination in public places as far as the Government's sphere of influence was concerned but, in regard to private premises, the Government was averse to legislating to enforce integration or compel multi-racialism.

"The fourth point gave rise to the problem as to how the feeling of the majority of the people could be decided to the satisfaction of the British Government. The views of the majority of the Europeans were not doubtful and as the Government believed, it had already demonstrated at the Domboshawa Indaba the extent to which it enjoyed the support of the tribal Africans in its bid for independence. The British Government, however, had rejected this method.

"The Secretary of State did not rule out the possibility of the political pulse of rural Africans being taken through traditional consultative processes rather than through the ballot box. His mind was not closed on this although both the major Parties in Britain would undoubtedly require something on a wide scale and with a broader base than the Indaba held last year. He could not agree with a remark the High Commissioner had made earlier regarding the African nationalists representing nobody but themselves. It would admittedly make things easier for both Governments if only this were true but his own experiences in Rhodesia last February had convinced him that the nationalists enjoyed a wide measure of support in the urban areas and this was the factor that neither Government could afford to ignore.

"Discussion then turned to the fifth point of principle. The High Commissioner said Rhodesia's record spoke for itself. White Rhodesians could be trusted – it was in their own interests to act honestly and honourably since it was their future that was at stake and it was they who would have to continue living with the problems of the country.

"The Secretary of State did not doubt our Prime Minister's sincerity in this respect but Mr. Bottomley entertained misgivings concerning the intentions of certain elements within the Rhodesian Front.

"The British Government had to convince not only Parliament at Westminster but also the majority of the Commonwealth and responsible member countries at the United Nations that any settlement reached was fair to both major racial groups. He was prepared to defend his actions to the hilt to the Commonwealth and to the United Nations but only if a settlement could be shown to be reasonable.

"The High Commissioner felt that it would be unfortunate if a misunderstanding arose from each side waiting for the other to commit something concrete in writing and again urged the Secretary of State to submit proposals to Mr. Smith prior to his trip. Mr. Bottomley repeated that he and Mr. Smith had reached certain understandings during their private talks in February. He required a definite assurance – which he said he had not had – that our Prime Minister stood by the principles then discussed and which had now been outlined to the High Commissioner before any meaningful progress could be made in putting flesh on the bones. Mr. Bottomley asserted if he had been furnished with an assurance to this effect by, say, last March, Rhodesia would by now be on the very threshold of independence.

"The High Commissioner thanked the Secretary of State for discussing matters so freely and frankly. Brigadier Skeen was convinced that White Rhodesians could be relied upon, once they had gained their independence, to act generously and in the best traditions of their heritage as far as matters affecting African advancement were concerned. The credit for an act of statesmanship would then be Mr. Bottomley's and his Government's standing would be enhanced in the eyes of the British electorate and amongst the more responsible members of the Commonwealth.

"Mr. Bottomley said this might be true, provided things work out after independence as the High Commissioner thought they would.

It took two to make a bargain, however, and Mr. Smith's co-operation and his willingness to make certain concessions to his principles were essential ingredients to any negotiated settlement between Britain and Rhodesia."

It will be seen from this conversation that no reference was made by the Secretary of State to the discussions that had been held between our Prime Minister and Mr. Hughes in July, and apparently the specific suggestions to implement the five principles that had been put forward at that time were to be ignored. Another visit by Mr. Bottomley could only have the same result and more time would be wasted.

Mr. Bottomley's commitments together with the annual Labour Party Conference would not permit his departure to Rhodesia before 13th October, nearly a month hence, and I signalled back to this effect. We were now faced with a further month or more of delay.

On 22nd September I received the signal from Salisbury which stated that Mr. Smith intended to come to London for final discussions as early as possible and that I was to approach Mr. Bottomley with this suggestion.

I did so and found Mr. Bottomley receptive to the suggestion, but as the Labour Party Conference started that weekend and did not finish till the 2nd October which was a Saturday, the earliest that our Prime Minister could come was Monday, 4th October. I would be given a definite answer after the following day's Cabinet meeting.

Mr. Wilson's Cabinet were agreeable to this meeting and I signalled back accordingly, but warned Salisbury that the news should not be allowed to leak out till after the following Thursday when the rules of the Labour Party conference would preclude any debate on Rhodesia being brought up, to avoid jeopardising the negotiations by an unfavourable resolution.

I was informed that Mr. Harper, Minister for Internal Affairs, and Mr. Wrathall, Minister of Finance, would be arriving ahead on Wednesday, 29th September, and would be followed by Mr. Thompson, the Prime Minister's Private Secretary, on Friday. Thereafter the Prime Minister accompanied by Mr. Lardner Burke, Minister of Justice and Law and Order, and Mr. Clarke, Secretary to the Cabinet, would be arriving on Monday, 4th October.

As the first two arrivals would be in the middle of the Labour

Party Conference, I at once signalled back that their arrival should not be coupled with the independence negotiations. It was therefore announced in Salisbury that Mr. Harper and Mr. Wrathall were going to London in response to the High Commisioner's request for a ministerial mission to examine and report on reorganisations necessary at Rhodesia House.

The Press of course were sceptical about this announcement, and although they were unaware at this moment of Mr. Smith's imminent arrival in London, started all sorts of hares. According to them Mr. Wrathall had come to sound the City about financial matters in the event of an assumption of independence and Mr. Harper was an emissary of a junta of "Extremist" right wingers who had come to London to see there was no backsliding by Rhodesia in negotiations. When Mr. Wrathall went north to see some relatives, shortly after his arrival, the public was informed that he was in Blackpool as an observer of the Labour Party Conference.

In actual fact these two ministers, reinforced by Mr. Ravenscroft of the Rhodesian Public Services Board, who had arrived from Rhodesia, and Mr. Young of the Treasury, who was in England at this time, and was recalled from leave, spent the few days before the Prime Minister's arrival doing just what we had announced. They and their officials examined the organisation of Rhodesia House, together with myself and my staff, and produced a valuable report on measures necessary to streamline the work of the mission. Under normal circumstances it was unlikely that such a high level inspection would ever have taken place. As it happened, we were never able to implement the report that was prepared, but it is still available for the day when Rhodesia House reopens with full diplomatic status in London.

On the Wednesday night I had a telephone conversation with Sir Arthur Snelling of the Commonwealth Relations Office, who stated that the news of Mr. Smith's arrival would be released simultaneously next day from Salisbury and London. I was assured that by that time the subject of Rhodesia could not be discussed at the Labour Party Conference. I agreed and signalled Salisbury accordingly. The news became public next day.

Two other members of the Government had arrived in London, but on matters not connected with Mr. Smith's visit. One was Ian McLean, the Minister of Health, who was attending a Commonwealth Medical and Health Conference in Edinburgh with his Director of Health Services, and Mr. P. K. van der Byl who had arrived on leave in England. He was the Deputy Minister for Information and had already been on the Continent on duty in connection with his Department. So we now were to have no less than five ministers of our cabinet and a deputy minister in London at the same time.

Almost half the Government in Rhodesia was concentrated in the High Commissioner's Office, a unique event, which imposed no inconsiderable strain on our communications and clerical system. The Rhodesia House staff responded magnificently to this added work, and particular credit must go to the Information Section and to our three confidential typists and cypher girls, Misses Lee, Clark and Adlington.

Accommodation in London was difficult to find at this time. The Commonwealth Arts Festival was still going on and the Motor Show at Earls Court was commencing. Coupled with this we had to book accommodation for our Ministers under conditions of secrecy, usually under the cover of anonymous visitors to these two functions. We were able after trying 17 hotels and the services of an agency to get the ministerial delegation accommodated at the St. Ermines Court Hotel, whilst Honor and I put up Ian McLean in our small house.

Living as we do in a James Bond world where "bugging", as it is called, is often a fact, we decided that no conferences or work would be carried out except in the High Commissioner's office which was regarded as reasonably secure. After the office had been carefully examined, and a conference table placed in the centre of the room, upon which a transistor radio gently played the latest discordances from the Beatles and Rolling Stones, we were able to discuss the negotiations as they proceeded in hushed voices.

On one particular occasion when something of particular secrecy was discussed, the whole party moved into the ladies' cloakroom on the mezzanine floor, and the High Commissioner stood at the door and diverted the ladies to other female sanctums. I regretted that Bond and Pussy Galore were no longer available to undertake this task, as this particular and peculiar chore as janitor became irksome after the secret conclave dragged on into its second hour.

But I anticipate. The Blackpool conference passed without

reference to Rhodesia, and took up the main headlines. The weekend passed quietly and then on Monday our Prime Minister was due to arrive at London Airport.

The confrontation so long delayed between the Governments of first the Federation, and then of Rhodesia and the British Government, had at last come about. It was to be a decisive one, and I think that by now, at long last, the penny had dropped with the British politician. The Rhodesians meant business. The answer must be Yea or Nay and no procrastination would avail.

9. The Lighter Side

By now seventy-five of my one hundred and fifteen days had passed. The remaining forty were to be ones of intense activity, with a journey to Rhodesia and back, and filled with events of mounting drama. It is therefore time to pause and write of the lighter moments of a diplomat's life before I relate the more sombre and anxious ones.

One of the pleasures of a diplomatic life is the opportunity to take part as an honoured guest in the pageantry of English life which even in this egalitarian and modern age carries on as it has done for centuries. Banquets given by the City Livery companies are often the highlight of the many social events in which a diplomat takes part. Honor and I were fortunate in being asked to attend several of these. The ritual is very reminiscent in many ways of guest nights in regiments of the British Army, and to be privileged to sit at the High Table with several hundred guests and be part of these occasions is a never to be forgotten experience. The opening of Parliament is another, and this we were able to attend only two days before the Mission was closed.

But possibly the most inspiring experiences are the great religious ceremonies held in Westminster Abbey. We were able to attend the service commemorating the 25th anniversary of the Battle of Britain, and with other High Commissioners and their wives were seated in the stalls near the high altar with an unrivalled view of the service. Nowadays the service is televised and screens are placed in various parts of the Abbey, one happening to be a few feet from our seats. Here not only were we able to see what was going on throughout the Abbey, but occasionally had the peculiar experience of seeing ourselves as the cameras passed over the congregation.

On this occasion the Winston Churchill memorial was unveiled after the service by Her Majesty the Queen. It was pleasant also to arrive in one's own chauffeur-driven car and be conducted to one's seat, and to depart with the same ease; not having to endure the endless queuing that is inseparable from the present-day English life.

We were in London when the Commonwealth Arts Festival was opened. This was a busy time for most of the High Commissions, for they had teams of dancers and artists to look after, not only in London, but in the provinces, where these people were later to perform. We, in Rhodesia, had contented ourselves by sending an art collection from our National Gallery. This was entirely due to the initiative of its Director, Mr. Frank MacEwan and his wife, and it more than held its own with the other Commonwealth contributions and exhibits. Together with Denzil Bradley, my P.A., and Miss Wendy Lee, my secretary, we paid a visit to the exhibition and saw our country's contribution. It attracted a great deal of favourable comment and publicity, which was particularly welcome at this time.

Most of the great national institutions displayed a serried row of the flags of the Commonwealth countries, with the noticeable exception of the Rhodesian flag. My staff were indignant and pressed me to lodge an official and public protest against this obvious and invidious omission. Though sorely tempted I refrained because I wished to show up the contrast between our country and the host of new nations that had suddenly appeared on the Commonwealth scene. Should such an insult have been offered to their hyper-sensitive dignity, I suggested, without fail they would have rent the air with undignified and shrill complaints in the manner of the leprous beggar in an Eastern bazaar who shakes one fist at his benefactor whilst soliciting alms with the other open paw.

The opening day held more than seven functions for Honor and myself to attend. It started off with an opening ceremony in the Banqueting Hall in Whitehall, last known to me as the Museum of the Royal United Services Institute of which I had been a member. It was also the Chamber through which Charles I had passed to his execution. Here the multi-racial Commonwealth was displaying the variety of its costumes. We had been asked to attend in national costume, or failing that in morning dress. We were in some doubt as to what we should wear. The Singalese appeared in flared safron dhotis and bare midriffs – the Indians in saris, jodhpurs and Ghandi caps – the Polynesians in modified grass skirts and so forth. We finally decided on morning dress as we felt that the Rhodesian national dress of khaki shirts and shorts, and a cotton dress without stockings but with sandals, might present a drab appearance beside this riot of exotic colour.

73

After the opening by H.R.H. the Duke of Edinburgh, we went to the Anglican Church of St. Mary le Bow in the City where representatives of all the religions of the Commonwealth were meeting to worship some undefined Deity supposed to be common to all. It was an occasion that would have horrified our Calvinist ancestors, and in those far-off days would almost certainly have led us to be burnt at the stake on our return home.

Whilst Eastern music drifted from one of the crypts, interspersed by the soft throbbing of what I took to be a tom-tom, a bishop, no less, in mitre and full regalia entered and took up his seat on a throne facing us. This proved to be none other than the Most Reverend Joost de Blank, lately Archbishop of Cape Town. The Anglican Vicar of St. Mary le Bow compèred the service. The presiding Bishop was followed by a Mullah of Islam, a Jewish Rabbi, a Buddhist Monk, a Hindu Priest, the latter two in their native priestly garb, together with a Catholic and a non-Conformist. All in turn read prayers from their respective religious literature and hymns peculiar to each religion were sung or intoned with appropriate music from the hidden Commonwealth musicians.

I was interrupted during this interesting service by an urgent message from the Commonwealth Relations Office to which I dictated a reply and then returned to my seat.

We left the service with confused minds, and I remarked to my wife that the African personality cult had been ignored, and there would be shrill complaints from the African members of the Commonwealth because a witchdoctor complete with bones and wildebeest tail, and clad in ochre and skins, had not been invited to join the officiating clergy. I was later informed that the whole concept had been a great success and it was hoped that the following year the ceremony would be held in St. Paul's or Westminster Abbey. This serious omission will doubtlessly be rectified when that occasion arises, and thus avoid a rupture in the religious solidarity of the new Commonwealth.

Then I went on to the Mansion House where a banquet, the first to be served from its new kitchens, was being held for Commonwealth personages. The Duke of Edinburgh made a brilliant and witty speech, which was followed by others and then replete the guests hurried off to another ceremony, to which I had been invited, but had excused myself. I had many preoccupations in my office, not the least being a further meeting with the Secretary of State for Commonwealth Affairs at five o'clock. This was followed by a hasty change and then Honor and I attended three receptions at various embassies who were entertaining the Commonwealth visitors. As these receptions started at 6 p.m. and finished nominally at 8 p.m., one has only time to present oneself to the host, sip a single drink and then hurry to the next. At these functions one comes across one's colleagues from the newer nations of the world, many of whom have jumped from quite humble occupations to exalted rank in a matter of months or even weeks. There their diet was of the simple kind one finds in primitive societies, and the alcohol of the rawest variety.

They invariably thronged to all these receptions and enjoyed themselves hugely. I remarked to one of them that I found these receptions somewhat of a strain after a busy day. He disagreed violently and told me his main reason for attending was the ex-cellent food and abundant alcohol. His attention wandered to the far end of the room, so I felt it polite to pass on. Then I noticed him dive for the buffet where he was joined by three others who obviously shared his delight in the diplomatic life. They soon cleared the plates within reach and then turned to the drink. Glasses filled with various wines are either passed around by scarlet clad foot-men or wait in rows on a sideboard. It takes some acumen to dis-cover which particular tipple the glasses contain, but this was no problem to my new friends. They liberally added whisky, gin, sherry from all available bottles and quaffed this cocktail with delight. As one departed from each function for the next in line, one met these fellow diplomats on the doorstep in festive frame of mind while they waited for their respective Rolls-Royces. However, I noticed that by the third or fourth reception in an evening their numbers had thinned considerably. Possibly their office work had called them, though this I doubt. It may be that the pace had told on their capacity.

These invitations fell thick and fast, though occasionally there was an embarassing hitch. On one occasion a Communist country had sent us an invitation to a reception to mark the anniversary of one of its numerous revolutions. Never having penetrated behind the Iron Curtain we accepted, but the day before we were due to present ourselves, an apologetic telephone call reached Wendy Lee, explain-ing that owing to a "technical hitch" – this was the term actually used – the invitation had been sent in error. Obviously the Rhodesians as "Fascist beasts" were *non persona grata* to this particular mission, but I was sorry for the unfortunate junior official in charge of entertaining whose geography must have been at fault. I do hope he or she was not recalled to serve a term in the salt mines for sabotage.

Apart from several small evening receptions limited to about 40 guests and which were usually held in my office for trade delegations from Rhodesia to meet their opposite numbers, we gave two big receptions. Rhodesia House, though cramped, had three large apartments – the hall, the High Commissioner's office and the Reception Lounge. The latter is a big room, equal to any in the other mission buildings in London, which can accommodate over 500 people. The arrangements for these receptions were left in the most capable hands of Mrs. Thorn, the resident housekeeper, and Mr. Charlie Gladman, who is in general charge of the building. We did not employ catering firms with their uniformed footmen, but ran these functions with our own people. The whole staff was enlisted, especially the girls, and their duty was to serve refreshments and keep the guests circulating.

At most diplomatic functions it is assumed that everyone knows everyone, for the same people go to them all. As a result a newcomer to the diplomatic world has a dull time for the first few months. In Rhodesia House our receptions were attended by a much wider circle of people. I made a point of inviting not only visitors from Rhodesia who had signed the book, but many people in England from everyday life whom I had contacted. It was my aim to get Rhodesia and our way of life known to as many people as possible. The task of our staff therefore was to look after these guests and make the atmosphere less like that of a stiff diplomatic function and more like a Rhodesian sundowner.

I think this was popular, judging by the few refusals we had and the way in which our guests stayed the full period of the entertainment, possibly cutting the other functions of the evening.

The first entertainment was held on 21st September. The invitations sent out came near the 400 mark, and together with members of Rhodesia House and personal friends I had asked by word of mouth, nearly 500 turned up.

The Ambassador or High Commissioner as the case may be,

76

with his lady, greets the guests as they arrive, but with a number such as this the receiving, apart from the muscular effort of shaking hands, took upwards of an hour. We were able to join our guests at 7.15 p.m., an hour and a quarter after the doors had opened, and then after a brief 20 minutes with them, we were back in position to take the farewells.

We were thus only able to have the very briefest of words with many of our old friends whom we had not seen for 20 years or more. However, an amusing incident occurred. Two of my oldest friends, both of whom had been my company commanders when I was a second-lieutenant, joined me while I was talking to the Lord Chancellor, who had been to Rhodesia with Mr. Bottomley in February. Not knowing who he was, they launched into a passionate defence of Rhodesia, declaring that the British Government should give us our independence straightaway, and they declared that many thousands of others felt like them. I hurriedly introduced them to the Lord Chancellor, on whose lips I might have detected a smile, and explained the position he held in regard to this issue. I then excused myself and left them to tell him what the British public felt about the matter.

It proves that a policy of not confining these functions to the political and diplomatic world pays dividends.

Our second reception was arranged in a hurry. Whilst our negotiations were proceeding, I arranged a similar affair for the Prime Minister of Rhodesia and his cabinet colleagues on the 7th October.

Invitations were sent out informally to about 250 people, this time mostly to politicians and others interested in our affairs. Numerous Rhodesians visiting or residing in England were included on the list. As interest in Rhodesia was at fever pitch, and Mr. Smith was to be present, we had a number of frantic telephone calls from people who had not received an invitation, and felt they should be invited. Apologising for the omission, I invited them and soon the number swelled close to 400.

On this occasion there was a full house. No one was prepared to miss this treat, for it might prove to be a historic occasion. Sundry gentry of the Press sought invitations, for this to them meant business, a possible scoop, and not only pleasure. I was careful to ask only those whom I regarded as suitable and responsible, but nevertheless a few managed to slip in by devious means. Others were left baying outside the portals of Rhodesia House.

This occasion I think proved of value, for it gave a great number of influential people a chance to see and speak to our Prime Minister, as well as to the other members of our Cabinet. The impression they made was very favourable and to our advantage.

Apart from the receptions given by the High Commissioner, there were others given by members of the mission in their respective spheres of work. For example a highly enjoyable function was given by our military and air force liaison officers for the services, at which I met many old army friends, and our Chief Information Officer, Mr. Read, gave one to the Press. Here I saw a number of journalists whose articles I have subsequently read. Unfortunately the entertainment they received had not noticeably mellowed their attitudes to Rhodesia. Others, on the contrary, are our firm friends, and to them we owe our gratitude. On the whole I consider that the entertainment side of our work in Rhodesia House was of value and the money well spent.

It was my wife's duty to call on the wife of a diplomat after I had called on him. In most cases these were normal social calls, but some were on the female representatives of newly emergent states.

These new states do their diplomats well. Nearly all are bankrupt, yet nevertheless they keep well up with the Joneses – better in fact. One well-known and very vociferous state, with a budget deficit of millions, has a mission in London equipped with several Rolls Royce cars, and a representative's salary running well into five figures. But why should they worry? The Western World with its ever open purse will pay, and the long suffering taxpayer does not seem to object. With a British taxed pension I am unfortunately one of those taxpayers, and I viewed this particular ostentation with a jaundiced eye.

These lucky and favoured ones usually have a large mansion situated in the inner suburbs of London. The servant problem which plagued us along with others in the diplomatic world offers no difficulty to them. On being translated from their tropic shores, they are probably besieged by clamouring relatives and friends, only too eager to serve their fortunate relation in any capacity and thus be assured of endless supplies of Western food and drink at duty free prices.

Such was the case when Honor paid her calls. The once proud lawns and grounds of these houses were usually ploughed up and planted with maize in the traditional pattern of the home land. The pathetic little plants she saw, the pride and joy of their owners, were, in August and September, a few inches high. Alas for their hopes of maturity when the snows and frosts of December overtook them!

Having traversed this rural scene my wife was greeted at the door by the footman, clad in singlet and khaki longs, and ushered into the august presence of the hostess, who with native charm indicated an enormous piece of furniture at one end of the room. This proved to be a mammoth cocktail cabinet. A whisky and soda was the inevitable offering at 3.30 in the afternoon. This declined, tea or coffee was forthcoming.

Conversation was difficult in these circumstances, but was eventually centred on family affairs and carried out in English or French, with a variety of accents. When the conversation flagged, a tour of the maize garden was offered, or if it was raining, a sight of the maize in the conservatory which was always attached to these Victorian mansions. These plants seemed to be in better shape.

Sometimes a wife of ambassadorial rank from another mission or from Europe was staying in the house for a visit. Unfortunately these ladies were usually reclining in the garden with a can of beer and a transistor radio, and were loath to have their siesta disturbed by the demands of protocol. After the prescribed hour of the visit my wife bade her farewells and made her way to her car, being careful to avoid the empty beer cans that lurked in unlikely places near the exit.

The pattern seldom varied from this, but Honor began to wonder if the diplomatic world had perhaps changed from the times and novels of Disraeli and Ouida.

There is one great advantage that a diplomat enjoys. He can buy himself a personal car at a diplomatic discount that varies from 15 per cent for a British car up to 25 per cent for a continental car. In addition he does not pay purchase tax, nor the carriage to his home country when he returns. He naturally does not pay duty on its entry on return. In addition he gets cheap petrol in the host country.

Unfortunately motoring in England has lost many of its attractions with the tremendous amount of traffic on the road. Furthermore it requires more courage than I possess to drive a car in or out of London. Nevertheless I was determined to get a car at these vastly reduced prices and acquired a German Ford Taunus at about one half of the British retail price.

If his country is in the news, a diplomat has a deluge of invitations to speak at this or that society's meetings. I received several of these, but was not able to fulfil them all, because on two occasions I was back in Rhodesia for discussions with my Government, and on one occasion the subject was one on which I felt diplomatic misconstruction might be placed.

But any diplomat must be well versed in public speaking, and on any subject from the light to the serious. Furthermore he must be able to speak off the cuff and to frame his words and delivery to suit his audience and occasion. A chance sentence thoughtlessly spoken may undo months of patient diplomatic work and earn him a well-deserved reprimand from his Government, or in serious cases a sudden recall.

An amusing incident occurred at a function I attended and at which I was asked to speak. Sitting with me was a famous person for whom I have the greatest respect and admiration. He is also renowned for his forthright views, which do not always find favour with the establishment. As I got up to speak, he whispered to me, "Tell them that White rule is what is wanted for Southern Africa." After I had finished speaking I added: "I have been asked to tell you something by . . . , but as a diplomat I cannot repeat it with the Press present."

I know this was pusillanimous of me and I was ashamed of my reticence, but at that moment most delicate negotiations were going on and a remark such as that might have sown unjust suspicions in the minds of Socialist politicians. Furthermore the Press were there in numbers, pencils poised. Nothing daunted, my prompter jumped up and repeated his remarks, loud and clear, and there was an enthusiastic cheer and much laughter.

With some trepidation I opened the papers next day to see how the Press had twisted this incident to the disadvantage of my country. Nothing had been printed. I was surprised, but later heard that it had been printed in full in the Cape Town newspapers.

But these are only a few of the pitfalls of diplomacy. One must not only learn to speak, but to be able to think on one's feet while speaking.

Let us now return to more serious matters.

10. The Confrontation

On Monday, 4th October, Bill Harper, John Wrathall and myself drove out to London airport to meet the Prime Minister's aircraft. Len Thompson and members of my staff followed with the car we had hired for the party, with another for luggage. The V.I.P. lounge was besieged by newsmen and photographers and inside we were joined by the Chief of Protocol for the Commonwealth Relations Office, and the Minister of State, Mr. Cledwyn Hughes. As far as I can remember the aircraft was not late and Mr. Ian Smith, Des Lardner Burke and Mr. Clark, the Secretary of the Cabinet, landed, were duly photographed and ushered into the lounge where we all drank the inevitable tea or coffee. Arrivals in the early morning were offered these homely beverages, midday arrivals could have tea or alcohol, and night arrivals and departures had a fully equipped bar at their disposal – all on the British taxpayer.

After this the whole party drove in the three cars with a police escort of motor cycles to St. Ermine's Hotel. The P.M. and the three ministers and myself drove in RHO 1, with a special branch detective beside the chauffeur in front. It is inadvisable to discuss any confidential matter in a car and we kept the conversation to innocuous trifles, as was to be the rule everywhere except in Rhodesia House or when walking in the Park.

Having left the ministers at their hotel to settle in and later have lunch, I returned to Rhodesia House. A meeting with Mr. Bottomley was arranged for the afternoon. This was to be a purely courtesy call to arrange the first meeting for next day. The details of procedure for meetings were also arranged. I got my secretary to cancel all engagements for the week ahead and set about organising office space for the new arrivals.

Norman Heathcote departed to an upstairs office to carry on with the immense amount of routine work that went on unabated and I took over his office. The High Commissioner's office was cleared and made available for the Prime Minister and his colleagues. As the days passed and throngs of visitors sought interviews, I had to leave this new office of mine so that it could be used for these interviews and conducted my own in the reception lounge or the passage.

On Alan Izod's arrival two months before, we had been at our wits' end to find him some place to work. Now his problem seemed an easy one. Ravenscroft and Young were still working on the reorganisation of Rhodesia House, and this influx must have brought home to them the vital necessity for their investigations. Before this party left the following week, Mr. C. G. Tracey arrived to prepare for his team of lecturers.

Rhodesia House was bursting at the seams, and the Information Section was swollen by the arrival of a team from Rhodesia Television who operated in the Library and the Lounge. Next day Air Vice-Marshal Raff Bentley, our Minister in Washington, arrived from the States.

This formidable team from overseas was now assembled in London and was operating from Rhodesia House. A Prime Minister, five Cabinet Ministers, a deputy Minister, a diplomat from Washington, chief of an Information team, four senior civil servants and three Press men and their equipment.

On Tuesday they got down to business. During the morning the Prime Minister, Messrs. Harper, Wrathall, Lardner Burke, Clark, with Mr. Brice, the Political Counsellor from Rhodesia House, and Len Thompson and myself drove to the Commonwealth Relations Office, and after a preliminary session of tea and cakes we got round a table.

The opposing delegation consisted of Mr. Bottomley, Mr. Hughes, Sir Saville Garner, Permanent Secretary to the Commonwealth Relations Office, Sir Arthur Snelling under whose Department Rhodesia belonged, Mr. Watson of the Rhodesia desk, and three more junior British civil servants. The British High Commissioner in Rhodesia, Mr. Jack Johnson, completed the British team.

Proceedings started by the Commonwealth Secretary restating the British proposals which were in effect the five principles. The ball was then tossed to us. How were these to be implemented? Would we make our concrete suggestions? After considerable sparring we got round to the question of the blocking third or even a blocking quarter. The Rhodesian offer was an Upper House of Chiefs and notabilities, nominated by the Chiefs' Council and various organisations. This did not suit the British. They would prefer this house to be composed of elected Africans. This Upper House voting together with the Lower House on the entrenched clauses on the third reading of a bill, might, but only might, meet the British case.

But then the British dropped a bombshell. The unentrenched clauses as existed in the 1961 Constitution in their view needed to be safeguarded. To do this they required a blocking third in the Lower House as well. Uppermost in their minds all this time was the fact that all 50 A roll seats in the Assembly were held by Europeans and by Europeans of the Rhodesian Front at that. What they could not see was that the electoral system was non-racial, and that at that very moment, if the Africans bothered to register on the A roll, they could possibly win half a dozen A roll seats at any time.

It was the old error of trying to frame a constitution or an organisation on personalities and accidents of the moment. Such a constitution could never endure. It was in vain that this was pointed out to them. Furthermore, by this very suggestion they had departed from the 1961 Constitution, which had been agreed upon by all parties at that time. It seemed therefore quite obvious that the British were preparing to destroy this constitution which had operated for only three years.

The high hopes with which the Rhodesians came to the conference table began to fade. At this juncture the deadlock was averted by an invitation to a lavish lunch in one of the Government's hospitality houses in Carlton Gardens.

After lunch the dialogue shifted to the other principles. Here the Rhodesians offered to meet the principle of African political advancement by virtually throwing open the B roll to one man one vote. This was favourably considered by the British who hurried onto the question of discrimination and the Land Apportionment Act. Here no progress was made even when it was pointed out that this Act existed for the security of African tenure. This the British accepted, but pointed out that it was the European areas that they wished to have thrown open to all races. The Rhodesians pointed out that great areas of Crown land as well as certain previously European areas had already been handed over for this purpose but only a fraction had been taken up.

It was pointed out that more racial discrimination existed in the U.K. than the British themselves like to admit. This was a sore point to which the British gave a heated reply that legislation had

"But Mr Smith, if you were prepared to risk your life for Britain in 1941, why can't you commit suicide for Britain in 1965?". (From the "Sunday Express", October 10, 1965. Permission: London Express Service)

been passed to outlaw it. Nevertheless the fact was that legislation only exacerbated the situation, and only time could solve this particular problem, if it ever could.

This argument never got down to realities, for it was reality which the British politicians could not face up to, and they took cover behind a smoke screen of ideology which has not proved practical anywhere on earth.

We got no further that day, and returned to Rhodesia House to discuss this session. A further meeting was scheduled for the next day, which followed the same pattern. But from it emerged that whatever was agreed on the first four principles, and however liberal a solution was suggested, the new proposals would have to be accepted by the people as a whole. How, was the problem. The view that the chiefs represented the vast majority of the African people, was rejected out of hand by the British. In their minds the answer lay in a referendum. The absurdity of this exercise did not enter their minds – the African people would not have the slightest idea of what they would be voting for, whilst the few nationalist leaders and their followers would accept nothing but immediate power.

It was obvious that we were getting nowhere in these negotiations and however far we leant over backwards the British Government would reserve its position for further demands, with one eye on the Afro-Asian states and the other on America and the Communists.

A solution was only possible if a formula was arranged through which an African nationalist government emerged in Rhodesia within a couple of years. Even that might be too long to suit Britain's new masters in Africa and elsewhere.

It was now considered that a meeting on a higher level should be held. At this meeting all non-political advisers were to be excluded, with the hope that this meeting might resolve the deadlock.

Under the British system of Government the civil service has a major say in all matters of any long-term policy, and any departure from this policy would meet with objections and these would also be reinforced by the interlocking interest of other interested departments. To get radical decisions out of the politicians, with this dead weight of objection, was a major exercise.

Accordingly our four ministers and a secretary joined a similar team from the British side. The two Prime Ministers faced each other and this confrontation was on the highest possible level.

The same ground was covered again, but no progress was made. The final offer from the Rhodesian side was later published in the British Press. It was the most we could offer without handing over Rhodesia to immature and irresponsible rule, and delivering Africa south of the Zambezi to those influences which were taking over the rest of Africa.

A House of 12 Chiefs, all Africans, was offered to provide a blocking third mechanism to safeguard the entrenched clauses, and this would replace the unworkable referendum of the four races. Increased African participation in politics was made possible by extending the B roll franchise to all taxpayers. This meant that approximately one million Africans over the age of 18 would have a vote. This was far more liberal, on grounds of age, education and property than most European systems of franchise.

African nationalists and others were fond of talking about the four million Africans in Rhodesia. This was an inaccurate and misleading figure. There are under four million Africans and of these nearly half a million are foreign workers who are not citizens. In no country would such visitors have a vote. Of the remainder 2,600,000 were under the age of 21, a tribute to our health services since the war, and these again would have no vote in a country like Britain. This left about a million who were adult and citizens, and to all of these a vote was now available by right on the B roll or by qualification on the A Roll.

In addition the tribal African, nearly three quarter million out of the million enfranchised had a further representation through their chiefs. Surely these concessions were enough to guarantee African participation in government, a participation that would inevitably increase as they became more educated. It more than met the first two principles demanded by the British Government.

As regards the Land Apportionment Act: The Tribal Areas were sacrosanct in the 1961 Constitution. In the European areas more land had been thrown open for multi-racial settlement than could be taken up for many years and was already available for Africans. In addition in the European urban areas legislation already existed for the formation of multi-racial zones, where those who wished to experiment in this way of life could take up residence or do business.

Discrimination had legally been abolished in all public places and forms of transport for which the state was responsible. If any discrimination existed it was only in the private sector, and to force this by legislation was an infringement of the rights of the individual and could not be tolerated. Even in Britain such legislation is unworkable and has led to friction and distrust, which we wished to avoid.

On the last principle, which was the acceptance by the people as a whole of any agreement that was made, the Rhodesian stand was quite clear. It had been done already and under the 1961 Constitution as it stood, which had not included any of the foregoing concessions. The methods used had been the only ones practicable, namely a referendum of all A and B roll voters, and those as yet without a vote by consultation through their tribal chiefs. This latter method had been accepted by all previous British Governments on all issues affecting our constitution, including the acceptance of the 1961 Constitution. There was no reason to depart from it now.

These were major concessions and could meet all valid British objections, provided always that they were prepared to stand up to the Afro-Asian states and asserted for once their own British independence as had been the British way prior to Suez. We Rhodesians could do no more, and go no further than these very generous and realistic suggestions. However, it was abvious that the British were determined to establish immature African rule at the very earliest date possible, so that they could shrug off this responsibility without regard to the future well-being of the peoples of Rhodesia.

A deadlock ensued. We discussed the situation in Rhodesia House. There seemed no alternative to the assumption of our independence without the blessing of the British. All of us were well aware of the serious nature of such an act and the consequences that might flow from it. But, a man faced with certain death in the near future unless he undergoes a serious and maybe fatal operation which has a fair chance of success, has no option.

Having negotiated to what must be the bitter end, this decision was reluctantly taken. All that remained was a possibility of a last minute change of heart by the British Government, or some miracle of compromise that could avert this action. The matter had to be put to the remainder of the Cabinet and the caucus in Rhodesia.

The situation had also to be explained to the people of Britain, and the Independent Television was anxious to interview the Prime Minister. This was an opportunity to be welcomed and this interview took place. The interviewing panel consisted of three people, one of whom was inevitably hostile to Rhodesia, but Mr. Ian Smith dealt with the questions in a brilliant manner and put the Rhodesian case with honesty and integrity.

It was a resounding triumph and made a tremendous and favourable impression on the man in the street who had hitherto only been dimly aware of the situation in Central Africa. So great an impression did Mr. Smith make, that an interview arranged for the following day by the BBC was hurriedly cancelled only four hours before Mr. Smith was due to appear on the air. There is no doubt that the British Government was frightened by the growing support for Rhodesia, and was determined to stop it. A very lame excuse was offered that we had had our fair share on the air and could have no more time. In fact we had never been granted any time by the BBC, whilst programmes hostile to Rhodesia had been appearing for some time in the late night News Round-up.

Almost immediately after Mr. Smith's departure the B.B.C. granted Mr. Wilson a fully staged T.V. appearance, and this was a solo performance without hostile or penetrating questioning on British attitudes. We were not alone in feeling that the British Government had exerted strong pressure on the BBC to cancel Mr. Smith's appearance and we had definite evidence of the part Government officials had played in this.

I wrote a strong protest to Lord Normanbrook and published this protest in full to the Press who for reasons best known to themselves joined in this attack on the BBC, and so for the first time we had the majority of the Press on our side. The BBC's rather lame reply to my letter convinced no one and the public was left with the impression that their state controlled broadcasting and television had not come out well in this affair.

But in the meantime we held a mammoth press conference in the lounge of Rhodesia House. There must have been over 200 journalists present and here again our Prime Minister excelled, and made a wonderful impression.

Great crowds thronged the Strand outside Rhodesia House to catch a glimpse of him as he came and went, and the police escort, far from having to protect him from possible enemies, had their hands full controlling fervent admirers who had come to shake him by the hand. Many had come all the way from the north of England to do this. These demonstrations and the crowds outside Downing Street were all friendly, and our delegation was cheered on all occasions. There were no hostile voices, and only one lone placard, carried by the usual shaggy lay-about with the inevitable beard and straggling locks, demonstrated an opposing view.

This was not lost on the politicians and no doubt urged Mr. Wilson to try and get the ball in his court again by some dramatic gimmick.

Representatives of big business sought interviews with our delegation and myself, urgently warning us of the dangers of taking matters into our own hands. After Mr. Smith's departure a high-powered delegation of business interests, despite my advice, flew out to Rhodesia to assess the situation and add their warnings. They came back with information that the Rhodesians were determined and fully aware of the consequences of an assumption of independence, but were not to be diverted by economic threats from a course they felt was vital to their long-term security. This was reported back to the British Government, and had an immediate effect on their thinking.

The complacent idea, which had persisted so long, that Rhodesians were certain to capitulate against the forces that were ranged against them, as they had done under previous governments, now died a sudden death.

The British Government at last realised we were in earnest. Poor Britain, who had proudly managed her own affairs unaided for so long, took recourse to her allies and late enemies. Ambassadors sent Mr. Smith messages from their governments politely asking him to refrain from hasty action. Britain ineptly caused the Germans to do likewise, and this fact seemed to infuriate the British public and brought increased sympathy and support to our side. After all, Rhodesian servicemen had rallied to Britain's side in the last war against the Germans, and to call upon our late enemies to bring indirect pressure on these same Rhodesians, was really too much to stomach.

At this stage the battle for the public mind was going in our favour. From now on it was a struggle on both sides to capture and hold it.

The Prime Minister had decided to prolong his stay in the hope that a solution might still be found. He was invited down to Hatfield on the Sunday to visit Lord Salisbury, and had discussions with him. On his return he had visits to his hotel from the leading Conservatives, headed by Mr. Heath and Selwyn Lloyd. This gave rise to the idea of a treaty.

We had long pressed upon the British Government that we were people like themselves – their own kith and kin. We could be trusted to follow the 1961 Constitution to its logical conclusion, tied to no time limits, and as we lived in Rhodesia it would be folly for us to become reactionary and ignore the welfare of our African population. Our record over the years had already proved our good faith, for the health, wealth, economic standards and education of our African peoples had progressed far beyond those of any African country north of the Limpopo. If our word could not be trusted, we were prepared to put it in writing. Thus the idea of a treaty in which we would undertake not to go back on our existing constitution.

Another and final meeting followed with Mr. Wilson after the Conservatives had reported to him. This treaty, however, was unacceptable to the Socialist Government. It would not have suited their plans for an almost immediate African nationalist government, and it would certainly not have had the approval of the Afro-Asians, who had to be appeased at all costs.

The Rhodesian delegation now began to leave London. The first to go were the two Ministers, Bill Harper and John Wrathall. I took them out to the airport in RHO 1. It was a fine afternoon and as the car passed down the Mall and past Buckingham Palace, we speculated if this was the last time we would make this journey without the threat of a spell in the Tower of London hanging over us.

The Prime Minister and Mr. Lardner Burke and the two civil servants who accompanied them were the next to depart. Honor deputised for me at the airport as I was due to speak to the Monday Club, a Conservative one and formed after Suez by a group of M.P.'s and their supporters. They were very pro-Rhodesia, for like us they felt that a stand should be taken against the eroding standards of international conduct that had occurred since that watershed in history. The meeting was very well attended and a unanimous vote supporting Rhodesia was passed.

The fog had delayed the departure of the Prime Minister's flight, and Mr. Soref, Tracey and myself were able to drive out after the meeting and see the Prime Minister off. It was a cheerful party in the V.I.P. lounge, but the aircraft was further delayed, so we took our leave when he went in to dinner.

I am told that Lord Caradon had been summoned from New York to be briefed on the Rhodesian crisis. He appeared in the lounge on alighting from his flight, but as the Prime Minister rightly should not be disturbed at his meal, he waited for him to come downstairs. By then the aircraft was ready to take off, and so the briefest of greetings passed. Dire warnings from the mighty United Nations, which in any case were of no consequence, thus could not be delivered.

Then Air Vice-Marshal Bentley departed for Washington. Before he left he was called to an interview with Mr. Bottomley, where the latter heard once again the points I had been pressing on him for the past few months. Communications between London and Washington presented a difficulty, and we both felt that signals and letters from Salisbury through London to America were not exactly secure, especially while such an inquisitive organisation as the Central Intelligence Agency existed. We arranged for a courier service and the next week I sent one of my staff over to him with despatches. Whilst I sometimes felt out on a limb, he certainly was out on the very edge of the branch.

Rhodesia House became strangely quiet and I returned to my desk, as did other displaced persons. Only Mr. Van der Byl and Mr. McLean remained, the latter soon to fly home.

Then P. K. van der Byl flew off to Finland and the Scandinavian countries for a holiday mixed with business and was shortly to be recalled back to London.

11. The Ball Game

There were lighter moments during the period that our Prime Minister was in London.

We received a signal that certain members of the Rhodesian Opposition Party were coming to London in order to be present during the discussions. There seemed to be some confusion why they were coming and what purpose their visit would fulfil. Furthermore one of this party appeared to be coming as a private individual, and stated he was representing the views of the chiefs. The chiefs however disowned his credentials in this respect. The Leader of the Opposition was believed to be joining the party later, but in the event did not arrive.

The visit and the transport were thought to have been arranged by Mr. David Butler who had been the Leader of the Opposition in the last parliament and had succeeded Sir Edgar Whitehead in this post.

We had no information as to the exact time and date of the arrival of these three individuals, Messrs. Mkudu, Samuriwo and Kandengwa, but as they were Rhodesians I felt it was my duty to assist them in their stay in London. This was not entirely altruistic as I had information that the representatives of the rival and feuding African nationalist parties, then in London, were anxious to contact them and take them under their wing. Furthermore the Press and T.V. were hot on their trail, and would undoubtedly seek to make news and capital out of these innocents abroad, with a view to complicating the issues to be resolved during the negotiations.

However their travel arrangements had gone haywire, owing to break-downs and delays by their chartered aircraft. I had an emissary chasing round the various airports at all times of the day and night to meet these arrivals. Neither he, the Press nor the African Nationalists ever succeeded in meeting them. They had slipped unseen into England and disappeared into the sprawling mass of Greater London. However, through good friends in Scotland Yard we finally located them within hours of their unobtrusive arrival at a little known hotel, and I got them to come to Rhodesia House.

Here I gave them facilities to interview the Press under supervision and briefed them on the attitudes they should take up. They were, I hope, gratified by their reception, but what really took their interest was the bowler hat I was wearing when I met them.

I enlarged on the social significance of this article of headwear, and I regretted that few Rhodesians in London would wear it.

I never saw them again after this interview. Very little appeared in the Press about their activities, but I hope they enjoyed their jaunt to London. The only prominence the Press gave them was a large photograph of the trio being fitted with bowler hats at Locke's.

One day they silently left London, having accomplished I know not what, but at least one bit of advice I had given them, had been taken. I noted that the Rhodesian Press had published photographs of them alighting at Salisbury airport in bowler hats. This incredible sight attracted much notice and comment, and so when I returned to Salisbury about 10 days later, I descended from the VC10 in my bowler hat. To press comment on this eccentric behaviour I replied that "I had to keep up with the Mkudu-Joneses".

The British Government and the British public were now thoroughly awake to the real and imminent possibility of Rhodesia assuming her independence. The idea of a treaty having been rejected by the Socialist Government, they began to search wildly for some means by which the dialogue might be continued and dragged on. By such means they hoped that the issue might lose its interest to the British public, sympathy in Britain die down and the Rhodesian public lose confidence and determination on this issue.

I think this was now the one dominant political aim in Mr. Wilson and his advisers' minds. If by some means the issue could be prolonged and side tracked for some months, all the ground gained by the Rhodesians could be lost to them, and the *status quo* restored to the British Government.

It was now thought that an outside influence could be used to this effect. The following message was sent to Mr. Smith, and duly published to the world.

"Since our last meeting I have been considering whether there is still any way out of our present impasse. To the Commonwealth as a whole, no less than to our two countries, it is important that everything that is humanly possible should be done to devise a peaceful solution of the Rhodesian problem.

"At this crucial moment I therefore thought it might be useful to speak about these issues to Sir Robert Menzies, not only because he is the senior Commonwealth Prime Minister but also as a person for whom I believe that Rhodesians no less than we in Britain have great respect. He has told me that if you would be ready to receive it he would be willing to take part in a small Commonwealth mission of respected senior statesmen which could go to Rhodesia and examine the whole situation. We hope that the Prime Ministers of Nigeria and Ceylon and perhaps one other Commonwealth country would also be willing to take part. As yet however I do not know whether any of them apart from Menzies would be able to take part in such a mission.

"Please let me know whether you would be willing to receive such a mission. I know that you have in the past maintained that the question of Rhodesian independence is a matter for settlement between Britain and Rhodesia alone. We have supported you in this view. But in the crisis which has now been reached in our affairs it is possible that a collective Commonwealth voice might be able to produce proposals worthy of consideration. I earnestly hope therefore that you will not dismiss the suggestion which is genuinely meant as an attempt to open up new avenues of negotiation."

The reply which I received for delivery to Mr. Wilson ran as follows:

"At our last meeting on Monday, 11th October, you left me in no doubt that the British Government were not prepared to depart from their stand on the five principles, nor from their refusal to acknowledge any longer that the 1961 Constitution can be a basis for independence. You also made it clear that it was not your intention to deviate from your new demand, which caused us surprise and concern, for a blocking mechanism for normal constitutional changes – a demand which I regard as tantamount to a desire to interfere in Rhodesia's internal affairs. Moreover, the joint communiqué which we issued states in the penultimate sentence: 'Despite intensive discussion, no means have been found of reconciling the opposing views.' In view of these considerations it is difficult for me to appreciate what new avenues of negotiations could possibly have occurred to you in the twenty-four hours which had elapsed since our meeting. I regret, that, in spite of the fact that I stayed over in London for an additional two days, you did not discuss this matter with me before I departed.

"I agree with you that it is important that everything that is humanly possible should be done to devise a solution of the Rhodesian problem. Rhodesia has done its very best and has put forward constructive suggestions to meet the British Government on the five principles. But I must repeat my regret that the British Government have shown no disposition whatever to make similar advances to a common meeting ground, but have, in fact, moved back from their original stand.

"Of course, we have the highest regard for Sir Robert Menzies and he has, as you know, already been in touch with me, expressing his concern. Furthermore, on two separate occasions I have invited him to visit Rhodesia as a friend, and this invitation still stands. But I believe that with the best will in the world Sir Robert Menzies and any colleagues who might wish to associate themselves with your proposals would be so far from the issues involved that I certainly think they could not better any contribution made by you and the Commonwealth Secretary during the last week. As for us, we have explained our case completely to the British Government, which is the only Government that is responsible for our affairs. Moreover, it has taken us three years to complete this exercise, and, as was proved last week, in London, the British Government is still factually ignorant on certain aspects of our case. In the light of this I must say that I think the idea of a Commonwealth mission is not practical.

"As you yourself say, the question of Rhodesian independence has always been regarded as a matter for settlement between Britain and Rhodesia alone. We, of course, have always maintained that the Commonwealth has no jurisdiction as far as Rhodesia is concerned. It would, therefore, I regret to say, be quite impossible for us to reverse a principle and to commit ourselves to the decisions or recommendations of any Commonwealth mission. The responsibility for negotiating a settlement with us remains that of Her Majesty's Government. If it is now expected that we should listen to a collective Commonwealth voice it is indeed a pity that Rhodesia's right to attend the Prime Ministers' Meeting was withdrawn some years ago and that Rhodesia has been precluded from participating in Prime Ministers' Conferences, even when her own affairs have been under discussion. Up to the time of his exclusion the Rhodesian Prime Minister had been attending Imperial and Commonwealth Conferences since 1935. There is a further point; it is evident that you have already lobbied all other Commonwealth countries on the problem of our independence, and having taken their views I suggest that you are being less than fair to us to ask them to sit in judgment upon the Rhodesian case.

"A mission in keeping with your suggestion must have within its ranks people who have openly expressed themselves as enemies of the present Rhodesian Government and Constitution. Such an exercise must therefore lead to bitterness and resentment – something which is absent at the moment, and which would prove tragic to reintroduce. You will not have failed to overlook the pledge made in September, and confirmed again this month, by President Nyerere of Tanzania that he would withdraw Tanzania from the Commonwealth if Britain granted Rhodesia independence under minority rule within or without the Commonwealth. Since it is our determination not to accept independence under majority rule, the conclusion should be obvious. You will no doubt also have noted the statements made by Mr. Kamanga, Vice-President of Zambia, to the effect that the proposal for a Commonwealth mission on Rhodesia is "just a time-consuming device" and that Sir Robert Menzies is "no different from Mr. Smith". India, as well, has dissociated herself with your idea on the grounds that this is something to settle between Britain and Rhodesia. It would seem therefore that your suggestion is as unacceptable to certain other members of the Commonwealth as it is to Rhodesia."

Meanwhile in Rhodesia opinion had hardened for the Rhodesian people were now seeing for themselves once again the process by which the Federation had been dissolved. But once bitten, twice shy. At last they had realised that the British Government was not to be trusted. These manoeuvres had only one end in view: The wearing down of Rhodesian will and the loss of confidence in their government, the one government which had so far not betrayed their hopes and faith. If the British could succeed in this aim, it was the end indeed.

Majority opinion in Rhodesia had had enough. Impatience was growing, a certain loss of confidence was already apparent through what appeared to the public as delay and procrastination.

In actual fact there was no loss of will and determination. What Rhodesia needed in the coming show-down was the support of the British public. To retain this, it was essential not to be put in the wrong, to meet each British proposal on its merit and not to reject it outright and appear to British eyes as unreasonable and irresponsible. It was in fact a ball game in which the ball, which was the retention or gaining of British public sympathy, had to be in the right court before any final action was taken. With a player of Mr. Wilson's skill, a player who moreover had all the mediums of public information on his side, it was a difficult and skilled game. It was my duty to act as linesman and umpire at the London end.

With my staff I daily reported the shifts in public opinion to Salisbury, so that our side could act accordingly. This was the reason why our assumption of independence was delayed from the time of Mr. Smith's return to Rhodesia till 11th November. One whole month.

With Mr. P. K. van der Byl I discussed this whole question of public opinion, and knowing how short a time we could hold it in our favour without its becoming bored with the drama, we estimated that, barring the British Government suddenly meeting our terms, the final date was 11th November. We reported this assessment to Salisbury.

With our limited resources we had to continue presenting our case to the British public, and in this respect we received unstinted help from the Anglo-Rhodesian Society. This society had received a great number of fresh applications for membership, and to them we passed over the names of the thousands of sympathisers who had written or called on us. Many of these had sent sums of money to help our cause which we donated in turn to this society.

In addition Gerald Sparrow, an eminent lawyer and author, had received in response to a letter he had published a large number of replies. These, too, were passed over to the society. The Judge had been to see me to offer his help. I suggested that he should publish a booklet – entirely non-political and non-controversial –in which he could put the facts about Rhodesia. There was still considerable ignorance about our non-racial and very liberal franchise, and what we were doing and had done to further African education and welfare. The position of the chiefs and their indigenous and traditional, and very democratic way of representing their people was not yet fully understood. Armed with this data he wrote and published an excellent little brochure called "Rhodesia: An independent Presentation of the Facts", and this was distributed and put on sale.

We used all these facts as advertisements in the national Press, and published how far we had gone in meeting the British Government's demands over our independence. (These are given as appendices to this book.)

This period witnessed an intensive public relations campaign. Our team of seven lecturers were active in the field and thus we were vigorously keeping the ball in the Rhodesian court. Our opponents, the left wing and the Communist fellow travellers, were active against us, the BBC, disgruntled and smarting from our recent protests, was their active ally. However, these people in their teach-ins and T.V. presentations as usual overstated their case, thus losing their balance and dignity and, I think, as a result did our cause more good than harm. This was particularly so when they called in the African nationalist spokesmen to appear on television.

Mr. Kamanga, Vice-President of Zambia, had hit the nail on the head when he referred to a Commonwealth mission to Rhodesia headed by Sir Robert Menzies "as a time wasting device", though his reasons for objection were different from ours.

Further communications were passed between Salisbury and London in this game of battledore and shuttlecock. All were published immediately in the Press, and so rapid was the exchange that I was only just able to get them typed from the signal pads and cypher machines and hurried to 10 Downing Street before the dead line of publication in Salisbury, whose time was two hours ahead of London. Doubtless the High Commissioner in Salisbury was experiencing the same difficulty. The Press of course enjoyed the advantage of not having to cypher or decypher these letters, but could get them through in minutes on the telex machines.

Poor Wendy Lee, my confidential cypherette and stenographer, to whom this burden often fell, grew pink in the face with exertion as I stood over her with a stop watch and urged her to ever faster efforts on her electric typewriter.

The next message from Mr. Wilson to our Prime Minister, addressed through the British High Commissioner in Salisbury, went as follows:

"I have received with great disappointment your message of 18 October in reply to mine of 11 October.

"Successive British Governments have throughout sought to reach agreement on conditions on which Rhodesia could advance to independence. In our talks in London unfortunately we failed. It was for this reason that at our meeting on Friday, 8 October, I urged that you should consider alternative courses and I suggested specific ways in which progress might be made.

"In spite of a final effort at a further meeting on 11 October, you confirmed that there was no basis for agreement between us.

"Moreover, at London Airport, when the Secretary of State repeated what I had said to you, namely, that he would be prepared to come to Rhodesia at once if such a visit would help, you said that you did not see what more could be done.

"Because the consequences of an illegal seizure of independence would be so grave and so widespread, as soon as it became clear on the Monday morning that you ruled out any further discussions, I sought for any way in which this could be averted and negotiations could be resumed. I accordingly spoke to Sir Robert Menzies on the telephone during the course of Monday and the Commonwealth Secretary told you at the Airport before you left that I had done so and might be communicating a further proposal to you. It was, however, only during the course of that day and the next that I was able to consult other Commonwealth Governments on the subject.

"The Commonwealth mission was never contemplated as a negotiating body or as sitting in judgement. My hope was, however, that a Commonwealth mission composed of persons of eminence, experience and wisdom might be able to make a contribution in suggesting the lines on which further progress could be made between us. I can assure you that the proposal has received broad support from Commonwealth Heads of Government.

"You would not expect me to comment on, still less accept, the unwarranted comments which you make about the British Government, such as that we are 'factually ignorant'. But I must make clear that I cannot accept your contention that the British Government had moved back in any way from their original stand. Both the previous Administration and ourselves have made it plain that there would have to be an advance on the 1961 Constitution. The five principles were presented to you as our essential requirements if a basis for independence was to be negotiated.

"You accepted them as a basis for negotiations, and they have held the field throughout all the discussions from the spring until this month. I do not see what reason you had to expect us to depart from them. Nor is it right to say that we introduced any new demand on constitutional safeguards in our recent talks. During his visit to you last July the Minister of State explicitly said that, as well as a blocking mechanism for ordinary amendments to the Constitution, the question of safeguards for the entrenched clauses would have to be covered. These clauses include, of course, such fundamental safeguards as freedom of the Press and freedom of the individual.

"At this grave hour I would only add this, that we are open to any ideas, to any further way of seeing whether agreement can be reached between us. So far you have not responded.

"After the warnings you have received from two successive British Governments and in the past week from all three major political parties in this country, you cannot be in any doubt about the tragic consequences of the illegal and unconstitutional action which you have said you have in mind. Before any irrevocable step is taken I beg you yet again, even at the Eleventh Hour, for the sake of your country, for the sake of Africa and for the sake of future generations of all races, to pause before bringing hardship and misery, perhaps even worse, to your own people and to countless others far beyond your borders, who have no power to influence your decision but whose lives may be gravely affected by it.

"Since your message has been published I am issuing this message to the Press."

The Rhodesian reply, also published, came back as follows:

20 October. "I received your personal message of the 18th October from your High Commissioner when he called on me yesterday morning.

"You say that successive British Governments have throughout sought to reach agreement on conditions on which Rhodesia could advance to independence. The same is equally true of successive Rhodesian Governments. I agree that I accept your five principles as a basis for negotiations and that they held the field throughout all the discussions from February until this month. You say that you do not see what reason I had to expect you to depart from them. But I say that if you were negotiating for a settlement you could surely have reached a reasonable compromise with us.

"We have our principles as well, but we went beyond what we were originally prepared to do in an effort to satisfy to the best of our ability the implementation of your principles. The British Government, I regret to say, have not shown the same good will or desire to abandon fixed positions and, I must repeat, have in fact moved away from us.

"I note that you say that you are still open to any ideas and to any further way of seeing whether agreement can be reached between us. Well, here is my response to this appeal: It is that it would be reasonable and just for the British Government to grant Rhodesia its independence on the 1961 Rhodesian Constitution. This Constitution covers your five principles, if only you will admit it; they are enshrined there for all to see. This is the Constitution which was the direct outcome of a Constitutional Conference held in 1961 and presided over by the British Secretary of State for Commonwealth Relations. This Conference was attended by all the political parties and racial groups of the country. The Conference Report which became the foundation of the Constitution as finally drafted was subscribed to by the following:

The United Kingdom Government led by the Commonwealth Secretary;

The Government of Southern Rhodesia led by the Prime Minister;

The United Federal Party, which was the Government Party but was independently represented;

The National Democratic Party represented by Mr. Joshua Nkomo and the Reverend N. Sithole supported by Mr. Herbert Chitepo and Mr. T. G. Silundika;

The Central Africa Party;

The Coloured Community; and

a representative of the Chiefs.

"It is a significant fact that the majority of those subscribing were members of the African, Asian and Coloured communities.

"Rhodesia is being condemned not for what we have done, but for what others say we might do in the future. Therefore, at this grave hour, I repeat to you the suggestion I made to you at the London talks that the statesmanlike thing for you to do is to grant us our independence and to put us on trust to observe and to abide by the principles of the 1961 Constitution. Therefore, we again offer you as an earnest of our good faith a solemn treaty to guarantee our undertaking. Should there occur a breach of such solemn undertaking that would be the appropriate time for the British Government to take whatever steps thought fit.

"I believe it is my duty to impress upon you that no hardship and misery will flow from any action taken by the Rhodesian Government. If the unfortunate situation which you predict should occur it could only stem directly from the actions taken by the British Government and those whom you have induced to support you.

"We have made our decision on what our next step should be. Its implementation and the consequences which flow from it now depend entirely on your response to this appeal I now make to you at this eleventh hour."

As a result of the publication of these messages an impression was gained by the Press that the whole dialogue was about to be re-opened *ab initio*, and that the words "last minute appeal" contained in the Rhodesian reply of 20th October, meant that the Rhodesians were weakening in their determination.

The following signals reached me from Salisbury :

1. "Mr. Wilson has asked me (The British High Commissioner) to inform you (Mr. Smith) that he has received your letter and will send a reply as early as possible tomorrow 21st October after he has consulted his Cabinet which will be meeting at 10 a.m. London Time. (Copy) Message ends."
2. From Prime Minister to Skeen – "According to press reactions as published here this morning it would seem that both Wilson and the official opposition believe that my message of 20th October is a move to open the way for further negotiations. The purpose of my message was to give the British Government a final opportunity of saying whether or not they are prepared to grant Rhodesia

independence on the 1961 Constitution. The reference to a treaty is not a guarantee of political advancement for African majority but a guarantee that we would respect the 1961 Constitution. My message did not contemplate that there would be a resumption of negotiations unless the British Government give me, in writing, a categorical assurance that the constitution for independence will be the 1961 Constitution, with only such amendments as may be necessary for the transfer of power, and that all that would remain for discussion between the two Governments is the terms of a treaty to guarantee that Constitution.

"As it is important that Wilson should be left in no doubt about our attitude please ask for an urgent interview with him and place these views before him orally.

"I suggest you consider asking Wilson for his reply to my message of 20th October and also consider the advisability of your returning to Rhodesia tonight for discussions with me tomorrow or Saturday."

I obtained a meeting with Mr. Wilson at once and delivered the message.

It will be noted that I had been instructed to consider the advisability of returning that night to Rhodesia for discussions. There was more in this than met the eye, as I will relate in the next chapter.

While this correspondence was going on, Mr. Wilson suddenly decided to fly out to Salisbury. His intention was conveyed by a message through his High Commissioner in Salisbury, and the first I heard of it was through the Press, for by now this whole diplomatic exchange was being carried out through two channels, the two High Commissioners and the Press, the latter winning by a good margin.

There was some doubt if Mr. Wilson's visit would be acceptable to the Rhodesian Government, but by this astute move the British Prime Minister had placed a very skilful shot in our court and gained a breathing space in the battle for capturing the mind of the British public. By this move he restored his image to a great extent, an image that was slightly tarnished by the efforts we had made in the past two weeks to impress the public with the justice of our case.

He was also becoming nervous at the reports which were reaching him from Salisbury, not this time from his official sources, but through the more accurate views of returning businessmen.

103

"Mr Smith! Can't you die quietly like a gentleman? You're keeping us all awake!" (From the "Daily Express, October 11, 1965. Permission: London Express Service)

At the moment of my visit he was awaiting a reply to his proposed visit. It arrived while I was talking to him in the Cabinet Room at 10 Downing Street, and was brought at once by my P.A. I handed it to Mr. Wilson. It ran as follows:

"From Prime Minister to Skeen. Please deliver the following personal message from me to Harold Wilson *immediately*.

"I have received your personal message of the 21st October and I accept your suggestion that you should fly to Salisbury with the Commonwealth Secretary immediately. In view of this development I will reserve the whole of the coming week-end for our discussions.

"With regard to the remainder of your message, I wish to put it on record that I cannot accept the many inaccuracies contained therein. However, it is not my intention to deal with them in this message in view of your imminent arrival."

Mr. Wilson smiled as he read the first paragraph, and remarked that I could inform my Prime Minister that I had carried out his instructions with exemplary speed. In fact I could not have delivered the message more quickly.

Brigadier Andrew Dunlop who had just arrived in London with secret despatches and Mr. Van der Byl were awaiting me in my office when I got back from 10 Downing Street. We discussed this latest move, and none of us were particularly happy. All of us were well versed in the methods of the British Government and harboured few illusions about the cleverness of their politicians and the civil servants who advised and often dictated their moves.

We all saw in this a further fruitless series of discussions only to delay and weaken our resolution. I myself realised that this exercise would have to be gone through, if we were to retain any kind of support in Britain. To be obstructive and unready to meet Mr. Wilson half way would be to undo all our efforts at informing and enlisting British sympathy.

This point I put strongly to the two ministers, and they became resigned to the delay. But possibly only I, ever optimistic, thought that a miracle might occur through Mr. Wilson's taking note of the favourable image we were creating in Britain. After all, this is the chief task of a diplomat, and one does not like to admit failure till the last possible chance has gone.

However, it became obvious that Mr. Wilson was at that time less concerned with British opinion than that of the Afro-Asians and Americans. Our domestic issues were to become a pawn in the cold war once again.

12. The Salisbury Dialogue

A day or two before the events described in the last chapter took place, our battle for the public mind, which had been progressing favourably, received a rude setback. News, as was usual in these cases, reached us through the Press that Mr. Garfield Todd, a former Prime Minister of Rhodesia, and now a strong supporter of one of the African nationalist parties had been restricted.

He was due to appear in Britain at a teach-in at the Edinburgh university on the Rhodesian situation. These peculiar gatherings were a form of debate, an innovation from America, but they were debates without rules at which leftist individuals were able to let off their spleen unchecked at the object of their displeasure. The Americans had suffered one of these at Cambridge university over Vietnam, and now Rhodesia was a favourite subject.

The victim of these organised assaults was courteously invited to attend on the platform, in the role of a defendant, whilst a massive array of his opponents was marshalled alongside him, and care was taken that the audience was hostile.

The Press and T.V. appeared at these affairs where the uninhibited conduct of those present was guaranteed to provide headlines. It was even better than a Trafalgar Square rally for the police could not be present to spoil the sport, and there was a real live Aunt Sally in the presence of the defendant in this free-for-all debate. These teach-ins are a new form of weapon in the armoury of the leftist fellow traveller, and are becoming increasingly fashionable.

As High Commissioner for Rhodesia I was invited to defend my country at several. I always demanded to see who were to be the other speakers, and saw the old familiar names from Harold Soref's book "The Puppeteers". For good measure the London representatives of the banned African nationalist parties were always invited plus a representative from a Communist Party. Sometimes unrepresentative itinerant agitators were included in this list.

I invariably refused to appear, and I would not let my staff attend. Sometimes I briefed individuals who wished to take our part, but asked them to confine themselves to facts, not arguments, and to correct the most glaring untruths that were uttered from the platform and the floor.

Deprived of their prey these orgies of hate degenerated into what they really were, Trafalgar Square demonstrations, and little notice was taken of them by the public. Two of our team of lecturers were unwary enough to take part at teach-ins, one of which degenerated into a riot at which he could not speak.

A strong impression was fostered by the Press that Mr. Todd had been restricted in order to prevent him from attending at Edinburgh. This was quite false. Nothing could have done our cause more good than his appearance on the platform. His restriction had been decided upon several weeks before and was connected with activities that were politically subversive under the existing law.

We did our best to put the true facts before the public, but his restriction at this time did much harm to our public relations. Most fortunately the Archbishop of Canterbury saw fit to make his famous gaffe on the Christian use of force against my country, Todd was forgotten and opinion swung again in our favour. We were most grateful to His Grace, and I considered sending him a telegram to this effect.

The BBC was still smarting from our temerity in accusing it of anti-Rhodesian bias, and it now appeared that Miss Judy Todd, the daughter of Garfield Todd, was being brought from America by the BBC to take his place. I understand she read her contribution to the assembled throngs at the Edingburgh teach-in and the emotional response to beauty in distress was overwhelming, but one of those present informed me that he could not hear a word she said. Whether her arguments against the Rhodesian cause were accurate and valid did not matter to the audience – her appearance was enough. So are great issues prejudged by these intellectual liberals.

One must not judge Judy Todd too harshly. She is very young, and the young often allow their emotions to control their heads. She later departed, much quoted and photographed, to seek a martyr's place in Rhodesia. Fully hoping for a well-publicised trial and further notoriety as a restricted or imprisoned innocent, she landed at Salisbury airport and to her presumable disappointment was allowed to go her way unmolested and free.

At this teach-in our case was presented by Mr. Charles Allen – a brave man to face such a hostile and prejudiced audience. He stood up to it well, and gave as good as he got.

The last exchanges having failed to get any response from the British Government, the Rhodesian Cabinet and caucus realised that there was no possible hope of negotiating further. We had made every endeavour to meet the British Government by concessions and offers of written treaties. It was decided that we might have to assume our independence on Monday or Tuesday, 25th and 26th October.

Brigadier Andrew Dunlop, the Deputy Minister of Roads, was therefore sent to London, arriving on the 20th October to inform me personally that, failing this last minute appeal by Mr. Smith being successful, I was to return to Salisbury.

Closeted in my office he informed me of this decision, and to my surprise and dismay told me that the reason for my recall was not only for consultation or diplomatic withdrawal but for me to be available in Salisbury as a possible choice for the office of Governor or Regent when Sir Humphrey Gibbs vacated this appointment. It was assumed with reason that Sir Humphrey had given an assurance that in the event of an assumption of independence he would resign and retire to his farm.

I had my own reservations about becoming a candidate for this promotion, not from any personal objection, but because I considered that it would be improper for a High Commissioner to go straight from London to such an appointment. It would not in my view improve the image that the Rhodesians had created in England. Furthermore I was a soldier with a military rank, and it might smack too much of an army coup, such as was happening daily in those countries which I had been comparing unfavourably to my own.

The globe is littered with states headed by Colonel this, and Brigadier that. Not only has this been the invariable rule in banana republics, but the idea had caught on throughout the Middle East and the Arab states. Even in Asia one could not keep count of the Field-Marshals, Air-Marshals and Generals who kept popping in and out of such high offices like jack-in-the-boxes. I thought that Rhodesia should try to avoid this invidious comparison.

It now seemed certain that my days in London were over, and I booked a seat in a BOAC VC10 for Saturday night. This meant

108

that Honor and Julia would be left in London after the possible assumption of independence on Monday or Tuesday. In view of the fact that I might be selected for an appointment that would be most unlikely to find favour with the British Government, we decided that she must be out of the country by Monday.

Apart from any other unpleasantness that might befall her, her life would be made impossible by the Press. This was only too true as the future confirmed. To take her out to Rhodesia with me, was too obvious an indication of our intention, so I arranged for her to fly with Julia to Lisbon, ostensibly on a holiday with the Reedmans. After all, what could be more natural than that during my absence she should take up this long-standing invitation, rather than be at a loose end in London.

The following day was a busy one for Honor. She packed up frenziedly, and as much as weight allowed was packed for myself and Andrew Dunlop to take back to Rhodesia, whilst she and Julia took as much as the allowance permitted to Lisbon. The rest was bundled up and sent to Rhodesia House for onward transmission to Rhodesia, and we began to doubt if we would ever see this luggage again. Visas to Portugal were obtained, and two full fare tourist seats in the names of Mrs. and Miss Jones were bought on the Lisbon plane for Sunday.

On Saturday she departed by car for Cornwall, collected Julia and returned late that same night. It was a hair-raising journey for road visibility was nil for long stretches, and the Great West Road had an unusual crop of piled up cars that night. On Sunday after I had departed, she flew to Lisbon where she had a most pleasant stay with the Reedmans, though naturally in view of the situation that faced Rhodesia it was an anxious time for all of them.

Certain side benefits might have accrued from this melodramatic departure. It was known that the Portuguese were becoming worried by the apparent hesitation of the Rhodesians, for they had seen how the territories on their borders in Africa had one by one fallen to hostile African rule, aided and abetted by British pressures. Their security was bound up with our resolution to maintain civilised standards of international conduct with our neighbours.

The departure of the High Commissioner from London, and the simultaneous arrival under these secret arrangements of his family in Lisbon, might have given them some reassurance, for they would be well accustomed to read between the lines. It is more than possible that the British Security services might have had the same ideas, for little is hid from them and it might have given the added conviction that the Rhodesians meant business, and an effort had to be made to meet them, even if it were more apparent than real and genuine.

The Saturday afternoon before my departure I had attended the wedding reception of my Personal Assistant, Denzil Bradley to Miss Judie Stevenson. This wedding had been put forward on my advice in view of what I thought might happen in the near future. Denzil might be packed off unceremoniously to Rhodesia with his fiancee stuck in London. In addition, my week's stay in Salisbury provided an ideal opportunity for him to have his honeymoon undisturbed by thoughts of duty.

That morning I had arranged my own affairs and cleared my desk and office. Both were then handed over to P. K. van der Byl who would hold the fort till my return or, failing that, during the upheaval that would follow an assumption of independence. I had a feeling that in the latter event P.K. was not averse to a spell in the Tower of London, a situation he would meet with dignity for at times he presented an almost medieval example of sombre wit and elegance. By Friday a certain amount of urgency and tension had been dissipated by Mr. Wilson's dramatic gimmick of flying to Salisbury – his first visit to the African continent and to countries over whose destinies he had so much control.

An assumption of independence was not out of the picture, but at least a breathing space of a few days remained. I still did not know if I would be able to return to London, though I thought it unlikely. That would depend on the final talks in Salisbury and if the British Government would at this eleventh hour recognise the justice of our claim.

I was very tired when I left London on the Saturday. Honor had not returned from Cornwall when I left our house at 8 p.m., and I was worried about her and Julia's safety in the appalling road visibility that existed at that hour.

It took a long time to feel our way to the airport but mercifully the Press were not interested in what they took to be the routine journey by a High Commissioner flying to Salisbury, where it was natural that he should be available for consultation during Mr. Wilson's visit. After all, the British High Commissioner in Rhodesia had returned for the London talks during the previous week. And to my satisfaction there were only one journalist and one cameraman attending my departure. The V.I.P. lounge was almost empty.

In the VC10 were a number of journalists flying out to Rhodesia for what might prove to be a press jamboree. Several passengers who looked suspiciously like security officers and king's messengers occupied the seats near me.

I slept most of the way to Salisbury and arrived about midday of a most beautiful Salisbury day, with blue skies and balmy weather, a striking contrast with London. I felt the change of atmosphere at once and felt an immediate lifting of spirits. I was home again.

I was met by Mrs. Janet Smith, representing her husband the Prime Minister, Mr. Jack Mussett, the Minister of Local Government, a fellow citizen of Umtali, and my son and nephew. After greetings and a ginger ale in the lounge, I was accosted by the usual throng of journalists to whom I had little of importance to say, and whose attention was drawn to my London garb and in particular the bowler hat I was wearing. I passed a few jests about this and was then driven off to External Affairs by Mr. Wetmore, the Secretary, and Mr. Bowles the Under-Secretary. I had a number of secret despatches to deliver, and I gave them various messages from Rhodesia House. I was then driven to the Prime Minister's House, whose guest I was to be during my week's stay in Salisbury. I was to enjoy one of the most comfortable weeks as a guest and returned refreshed and restored to my work in London.

Mr. Wilson was due to arrive in Rhodesia on the following Monday evening. I was able to bring Ian Smith up to date with the situation as it appeared to me in London. I touched upon the question of a Head of State should our negotiations fail and gave him my views on this subject. The idea of our Head of State being called a Regent I had mentioned in a speech to the Monday Club in London. However, on giving it further thought, I suggested that initially this officer should have some vaguer title, less reminiscent of the Prince Regent of tarnished fame. In the event, the word was dropped and something of the kind I had in mind was adopted. Meanwhile the matter regarding this appointment was held in abeyance, and was not brought up till we had assumed our independence.

The following day a Cabinet meeting was held and I attended a part of this. I gave the Ministers my views on the situation in London, the state of public opinion, how we could hold this in our favour and how our crisis was affecting and would affect the political parties in England. That evening I drove out with other members of the Cabinet to greet the British party.

The African nationalists, assisted by their few but active European supporters, had been busy at their old game of intimidation. Unfortunate Africans were being forced, in many cases without food, and without regard to health and fitness, to tramp the several miles from Salisbury to the airport. Some were paid to do this, others came out of curiosity, but the vast majority came under duress.

Few people of British stock can understand how the many can be forced through threats by the few to do something they do not want to do. The normal British reaction to a threat is to do the opposite, as a way of asserting one's independence. Even if the action meets with their approval, a threat is often enough to make them take the opposite course. But African thought processes are quite different from those of the European. This is a fact which the liberal politician cannot absorb.

For thousands of years the African has been at the mercy of the stronger individuals and tribes. Of all the races in the world the African has provided the slave in past ages. For example the invaders of the American continent could not force the Red Indians and the Caribs into slavery, but had to import Africans for this purpose.

Fear of violence and fear of witchcraft are the most powerful factors which operate on the lives of the average African. Against the person who uses these two weapons, they appear to be powerless and as helpless as a rabbit in front of a weasel, and they do not seem to be able to combine in their numbers against those more forcible individuals who seek to intimidate them. This trait in their character is the result of history and is seemingly ineradicable.

So several thousands of these people trekked out patiently to line the exits from the airport. One wretched African woman with her child had been forced out of her home early in the day and was placed on the airport balcony by her intimidator to stand there for long hours without food or water. Confessing her plight to sympathetic Europeans, she was duly fed and looked after by them. The African nationalist who had forced her to the airport was quite indifferent. Such were the people to whom Mr. Wilson was aiming to deliver the average African in Rhodesia.

112

The landing was scheduled to take place at 7 p.m., and the aircraft was overhead and circling to land at this time. We began to wonder if this delay was deliberate to coincide with the closing of the factories and places of work so as to allow the organisers of the demonstration to get the maximum numbers assembled. There were rumours that members of the High Commission staff had a hand in this welcome to their Prime Minister.

As it turned out, these throngs of African onlookers were too bored and tired or indifferent to spark off the rousing demonstration that was required, and Mr. Wilson drove into Salisbury through curious, silent crowds with only an occasional activist waving a placard or shouting a slogan.

The European population ignored his arrival and only a few white faces were seen in the crowd, mostly belonging to expatriate missionaries and students from the lunatic fringe of the university.

The Press however headlined these crowds, magnified their numbers and tried to draw inferences from the reception. Even their skilled pens could hardly paint a picture of wild enthusiasm for Mr. Wilson.

The British Prime Minister and his Cabinet colleagues were to stay at Government House. The overflow of his vast entourage which had arrived before him or with him in his RAF Comet were being accommodated by the High Commission and in the hotels. In addition to these people, journalists had arrived from all parts of the world and a great number of these congregated in the Ambassador Hotel. This is a multi-racial hotel in the heart of Salisbury, but they omitted to mention this fact in their despatches. The very fact of its existence should have dispelled some of their fond illusions about discrimination in Rhodesia.

It appeared that the British Prime Minister wished to meet what was called "all shades of opinion". Some of these "shades of opinion" represented only their individual selves, but all were welcome. In this respect it should be pointed out that the Rhodesian Front represented the bulk of European opinion.

Their chairman, Colonel Mac Knox, issued a statement that the Front had no wish to represent its opinion to Mr. Wilson. Mr. Ian Smith held the Party's confidence and he would speak for them. The European Trade Unions made a similar statement, whilst the bulk of the Africans were represented by their chiefs. These men obtained a short hearing from the British Prime Minister, but what they said might not have received a favourable hearing.

So, for the next two or three days the various delegations to whom the British Prime Minister gave untiring audience were those who represented minority opinion. The African Nationalist leaders and Mr. Todd were brought out of restriction and spent quite a bit of time with Mr. Wilson. Some of Mr. Wilson's entourage were able to get away from the enclosed atmosphere of Government House and saw something of Rhodesia, notably hospitals, factories and welfare centres which were quite an eye-opener to some of them.

There were one or two meetings between Mr. Smith and his Ministers and Mr. Wilson and Mr. Bottomley, but there was no record or statement of what passed at these encounters.

Meanwhile it transpired that the Chief Justice, Sir Hugh Beadle, had suggested a formula by which the deadlock could be resolved. The initial suggestion, which appeared to find favour with Mr. Wilson, was a Royal Commission – that stand-by of all Governments who wish to postpone or shrug off some unpleasant issue. This Royal Commission was expected to evolve a new constitution that would be acceptable to the country at large. As the majority of the country stood by the 1961 Constitution with the concessions already offered in London, this meant that the Royal Commission's task was to evolve something that was also acceptable to the minority views which had been besieging Mr. Wilson for the last few days.

Like the Monckton commission, this commission would be a godsend to the British. It could delay the issue for years and in the end its recommendations could be ignored, if by some fluke they were acceptable to the Rhodesian electorate. This was a non-starter, but the indefatigable Chief Justice had not given up.

On Thursday, 28th October, the Prime Minister of Rhodesia gave a dinner at his house to the British Ministers and senior civil servants. His own Cabinet and senior civil servants attended, as well as the two High Commissioners, myself and Mr. Johnson. Twenty-four of us sat round the table. The wives of the Rhodesian guests were present, but dined separately.

This was to prove a historic occasion, and I suggested to Janet Smith that a menu card should be passed round for the signatures of those present, as is often the custom in England on special occasions.

114

This was duly done, and amongst other signatures it bore that of the two Prime Ministers. I hope she still has it in safe custody, for now that the two opposing parties are not on speaking terms, it will become a most valuable possession.

Whilst Mr. Wilson was signing, one of us jokingly warned him that a document with carbon paper was concealed under the cardboard, and that it gave us our independence. The other signatures were merely witnesses. This was a jest well taken.

The Press made much of this dinner party. Many journalists were gathered outside the gates of the Prime Minister's grounds eagerly hoping for some dramatic story, but all they heard was much laughter, and the loud voice of some raconteur. From this they reported that high words and angry scenes had filled the dining-room. It was also stated that Mr. Wilson had outlined the sanctions he proposed to institute if Rhodesia declared her independence, oil embargoes being mentioned. If any such threats were uttered, I can vouch for it that they were not mentioned during dinner, although they may or may not have been touched upon in individual conversation during the pre-dinner drinks in the drawing-room.

The dinner itself was a most friendly and convivial affair, at which everyone enjoyed himself. After the loyal toast had been drunk and cigars had been handed round, the company added to its repertoire of after dinner stories at which Lord Graham, the Minister of Agriculture, as usual excelled himself. Mr. Wilson himself told one or two amusing stories that were passing round the Commons, and one story which touched the initials P.M., which were shared by two of us present, raised very considerable and ribald amusement.

The party broke up late and the guests departed with nothing of importance decided, except a demonstration that the two opposing parties to this dispute answered to that much derided phrase "kith and kin" and in all common sense should have mutually agreed that wider British interests would best be served by allowing the Rhodesians to uphold British values in this part of Africa. There were more discussions next day.

The day after my arrival I had travelled down to the Eastern Districts and spent a night with my son on our property. Here I met my family and a few friends and heard what they were thinking about things. Without exception they reported that nothing in their opinion would come out of Mr. Wilson's visit except delay and the sooner we

115

took our independence the better. This was the general feeling throughout the country.

Many were actually hostile to the delay and expressed a view that our Government was weakening and going the same way as had led to the dissolution of the Federation. I tried to explain to them how necessary it was for us to show our good faith to the bitter end so that in our eyes, and those of the British public, we would be free of reproach.

I spent only one night at home before I returned to Salisbury on the Monday. I was to pay one more very brief visit before I flew back suddenly to London.

13. The Ball Game Continues

No particular progress had been made by Friday, and the idea of a treaty was not acceptable to the British, although the 1961 Constitution and the concessions already offered would almost certainly have been accepted by any British Government a few years previously.

There is little doubt that strong Afro-Asian pressure was being exerted on the British Government. These nations were in full cry at this moment, and determined that a solution short of immediate African nationalist rule should not be found. The Americans, nervous of their position in the African world and heedful of the growing power of their Negro vote, together with the Communist world were no more helpful.

The British were not strong enough to stand up to this pressure. Their only hope now lay in some form of delay, and in the seeds of the idea of a Royal Commission lay the chance of buying this time. If this issue could be postponed till the next British election, or better still till the next Commonwealth Prime Ministers' Conference in June, all might be well for them.

At that time, having abdicated their position as head of the Commonwealth, they could hand their responsibility for Rhodesia over to the Commonwealth Secretariat – already being formed – and have a splendid alibi with their electorate.

One could well imagine how the Rhodesians and their 1961 Constitution would fare with the new Commonwealth's nine new African states, backed by the Asian members and, who knows by then such powerful independent nations as Mauritius, the Seychelles and St. Helena.

The ball was back in the British court. We had received Mr. Wilson with courtesy, demonstrated how peace and calm reigned in the country and how solidly the bulk of the population was behind Mr. Smith. We had given every facility to the British to sound opinion and had gone to great lengths to bring the African nationalists to his door for consultation and for him to judge their capacity to rule. We had again

117

offered the concessions put forward in London and were prepared to put our good faith on paper in the form of a treaty.

Mr. Wilson then requested to be allowed to appear on our T.V. and Radio and make an appeal to Rhodesians. He had brought out to Rhodesia the usual apparatus for his T.V. performance and the technician employed for this carefully staged appearance. We in turn offered him exactly the same facilities that had been given Mr. Smith in London, namely an appearance before a panel of Rhodesian journalists.

This did not suit him. He required a facility that Mr. Smith had been denied by the BBC, namely a solo performance such as he had given the British public on Mr. Smith's departure from London. I was a member of the Cabinet sub-committee that considered the whole question, and on hearing of his refusal, we went so far as to offer him RTV facilities in London, with the same panel appearing there with him in the BBC studios. This suggestion was declined by his press and information team. Instead he decided to hold a press conference on the eve of his departure next day.

Meanwhile the Chief Justice was still trying to revive the idea of a Royal Commission, of which he was to be the chairman, if not in its original form then in some other. He was very disturbed at the legal and economic consequences of a declaration of independence and was striving to avert it by all the means in his power. I wondered if he realised what the real intentions of the British Government were, and how an African nationalist government could destroy our economy and legal procedures to a far greater extent, as has happened in Ghana. Whilst I respected his sincerity, I deplored his lack of insight into the methods of the British Government, and later in London, I tried to put him wise on these.

As a result of his activities a last minute meeting was arranged at 9 o'clock that Friday night in the Prime Minister's House. This was a very full meeting at which the whole Rhodesian Cabinet and the entire British delegation were present. I attended this last confrontation between the two parties because my opposite number, the British High Commissioner, was present. There must have been over thirty of us seated round the Rhodesian Prime Minister's dining-room table. It was a hot night and most of us took our coats off. Like the words in the song, the old familiar dialogue went round and round. Mr. Wilson has described his version of what passed in the room and it was recorded in the Hansard of the House of Commons. There is some exaggeration in his description of the hate-filled faces of some individuals who he alleged were hell-bent on a declaration of independence at all costs. To my recollection the Rhodesian Prime Minister and his colleagues displayed an endless patience as they tried to demonstrate their goodwill. But it was to no avail. We were up against a brick wall of British political self-interest in which our long-term interests were of no account. I well remember our Prime Minister saying to Mr. Wilson that this issue might be vital to his political future, but to Rhodesians it was vital to their very lives and existence.

Finally at literally five minutes past midnight, after three hours of talk, Mr. Wilson referred again to the Royal Commission. He inferred that from some very recent conversation he had misunderstood the formula put to Mr. Smith. The ball had been very quietly and skilfully tossed to our Prime Minister. The Royal Commission now appeared to be the means of ascertaining opinion under the fifth principle, and was not to be charged with the task of framing a new constitution. Argument developed on this theme and what eventually emerged was a Royal Commission of three. One Rhodesian, one Briton both under the chairmanship of the Chief Justice, Sir Hugh Beadle, who also had the qualification of being a born Rhodesian and a British Privy Councillor. A neatly balanced team, or so it seemed.

This commission would be charged with framing its own terms of reference about the methods of ascertaining Rhodesian opinion, and these in turn were to be agreed to by both Governments. After this the commission was to sound opinion by these agreed methods.

There was no discussion on what would happen if the commission of three were not unanimous, but this issue was brought up again later. The British stated that we had agreed to the commission making a unanimous report. Presumably there were minutes to support or deny this argument. I must confess I do not recollect any agreement on this point. I was not taking the minutes for at least four scribes were busy at this task.

Finally there had to be agreement on the constitution that was to be put to the people. Broadly this was the 1961 Constitution with the concessions made in London. To this would be added such amendments as were legally necessary to frame a constitution of independence from Britain. As it was thought that this would be a simple task for the lawyers with no political complications, an arrangement was made for the British Attorney-General and Mr. Bottomley to work on it the next day and Sunday, and then to follow Mr. Wilson to London.

The British party then departed to their beds, and we Rhodesians were left to ponder on this sudden and apparent capitulation by the British. As the 1961 Constitution had already been accepted by a referendum and an indaba a year before, and we knew that the vast majority of the Europeans and Africans would accept it again with the new amendments which were even more liberal than the original constitution, the whole thing seemed too good to be true. Indeed it was, as we found to our cost during the following ten days.

Meanwhile we drafted a communiqué on the final result of this discussion and retired exhausted to our beds. Some of the more wary and wiser amongst us scented a trap, but still we hoped. It was quite untrue to assert, as Mr. Wilson did later, that there were elements in the Cabinet who were determined on a declaration of independence for its own sake. We were doing our utmost to avoid taking this course, except in the very last resource, and then for the sake of our survival as a civilised country.

The following day Mr. Wilson and the bulk of his entourage departed for England via the capitals of the West African Commonwealth states, presumably to soothe their rage at this apparent betrayal of their designs and explain the British motives behind the new proposal.

Sir Elwyn Jones, Mr. Bottomley and the British High Commissioner in Salisbury got down to work with the Rhodesian team which consisted of Messrs. Dupont, Harper, Rudland, Lardner Burke, Maclean and for a brief session, the Prime Minister. Their task was to draft the constitutional proposals on which the Royal Commission would work. I excused myself from this meeting, at which I was entitled to be present owing to the presence of my opposite number.

A communiqué had been issued by Mr. Wilson after a press conference with the journalists assembled in Salisbury. In certain respects it did not tally with the one we had issued the night before and our information sub-committee examined it with care.

The first doubts began to be sown in our minds about British intentions. The first meeting to draft the proposals for the Royal Commission ran into difficulties, for it began to appear that the British wished to go far beyond the concessions already agreed.

Meanwhile the Prime Minister was due to attend a public meeting at Rusape that evening. As Rusape was on the way to my home, I took the opportunity to attend this function, and my son and I drove down that afternoon. It was very well attended and I met a great number of my friends, and I was able to tell them about the situation in London. The Prime Minister spoke at length about the new developments and the Royal Commission, and was able to get support for the idea. There were many who were suspicious of the whole thing, especially when they heard that the final answer would delay the issue for at least two months, but they were prepared to accept the good faith of the British Government if the exercise was allowed to proceed without further concessions being incorporated in the constitution and the end result was accepted without quibble by the British.

Alas this was not to be. No agreement was possible at the meetings of Mr. Bottomley and our Ministers, and it appeared as if the negotiations on our constitution were to be reopened afresh.

I returned home after the Rusape meeting, arriving at our house about midnight and went to bed. Next day I visited some friends and was due to lunch at my mother-in-law's house. Just as we were starting lunch I had an urgent telephone call from Mr. Rudland in Salisbury. I was asked to return to Salisbury at once, see him and Mr. Ian Smith, and then fly back at once to London, where I was to report to Mr. Wilson next morning.

My son and I dashed back to our house, packed and were on the road in twenty minutes. It was then 1 o'clock. Driving at speeds far in excess of the speed limit on a road that was mercifully empty, we reached Salisbury at 4 o'clock. Here the Prime Minister gave me a written statement to Mr. Wilson. It was written in longhand, there being no time to type it. It ran as follows:

"From Rhodesian Prime Minister to British Prime Minister, 31st October 1965.

"The talks ended here this morning without managing to bring the two sides any closer. After you departed no progress was made, I regret to report.

"As we agreed here on Friday night, there is no point in the

121

"D-down on your knees – you f-frightened little man of Salisbury!" (From the "Sunday Express", November 14, 1965. Permission: London Express Service)

Royal Commission starting, unless the proposed constitution is acceptable to the Rhodesian Government. Otherwise, the exercise would be a useless one.

"Even though our proposals may not completely satisfy the British Government, I believe that we should now leave it to an impartial arbitrator – the proposed Royal Commission – to determine whether our proposals are acceptable to the people of Rhodesia as a whole. If the Commission finds in the affirmative, then, in all justice, no one will have any right to stand in our way.

"I would remind you that last year I made an agreement with your predecessor that Rhodesia could have independence on the 1961 Constitution, if it could be proved that this was acceptable to the people of Rhodesia as a whole. Unfortunately, we differed over the mechanics of testing public opinion in Rhodesia. Under this proposed scheme the Rhodesian Government has agreed to additional liberal concessions in your favour.

"Therefore, if you are unwilling to accept the proposal now put to you, this means that you are departing, in principle, from the agreement which I made with your predecessor last year. As for the mechanics of carrying out the exercise, we have already agreed that this should be a Royal Commission. Hence we have overcome the difficulty which arose between your predecessor and myself."

122

What had happened was that the meetings between our Ministers and Mr. Bottomley and Sir Elwyn Jones had broken down at the very first hurdle, which was the form of the constitution that was to be put to the people by the Royal Commission.

At the midnight meeting which I have described, it was understood that this constitution was to be the 1961 Constitution and in it were to be inserted the concessions already made in London by the Rhodesian delegation. The other amendments were purely consequential legal adjustments to make this constitution an independent one.

What had transpired was that the whole issue had been reopened by the British Ministers who required still further concessions. Again the Rhodesian Ministers tried hard to meet the British objections, and were even prepared to provide a formula over the fade-out of the B roll seats, as time and education provided more Africans who were eligible to vote on the A roll.

My task was now to try and prevent this fresh deadlock by asking the British Prime Minister to allow the Royal Commission to go ahead on the constitutional proposals that were acceptable to the Rhodesians. After all, it was for the people themselves to decide what constitution they wished to have and if it was acceptable, what possible right had the British to refuse it. This was common sense democracy.

It was now more obvious than ever that it was not Rhodesian opinion that interested Mr. Wilson, but that nebulous concept of world opinion, and in particular the opinion of the Commonwealth leaders in Africa and Asia. We Rhodesians were now leaning so far back to help the British that we were in real ranger of toppling over.

Let this dispel once and forever that the Rhodesian Government were an intransigent lot who were determined not to meet British requirements. The result of the abortive meetings over the week-end are given below. I took a copy with me to London.

INDEPENDENCE OF RHODESIA
PROPOSED ROYAL COMMISSION

1. At the meeting of British Ministers and the Rhodesian Cabinet on 29 October the two Prime Ministers discussed proposals for an independence constitution for Rhodesia which might be put before a Royal Commission to be appointed to ascertain whether such proposals would be acceptable to the Government of Rhodesia; and the British Prime Minister accepted the importance of this. The two Prime Ministers agreed that the Commonwealth Secretary with the Attorney-General and Rhodesian Ministers should explore the extent of agreement on such proposals which can be reached and should identify the points of disagreement.

2. The results of our discussion are as follows:

(a) *Ordinary Constitutional Amendments*

Rhodesian position

The Rhodesian Government consider that the present provision that the clauses of the Constitution, other than those specially entrenched, may be amended by a two-thirds majority in the Legislative Assembly, should be continued into the independence constitution unaltered.

British position

The British Ministers suggested that, while this two-thirds provision should be maintained, the B Roll seats in the Legislative Assembly should be increased to provide a "blocking third" for the amendment of these clauses. This proposal is unacceptable to the Rhodesian Ministers.

(b) *Amendment of the Specially Entrenched Clauses*

Rhodesian position

The Rhodesian Ministers regard the present provision for amendment of the specially entrenched clauses by four racial referenda as unworkable. They would however allow this provision to continue into the independence constitution provided an acceptable

124

alternative was introduced for the present arrangements, set out in Section 109, whereby in lieu of these referenda a Bill may be submitted to Her Majesty for Assent. The Rhodesian Ministers propose that, in place of this procedure, a House of 12 Chiefs should be established which would vote with the Assembly on the third reading of any Bill seeking to amend the specially entrenched clauses. The Rhodesian Ministers consider that the 12 Chiefs, added to the existing 15 B Roll members, would provide a predominantly African "blocking third".

British position

The British Ministers do not regard these proposals as providing an acceptable substitute for the present Section 109 procedure and point out that the sole constitutional safeguard would be a margin of two votes. They suggest alternative procedures for the amendment of specially entrenched clauses, to replace the two alternative procedures in the present Constitution.

The first of these would require that a Bill to amend a specially entrenched clause should receive a two-thirds majority in the Legislative Assembly and should then be submitted to a referendum of the electorate, provided that the electorate on the B Roll had been increased to include, say, all adult taxpayers.

The alternative procedure would be that an amending Bill should receive a three-quarters majority in the legislative Assembly, provision having been made for an increase in the B Roll seats to provide a "blocking quarter". Thereafter, before the Bill became law, a fixed time should elapse during which the validity of the Bill could be challenged by any Rhodesian on the grounds (a) that the Bill discriminated or had the effect of discriminating unjustly between the races; (b) that it failed to pay proper respect to the rights and freedoms of the individual. The question of the validity of the Bill would be determined by the appellate division of the High Court of Rhodesia with an appeal as of right from the decision of that court to the Judicial Committee of the Privy Council.

The Rhodesian Ministers find the first of these alternative procedures (i.e. approval by a two-thirds majority followed by a referendum) unacceptable. They are prepared to consider the second alternative, provided the additional two seats necessary to enlarge the B roll to a blocking quarter are filled by Chiefs, who on appointment to the Legislature would cease to receive any Chief's subsidies, and provided the reference to the High Court is strictly limited to the question whether the Bill "discriminates unjustly between the races".

The British Ministers consider that the additional two seats on the B Roll should be filled by members elected on the B Roll.

Additions to the Specially Entrenched Clauses

Rhodesian position

The Rhodesian Ministers are not prepared to agree to the further entrenchment of any clauses in the present constitution, with the possible single exception referred to below.

British position

The British Ministers suggest the special entrenchment of Chapter III of the Constitution which is not now specially entrenched in the Constitution. This Chapter relates to the delimitation and number of constituencies and electoral districts. Without such special entrenchment, it would be possible, by a two-thirds majority, to amend the clauses governing the number of A or B Roll seats.

The Rhodesian Ministers cannot accept the special entrenchment of these clauses. They would, however, agree to the special entrenchment of the provisions governing the total number of B Roll seats, provided a "fade-out" arrangement was introduced into the independence constitution, under which any reduction in B Roll seats would be dependent on non-Europeans winning A Roll seats. The Rhodesian proposal is that for each A Roll seat won by a non-European, a B Roll seat would be abolished. This is unacceptable to the British Ministers. They consider that if an arrangement of this kind were to be introduced, it ought at least to provide that two A Roll seats would have to be won by non-Europeans before a B roll seat was abolished. Additionally, the British Ministers have doubts about this proposal on practical grounds e.g. the difficulty of definition or of subsequent electoral reversal.

126

The Franchise

Rhodesian position

Provided the remaining provisions of the Constitution satisfied their requirements, the Rhodesian Ministers would be willing to extend the franchise on the B Roll to qualified indigenous adult taxpayers.

British position

Provided the remaining provisions of the Constitution satisfied their requirements, and subject to the reasonableness of the proposed qualification, the British Ministers would accept this.

Consequential Amendments

Rhodesian and British Ministers are satisfied that no serious problems are raised by the sequence of amendments, of a consequential nature, which would be necessary to convert the 1961 Constitution into an independence constitution.

Submission of this report

It is agreed that this joint report will be submitted by the British and Rhodesian Ministers to their respective Governments."

After a quick briefing by the Prime Minister I just had time to change, pack and hand over Honor's and my surplus luggage to my son's care. The subsequent lack of these garments proved to be an embarrassment to our social duties in London during the next fortnight, but we were in two minds whether to send for them or not. These suitcases reposed in the care of External Affairs till we returned to Rhodesia, for the situation in London never clarified sufficiently for justifying their despatch to London.

I was seen off at the airport on this Sunday, 30th October, by Mr. and Mrs. Rudland and my son and nephew, and was back unheralded and unmet at London airport in the very early hours of Monday morning. I got an airport car to take me straight to Rhodesia House, where I called up my personal staff from their beds and asked them to come over to the office as soon as possible.

I had the various documents typed and asked Denzil Bradley to obtain an urgent appointment for me with Mr. Wilson. In the meantime, since Honor was still in Portugal and our house was shut up, I took a room in the Strand Palace Hotel, had breakfast and a bath and changed into my London clothes.

At 11 o'clock sharp I was at 10 Downing Street where I saw Mr. Wilson. I explained the situation and asked him for an early reply, if possible by Wednesday, as to whether the Royal Commission should go ahead on the terms outlined by Mr. Smith. He agreed that the matter was urgent, and I got the impression that he would decide and make an announcement in the House of Commons on Wednesday afternoon. I cabled back to Salisbury accordingly.

Should his answer be favourable, there were still two more hurdles before this whole exercise of a Royal Commission could commence. Firstly the composition of the Royal Commission had to be decided. There was no disagreement over the appointment of Sir Hugh Beadle as the chairman, and the Rhodesian member would be selected by the Rhodesian Government. Various names were already being mentioned by the Press as to who the British representative would be, the name of Mr. Malcolm McDonald being the favourite. This hurdle passed, the next would be the agreed method of consultation of the people of Rhodesia by the Commission. As the whole object of this Commission was to provide a means other than a referendum, it was anticipated that this would be the hardest one to cross.

My next task was to seek an interview with the Conservative leaders and inform them of the situation as it faced the Rhodesians, so on Tuesday evening I saw Mr. Heath, the Opposition leader, and Mr. Selwyn Lloyd. To them I put the fact that during the previous year we had understood that Sir Alec Douglas Home was prepared to grant us independence on the 1961 Constitution provided that we could show that the people as a whole accepted it. They denied that this was so, but I pointed out that we would hardly have held a referendum and a chiefs' indaba, if such had not been our impression.

I also told them that we required an answer by Wednesday on the Royal Commission, and if it should proceed with its work on the terms of reference outlined to Mr. Wilson in the letter I had delivered to him. They considered that the British Government was being unduly rushed by the Rhodesians in this matter and advised patience. I informed them that we had been very patient for a great number of years and were entitled to a quick answer.

It was not a satisfactory interview and heralded the beginnings of the bipartisan approach to the Rhodesian crisis that we have heard so much about. In view of the Conservatives' past record in negotiations, it would seem that they were initially committed to such a policy, and could not reverse it overnight. It is still to be seen if the pressures of public opinion and electoral advantage may modify and change this approach, though it will have to be a gradual change, and may take some time.

I reported back to Salisbury, and settled back into the routine work of Rhodesia House. It now seemed, if all went well, and the British did not hedge on the details, that a reasonably peaceful two months lay ahead till the Royal Commission published its findings.

Honor had returned from Portugal the previous day, and we once more took up residence in Chelsea. Owing to the uncertainty of things we decided to keep Julia with us for a few days before returning her to school in Cornwall. After an initial day of panic, with reminders of our three weeks' servantless purgatory, Franca, our daily, turned up, and all was quiet on the domestic front.

14. Intervention by the Sidesman

Mr. Bottomley had returned and presumably reported on what had transpired in Salisbury after his Prime Minister's departure. He had returned via the East Coast of Africa where he visited the various heads of state of the African members of the Commonwealth and presumably also reported their reactions.

It might well have been that the African states were alarmed when Messrs. Wilson and Bottomley explained the function and aims of the Royal Commission, lest the Commission should find that independence on the basis of the 1961 Constitution was acceptable, as was most likely, to the majority of Africans and Europeans in Rhodesia. They might have expressed their displeasure should such a thing occur. This is a matter for speculation, but it is a speculation more than justified by recent events, and it might well have caused some quick re-thinking on Mr. Wilson's part for on Wednesday afternoon Mr. Wilson made a statement in the House on his visit to Rhodesia and the subject of the Royal Commission. I give it in full here, because it shows that Mr. Wilson had departed in many respects from what we in Salisbury had understood to be the situation in regard to the Royal Commission.

"With permission, Mr. Speaker, I should like to make a further statement on Rhodesia.

"On Monday I said that the two Governments had agreed in principle to recommend to Her Majesty the appointment of a Royal Commission for the purpose of testing the acceptability to the Rhodesian people as a whole of a draft independence arrangement which, we hoped, would be agreed between the two Governments and would be based on the 1961 Constitution with such amendments *as we might consider necessary*. I went on to say that the two Governments were in discussion to see whether it was possible to agree on the content of a document which the Royal Commission could take for this purpose.

"My right hon. Friend the Secretary of State for Commonwealth

Relations and my right hon. and learned Friend the Attorney-General have now returned and reported on their discussions. It is now clear that there is no prospect – and the House would realise from what I said on Monday the kind of issues involved – of agreement being reached on the amendments which should be made to the 1961 Constitution as a basis for use by the Royal Commission.

"In these circumstances we have had to consider our position. This we have done with a deep sense of the responsibility lying upon us for ensuring that this House, before there is any question of its being asked to take a decision about independence, should have before it an authoritative statement of the views of the Rhodesian people as a whole on particular proposals for independence.

"Mr. Smith considers that independence on the basis of the 1961 Constitution is acceptable to the Rhodesian people. Neither we nor our predecessors have been able to accept this as a fact without the most rigorous proof being forthcoming.

"In this connection I must refer to statements made yesterday by Mr. Smith about the discussions he had with my predecessor, the right hon. Gentleman the Member for Kinross and West Perth, in September 1964. Mr. Smith said that he had made an agreement with my predecessor that Rhodesia could have independence on the 1961 Constitution, if it could be proved that this was acceptable to the people of Rhodesia as a whole.

"I want to make it clear that we do not accept this interpretation and we have so informed Mr. Smith. The right hon. Gentleman made it crystal clear again and again that the British Government had as yet no evidence that the majority of the population supported the Rhodesian request for independence on the basis of the present constitution and franchise, and indeed in the final agreed communiqué, the following statement occurs: 'The British Prime Minister said that the British Government would take account of any views which might be freely expressed by the population on the issue involved; but he must make it plain that the British Government reserved their position.' Against that background and unequivocally reconfirming the statement I have just quoted, the British Government have decided and I have so informed Mr. Smith that we are now prepared to agree, subject to certain conditions I shall outline, that the Rhodesian Government's constitutional proposals

131

should be put to the test of acceptability to the people of Rhodesia as a whole.

"But if this is to be done it must be known that we ourselves disagree with these proposals for the reasons I stated on Monday and which I will not weary the House by repeating. Indeed Mr. Smith himself recognised in his broadcast on Monday night that we disagree with them.

"Second we continue to hold the view that the Royal Commission, before canvassing the views of the Rhodesian people as a whole, should submit for approval by both Governments a unanimous interim report on how they would propose to determine acceptability. If the Royal Commission's suggestions for this purpose were approved, they should themselves supervise whatever procedures were adopted in order to implement their findings.

"Third when the Royal Commission have completed the process of ascertaining the opinion of the people of Rhodesia as a whole, they will submit a final report *which we have agreed must be unanimous. The British Government cannot of course be expected to commit themselves in advance to accept that report,* particularly as in any case the eventual decision rests with Parliament alone.

"But I must also inform the House that we have made it clear to the Rhodesian Government, and I do not want there to be any misunderstanding about this here, in Rhodesia, or anywhere else, that if, in the event, the Royal Commission's finding showed that the Rhodesian Government's proposal was unacceptable to the people of Rhodesia as a whole, *the British Government reserve their freedom of action as to the future course to be followed.* We would feel free to pursue other means of dealing with the problem such as reviving our earlier suggestion of a Royal Commission with the substantive task of *devising a new constitution for Rhodesia, or our proposal that the issue should be remitted to a Constitutional Conference.*

"I greatly hope, Mr. Speaker, and I am sure the House will share this hope, that after all the efforts that have been made in these past few weeks to secure a solution fulfilling all the requirements with honour and justice, that what I have said will enable us to go ahead with the Royal Commission, on the principle of which we agreed last week, and that the Royal Commission can get down to its vitally important work without delay.

"If what I have said is unacceptable to the Rhodesian Government

– though I am sure the whole House would find it difficult to believe that this could not be acceptable to them – I have one last alternative proposition which I have put to Mr. Smith, as a fall-back on which agreement could still be reached. We should still be willing, as an alternative, to agree that the Rhodesian Government's Constitutional proposals should be submitted to the test of a referendum of the whole of the Rhodesian people, provided that it was conducted without restriction on free political activity by all sections of the community, was subject to adequate impartial supervision, and that it incorporated stringent safeguards against intimidation from any quarter.

"I will, of course, keep the House fully informed of any further development."

Two salient points arose out of this statement. Firstly and most important the British Government did not commit themselves in advance to accept the report of the Commission. If it happened to be favourable to the Rhodesian Government, it could be ignored like so many findings of a Royal Commission. It would of course have been easy for the two parties to have pledged themselves in advance to vote in favour of the findings of the Commission, and this would not have prejudiced the sovereign right of Parliament to a final decision. This they did not do.

Thus the whole exercise could have wasted up to three months, without purpose, except to delay the whole issue further.

The second point was the insistence on unanimous recommendations by the three commissioners. Here again lay another uncertainty which made Rhodesians suspicious. Should the third, and presumably British nominee, decide in the interest of his Government that this matter should not be so easily resolved, he could bring the whole exercise to nothing and lay the way open for the British Government to demand a referendum, or failing that a Constitutional conference.

A copy of this statement in the House was sent in advance to the Rhodesian Government in Salisbury. There was, however, a significant omission in the public statement which was published in Britain. In the statement issued in Britain it stated, as will be observed: "The British Government cannot of course be expected to commit themselves in advance to accept that report." In the statement sent to Rhodesia, these words were preceded by: "I take it that although this report would obviously carry the greatest weight and there would have to be very compelling reasons for you to reject it, you would not be willing to commit yourselves (in Rhodesia) to accept it in advance irrespective of its nature."

This of course was an unwarrantable assumption, and appeared to be a *quid pro quo* alibi, to be concealed from the British public and the Commons. I cabled to Salisbury to point out this omission in the British statement.

What had appeared plain sailing in Salisbury the previous week, was now becoming hedged with imponderables and doubt. Suspicions in Rhodesia hardened into a certainty that the British were up to their old games again, and the sorry tale of the Federation was again unfolding itself before their eyes. Now all hinged on the British reservations about accepting the final result of the Royal Commission's work.

The following communications then passed between London and Salisbury, and both were released to the Press.

From the Rhodesian Prime Minister to the British Prime Minister and delivered by our High Commission to 10 Downing Street.
6th November, 1965.
"I have received your personal message of the 3rd November, 1965. (The statement in the Commons version sent to Rhodesia.)

"I first deal with your suggestion that I do not correctly state the position regarding agreement with your predecessor. This I fail to see – in fact, I think you make a distinction without a difference. It is correct that Sir Alec Douglas-Home was not convinced that a majority of the population supported our request for independence under the 1961 Constitution, but I am quite clear in my mind that Sir Alec also accepted that if the case could be proved he could not deny our claim. All I sought was that you should do the same. It was your suggestion that a Royal Commission be established to determine acceptability. If it found opinion in our favour what conceivable grounds exist for denying the validity and justness of our claim?

"You say in the fourth paragraph of your letter: 'I can now tell you that the British Government agree that the Rhodesian Government's own constitutional proposals should now be put to the test of acceptability to the people of Rhodesia as a whole.' You then go on

134

to hedge this acceptance with such conditions as to make it difficult to believe that it can be seriously intended, as I now show.

"(a) You wish to be free to state publicly that you disagree with the proposals. This you have done, but you also require that the Royal Commission, in the process of canvassing opinion in Rhodesia, should make this clearly known. In other words, the Commission would become a forum for argument and dispute on the merits of the relative proposals. It would thus find itself the centre of a maelstrom. Undoubtedly, advocacy of the British Government's proposals (which would not in fact be part of the submission of the Commission) would become a potent and distracting factor. Its effect would simply be to convert it into a constitutional conference, and in dealing with emergent and, in some cases, primitive people, through an interpreter, the confusion of thought caused could provide no significant answer at all.

"(b) You require that the Commissioners should submit a unanimous report on how they would propose to determine acceptability. This shows a singular lack of confidence in the Commission which, if it is to be entrusted with the task, is surely competent to fulfil it. You have expressed your supreme confidence in the Chairman of the Commission and it seems strange that you should now question his ability to guide the Commission in its fundamental approach.

"(c) You require the final report of the Commission to be unanimous. I accept that you made this point in our discussions, but I remind you that you did not obtain my agreement. If a Commission is unable to agree on a unanimous report it is customary to have a majority and a minority report. It would be wrong to demand of such a Commission unanimity of thought before it had even set about its task.

"(d) You then go on to reserve your position and indicate that you cannot be expected to commit your Government in advance to accept the report of the Commission and that in any case the eventual decision rests with the British Parliament alone, yet in paragraph three of your letter you condemn the proposals. Thus, at the very outset it appears that there is no likelihood (whether or not the Commission's report is unanimous) of your accepting its conclusions and advocating its acceptance by Parliament unless the proposals and conclusions are entirely satisfactory to your Government and accord

135

with your inclinations, irrespective of the wishes of Rhodesians. *We, for our part did not and would not have reserved our position had the Commission been allowed to function as we envisaged.*

"The proposals contained in paragraph five of your message regarding a Royal Commission to make recommendations for a new Constitution for Rhodesia are not acceptable to me and this was clearly indicated to you when you were in Salisbury.

"Similarly, your suggestion in paragraph six that the Rhodesian Government's proposals be submitted to the test of a referendum of the whole people of Rhodesia is quite outside the scope of the proposals made by the Rhodesian Government. Such a suggestion at this stage would be a negation of the understandings reached with you.

"The conditions you have imposed in your letter are clearly designed to reinstate your original proposals which we rejected and to defeat the whole object of our counter proposals, with which you concurred.

"I therefore regret to tell you that the only conclusion to be derived from your letter is that it is tantamount to, and can only be interpreted as, a rejection of the proposals agreed with you in Salisbury. I also regret to say that the impression you left with us of a determined effort to resolve our constitutional problems has been utterly dissipated. It would seem that you have now finally closed the door which you claimed publicly to have opened."

This message was to be published in Salisbury at 12 noon Rhodesian time.

To this message the British replied as follows:

1. "Thank you for your message of yesterday. It creates a difficult situation.

"2. The purpose of our present exchanges is to try to get a Royal Commission set up. No doors are being closed by me. You will recall that, when I originally put forward the idea of a Royal Commission with wide terms of reference, you made an alternative proposal for a Commission with a narrower task. In the light of certain safeguards which I was clear at the time that you were prepared to accept, I agreed to a Royal Commission being set up upon the basis you wished. Subsequently, it became clear that we could not agree upon the content of the proposals which the Royal Commission should canvass; and even on this point, as I explained in my statement in Parliament last Wednesday, I was prepared to meet you by agreeing that the question to be put to the people of Rhodesia as a whole should be the acceptability of your proposals alone.

"3. But one of the conditions which would be required for this purpose would be that it should be publicly known that we did not agree with the proposals to be canvassed by the Royal Commission. Our position has now been made clear by my statement in Parliament; and it is now for the Commission to ascertain, on this basis, what the people of Rhodesia as a whole really want, provided that they are free – and the need for this has been highlighted by the declaration of a state of emergency in Rhodesia – to express their views without intimidation from any quarter.

"4. I am more concerned about what you say on the unanimous nature of the Commission's work. I made it clear at our final meeting in Salisbury that the Commission would need to proceed on the basis of unanimity; and you agreed that this would be essential if their work was to carry conviction. Indeed, it was only your acceptance of the principle of unanimity that made it possible for me to entertain your proposal of a Royal Commission with narrower terms of reference.

"5. Now I turn to the question of an interim report. I would be prepared to consider how far we could perhaps distinguish between an interim report on procedure and a final report on substance. One idea which we might consider so far as the interim report is concerned is that it might be made clear to the Commission that if at any time any one of their members felt that he needed to refer back to the two Governments for further guidance, or if the Commission as a whole, while unanimous on their recommendation as to the method to be used, felt that they should first report back to the two Governments, they should be free to do so. There might be other ways of tackling this problem.

"6. But as regards the Commission's final report recording their views as to the acceptability or otherwise of the 1961 Constitution as a basis for independence, clearly this report must be unanimous if it is to do what we both require of it. I must repeat that the rights of the United Kingdom Parliament, with whom alone it rests to take the ultimate decision about the terms on which Rhodesia should proceed to independence, must be fully observed. I made this very clear in my statement in the House of Commons on 3 November; and you will see from the exchanges recorded in Hansard that this was regarded by the House as a whole as being of the greatest importance. Indeed, I do not believe that Parliament would accept the Royal Commission procedure on any other basis although, as I said in my earlier message, the Commission's report would obviously carry the greatest weight and there would have to be very compelling reasons for either of us to reject it.

"7. I must take this opportunity to comment once again on your claim that Sir Alec Douglas-Home agreed in September, 1964, that Rhodesia could have independence on the basis of the 1961 Constitution, if it could be proved that this was acceptable to the people of Rhodesia as a whole. I stated your claim in these terms in the House of Commons on 3 November and made it clear that the present British Government did not accept it. You will see from Hansard that Sir Alec Douglas-Home said, 'May I be allowed to confirm the interpretation which the Prime Minister has put on the talks of 1964.' Moreover he went on to say, 'It seems to me important that this should be done. We were not satisfied at the time that there were sufficient safeguards against retrogression in the position of the Africans and we were not satisfied either that the proposals before us for ascertaining the will of the people of Rhodesia were sufficiently defined.'

"8. I am bound to tell you also that public and Parliamentary opinion in the United Kingdom has been profoundly affected by the fact that, even since my last message, your Government has, abruptly and without warning, declared a state of emergency. The United Kingdom Government and Parliament will now need to understand more clearly precisely how a Royal Commission would – and indeed, could – operate in the circumstances of restriction on freedom of expression which the state of emergency is creating in Rhodesia. I feel therefore that we must have an objective and first-hand opinion on this question.

"9. We have already agreed that the Chief Justice of Rhodesia, Sir Hugh Beadle, should be the Chairman of the Royal Commission; and we have both expressed our full confidence in him. Since both you and I discussed with him in Salisbury how the Commission might work and since I understand that you have had further conversations with him since my departure, I suggest that he should now come to London to discuss with my colleagues and myself how the Royal Commission will work in the light of your announcement on Friday. I should like at the same time to explore further with him the other issues of procedure which I have mentioned in this letter, including the suggestion which I have outlined for dealing with the question of an interim report.

"10. I believe that after my further discussion with Sir Hugh Beadle it might be useful if you and I met again, preferably at some convenient meeting place, such as Malta. We could then decide not only the outstanding questions involved in getting the Royal Commission to work but also the action to be taken after they have presented their final report, consistently with my own explicit undertaking to Parliament."

Mr. Wilson, after publication of this last message, and intent on preserving his image with the British public who were now beginning to lose interest in this long-drawn-out drama, announced a theatrical move, or what the vulgar called a 'gimmick'. He proposed a meeting between himself and Mr. Ian Smith on the neutral island of Malta. On the face of it this sounded fine – a neutral territory outside Africa and England.

There was a theory in political and journalistic circles that Mr. Smith was a prisoner of extremist and irreconcilable elements in his cabinet, caucus and party. By detaching him from these "reactionary" elements and the atmosphere of Salisbury, it was thought that he would become more receptive to the British point of view.

It would have been far easier for Mr. Wilson to invite him to London for these further discussions, but this was the last thing the British Prime Minister desired. He had occupied the London scene alone now for two weeks, and the arrival of Mr. Smith in London would spark off another outburst of public sympathy for Rhodesia and counteract the intensive campaign being carried out against us on T.V. and in the Press, and greatly assist us in Rhodesia House in the efforts we were making to present our case.

I signalled these thoughts to Salisbury and suggested that if a further meeting was contemplated, insistence should be made on London as the rendezvous. However, Mr. Wilson's last message had in no way made it likely that a further meeting would bear any fruit, since it lacked any hint of an accommodation on the points at issue.

A communiqué, that was to be the final one as it turned out, was sent to me to deliver to the British Government. It read as follows:

8 November, 1965.

"Thank you for your message received yesterday evening.

"In paragraph four you claim that I agreed that the Commission would have to be unanimous in its report. I am quite clear on this point, and I am supported in this by all of my colleagues who were at the meeting, that while you did say that in your opinion the Commission's findings would have to be unanimous in order to carry conviction, we did not agree to accept unanimity.

"Your last message, to my mind, merely confirms, in different language, the attitudes which you adopted in your message of 3rd November. I have analysed your latest message very carefully and have compared it with your message of 3rd November and my reply of the 6th November, and it is clear that you have taken the matter no further forward.

"Even if we were to agree on the procedure and substance of its work, you have again made it abundantly clear that you are not prepared to accept in advance the decision of the Royal Commission, that you are not prepared to agree that the Commission should be free to submit a majority report, and that you are not prepared to commit your Government to advocating its acceptance in Parliament. These three points are fundamental. I regret to say, therefore, that the only conclusion must be that we are back in the position we reached at the end of our talks in London, when we both agreed that the views of our respective Governments were irreconcilable."

This message was published at 18.00 hours Rhodesian time.

Thus the meeting at Malta did not materialise. It was not surprising that it did not take place. On Friday I had received a signal that a state of emergency was to be declared in Rhodesia. Some journals at once seized on this as a sign that an assumption of independence was imminent.

Sir Hugh Beadle jumped into the news. The Press reported that he was coming to London as an emissary for Mr. Smith in order to finalise arrangements for the Royal Commission by resolving the deadlock over the questions of unanimous reports and their acceptance by the British Government. At no time had the Rhodesian Government flatly rejected the Royal Commission. It only wanted clarification of these two points. Thereafter it was fully prepared to go ahead with the whole exercise.

Mr. Wilson nevertheless, in an effort to place the blame on the Rhodesians, made the following announcement in the Commons.

"Honourable Members will have seen the message which I received from Mr. Smith on Saturday amounting to a flat rejection of the proposal for a Royal Commission. They will have seen also the terms of my reply on Sunday when I repeated what I believe to be the views of the whole House – that we cannot here and now in advance of the Commission prejudice the rights and indeed the duties of Parliament at the end of the day.

"The House will have noticed too the deep concern which I expressed in the Sunday message – and I am sure that concern is shared by the whole House – about the declaration of the State of Emergency last Friday and its possible effects on the ability of the Commission to obtain a free expression of the views of the people of Rhodesia as a whole. It is for that reason that I suggested that Mr. Smith with Sir Hugh Beadle, whom both of us agreed to recommend as Chairman of the Royal Commission, should come and discuss these matters in London preparatory to a further meeting which I would propose to have with Mr. Smith.

"I think that the House is aware that Sir Hugh Beadle made his wise advice available to both Governments during my stay in Salisbury and that he has been in regular consultation with the Rhodesian Prime Minister since I left Salisbury. All of us welcome Sir Hugh to this country not only for his sagacity, judgment and humanity, but also as a man with the courage of a lion – and it will be needed in this situation. I have already seen him for a brief discussion this morning and I intend to have full discussions with him later today and tomorrow. I hope that it will then be possible for Mr. Smith to agree to a further meeting. I do not think that the House will expect me to say more at this critical stage, and I assure the House that we have reached an extremely critical stage.

"I agree that it would have been agreeable to have had the agreed Minute to which the right honourable Gentleman referred, but the meeting which my right honourable Friend and I had with the Rhodesian Cabinet was very difficult. The right honourable Gentleman underrates the difficulties of a meeting with a Cabinet already set for U.D.I. within a matter of hours if we had not put these proposals. We had the greatest difficulty getting discussions on the new plan. There is a lot the right honourable Gentleman does know and a lot more I can tell him. I do not want to prejudice the position further by going into this, but when I say that we still have not got agreement about the Minutes of the right honourable Gentleman's discussions with Mr. Smith in September 1964 – and we are most anxious to publish these discussions to which the right honourable Gentleman has generously and very fairly agreed – the right honourable Gentleman will appreciate our difficulties in the very difficult situation a week last Friday."

Meanwhile our campaign for the public's support was continuing and at considerable expense we were inserting advertisements in all the leading papers. These were factual statements which published our non-racial franchise, details of African educational facilities, a subject on which the Press were critical and ignorant, and our case in general. This was essential as the majority of the Press were frankly hostile or lukewarm towards Rhodesia.

There were three big national dailies with very large circulations which published the truth about our affairs, as well as several monthly and weekly reviews, to some of which we contributed articles. We also were distributing brochures and pamphlets in large numbers as well as stickers for cars which read "Support Rhodesia". The distribution was not carried out direct but through organisations and groups of people who were dedicated to our cause.

One day I was summoned to the Commonwealth Relations Office to see Mr. Cledwyn Hughes. The object of this interview was to ask me to stop distributing these propaganda pamphlets as it infringed diplomatic protocol. I did not argue the point but my counsellor took this opportunity of asking the CRO to take some action, now delayed for several months, over hostile articles which had been distributed by an African mission in London and which had attacked us fiercely.

We had only presented facts favourable to ourselves, the normal task of a diplomatic mission, in fact its *raison d'être*. These others

"This should bring Mr. Smith to his knees pretty quickly." (From the "Daily Express", November 15, 1965. Permission: London Express Service)

had attacked another mission's country in the host country. However, what is sauce for the goose is not sauce for the gander, and we had the disadvantage of having white skins.

I gave an immediate undertaking to Mr. Hughes that we would cease from issuing these stickers and brochures, and trusted he would then take immediate action about the other offending mission. I gave this undertaking with an easy mind because our stocks had become exhausted the day before. There were a few dozen stickers left in Rhodesia House and I unctuously informed him that I would burn all existing material. I did so on my return. A single match and a metal waste-paper basket sufficed for the task.

On the week-end of the 6th November, C. G. Tracey and his team left for Rhodesia and on that Sunday P. K. van der Byl was summoned back. The ranks in London were thinning.

There was some doubt about Sir Hugh Beadle's credentials to speak for the Rhodesian Government, but I received a signal that he was coming to London in his private capacity on a visit believed to have been sponsored by the High Commission in Salisbury. As such, I was instructed to take no official cognisance of his arrival and activities.

Nevertheless I felt that a Rhodesian of his standing, and one whom I knew personally through serving with on a statutory board at home, should have some assistance in his personal capacity on

143

arrival. I was about to arrange a car for his use and book him accommodation as a matter of courtesy, when I heard that all these facilities were being provided by the British Government. I felt I should have a private word with him on his arrival and despatched the newly arrived Jack Brendan of our Information section to hear what the Press had to say to him, and to invite him to visit Rhodesia House at his convenience.

The Commonwealth Relations Office were doing Sir Hugh a high honour. Two Ministers met him in the V.I.P. lounge at the airport and a resplendent car was at his disposal. An amusing incident occurred here. Jack Brendan noticed that a British official was about to place a Rhodesian car flag on the car. According to strict diplomatic protocol this standard may only be flown by a car in which the High Commissioner himself, or the visiting Head of State or Prime Minister of its country is riding. As Sir Hugh Beadle was neither of these and was moreover in London in his private capacity, to place this flag on his car was strictly against the rules of protocol. It might also give the false impression that he was representing his country. Possibly this was the impression the action was intended to create. I don't know.

Anyhow, Jack Brendan with keen observation and quick wit pointed out these facts with quiet discretion, the offending flag was put away and I hope the incident passed unnoticed.

Later that morning Sir Hugh Beadle came over to Rhodesia House. He was not able to stay long as he was due for a series of meetings with the British Prime Minister and other members of the Government. His laudable object, as he put it, was to act as honest broker in getting the Royal Commission of which he was to be chairman, off the ground.

I tried to warn him about dealing with British politicians. I pointed out that not for nothing was Britain called 'Perfidious Albion', a term I had resented when I was a servant of the British Government, but which now with age and reflection and from the other side of the fence, I regarded as well justified. After all, how had Britain, a comparatively small country in the world, managed since Elizabethan times to maintain a pre-eminent position amongst other nations, unless it was through the skill of her diplomacy, and through principles of negotiation which had been evolved during the centuries and nurtured and polished by her permanent civil service throughout all these years. We colonials, and since 1947 I included myself in this select company, held a false image of the mother country and the ideal of British conduct, that had been extolled by writers like Kipling and others.

"Get it in writing," I advised, "and have it witnessed." I think Sir Hugh Beadle was shocked by this cynical advice. I could do no more than warn him to be careful and once again expressed the view that the whole exercise of the Royal Commission was to waste time and wear the Rhodesians down. If he could get the two points at issue over the Royal Commission sorted out to our satisfaction and put down on signed paper, he would have accomplished much, and his visit would have been worth while.

I saw him again next day when he informed me that he thought he had made some progress and was due for another meeting with Mr. Wilson that afternoon. He suggested that he might stay a day or two longer, but this would only prolong the agony, so I strongly advised him to return that night.

He took my advice to mean that an assumption of independence was about to be declared and hurried off to his appointment. Later that afternoon he telephoned me to say that he had managed to get some satisfaction out of the British Government. I asked if he got it in writing. When he replied "No" I remarked that it was no good.

I was relieved that he was returning that night to Salisbury. If a declaration of independence had been issued while he was in London, matters might have been difficult for him and myself. In the event he was still in his aircraft on the way back when our declaration of independence was made at 11 a.m. on the next day.

During this day I received a signal from Rhodesia asking me to make sure that a press statement issued by the Prime Minister in Salisbury was brought to Mr. Wilson's notice and that of the public.

It read as follows:

"How many times have Mr. Wilson and I tried to find a solution to our problems, how many times have we had positive proof that the differences between us are irreconcilable. I think the time has come when the only honest course open to us is to inform the people of the truth. I would say to Mr. Wilson, 'If we allow the position to continue, we are being deceitful and misleading the people of Rhodesia'."

I took the necessary steps required by this signal.

It was obvious from this message that the Rhodesian people, who were prepared only a week before to allow the Royal Commission to work out its task were now becoming disillusioned by the British Government's apparent hedging and going back on intention. Trust in the British Government, long dissipated through the years of the Federation and after, had completely vanished. Hope after hope had been dashed and trampled on.

I was then asked for my assessment of the position in Britain. I was able to reply to this at once because a constant stream of people from all walks of life had discussed the position with me. I sent the following signal:

"The press reaction is that the brink is approaching. General responsible opinion is that Wilson is gaining ground and time by continuing dialogue. Further hedgings and delays are certain if the Royal Commission gets off the ground. Public opinion is getting bored. Time is not, repeat not, on our side. If action is taken general opinion is that nothing dramatic should happen."

The last sentence referred to the position of the Governor in Rhodesia. Our friends were worried lest he should be arrested and marched off under guard and the Union Jack ostentatiously pulled down. I had assured them that nothing of this kind was likely to happen, and in the event of a declaration of independence any action taken would be done in as gentlemanly a fashion as possible.

That day, Wednesday 10 November, brought a special bag from Salisbury. It contained a letter of loyalty to the Queen from Mr. Smith and his Ministers. I was instructed to take it to the Palace for immediate delivery to Her Majesty's hand. Now this is not an easy task. By diplomatic usage a letter to the Monarch has to be delivered through the Foreign Office by Embassies, and through the Commonwealth Office by High Commissions.

I did my best however and rang up the Palace and said I had a letter to deliver. I was told that Her Majesty could not receive it till 5 p.m., and I would get a reply on this point by 3.30 p.m. At 3.30 p.m. as I had expected, I was informed that it must be sent to the CRO for onward transmission to the Palace. This was duly done. At 5 p.m. we rang up to enquire if the Queen had received it. She had not done so, but further enquiry elicited it was still at the CRO, where it was being dealt with. Further enquiries, after our threat that the news of the message would be released to the Press, brought forth an answer that the reply would be forthcoming that evening and that both letters would be published.

Up to this stage, of course, Her Majesty had never come into the affair at all. These missives were being dealt with in Whitehall, not Buckingham Palace.

I endeavoured to get a telephone message through to Salisbury in order to inform them that I was not being successful in getting this letter into the Queen's hand as instructed. A mysterious defect had by now developed in the telephone system from Rhodesia House to Salisbury. I tried from my flat to get through to a private number in Salisbury, but here again the lines appeared to be blocked.

Honor and I then attended our last diplomatic function at the Swedish Embassy where the doyen of the Corps was making a presentation to which we had subscribed. It was a 6–8 p.m. reception, and many prominent members of the political world were present. They eyed us with well-warranted speculation, but our conversation was limited to social trifles and the crisis was never mentioned.

On my return to my office at 8.30 p.m. I waited till my P.A. got through again to the CRO. This time we were told that Her Majesty would receive our letter, and presumably the reply for her approval. The time given for this was 9 p.m. I tried again to get in touch with Salisbury and found that the lines had suddenly become clear.

I reported this drama, and noted the whole affair when the question of loyalty to the Crown came up at a later stage. It appeared that loyalty to the Crown was a constitutional formula, quite separate from loyalty to the Queen's person, and in fact was no more than loyalty to the ruling party in England at the time. This was not generally understood by Rhodesians at the time, but later, through recounting this incident, they became aware of it and it eased their mind and conscience so that they were able to give their whole-hearted support to the Rhodesian Government – their own Government and the Queen of Rhodesia.

We in Rhodesia House were not aware that the crisis was upon us, and that our country would declare its independence next day. However, we realised that it could not be long delayed. The bitter fruits of British double talk and double dealing were to be picked at last.

15. Diplomat in Difficulty

Unknown to us in Rhodesia House there had been a telephone exchange between Downing Street and the High Commission in Salisbury, from which it appeared there had been last minute messages between the two Prime Ministers. Much has been made of these in the Press and in the House of Commons, but here again the fact stood out that whatever offers Mr. Wilson had made, if any, nothing was put in writing.

All along, throughout the years, the British tactics had been to ask the opposing parties to state their requirements in writing, whilst the British reserved their position and took refuge in verbal replies, which could be conveniently repudiated or forgotten. By now all trust in the British Government had gone. No verbal assurances were worth the breath that uttered them. This is the tragedy of all these negotiations from Federal days onwards.

I had an important engagement on Thursday, 11th November, namely to be present at the annual ceremony beside Westminster Abbey in the Field of Remembrance. This was organised by the British Legion and the British Empire Service League, as we continue to call this organisation in Rhodesia. It is not to be confused with the Laying of Wreaths at the Cenotaph, which takes place on the nearest Sunday to the 11th November and which this year was to take place on the 14th November. Her Majesty the Queen Mother attended by the President of the British Legion was present at this ceremony, which is quite informal.

Before leaving Rhodesia House I looked into our information office to glance at the telex. As I watched it ticking away, I saw the words "U.D.I. declared in Salisbury". The time was exactly 11.15 a.m. So the die had been cast. I made my way out of the staff entrance, through a throng of curious journalists, none of whom were at this moment aware of the news, and we drove off to the Abbey.

Here I met members of the Rhodesia House staff and quietly passed the news to them. We went about our business planting the tiny crosses with their poppies in the appropriate plots, and then listened to the short service. None of those present had as yet heard the news, and I did not mention it to our service friends who were present.

I had not seen some of them since my arrival in London, and was at a loss what to say when I received pressing invitations to visit them. Amongst those at the ceremony was Major-General Sir Richard Dimoline who had close associations with Rhodesia and was a friend of our country. I was very shocked to hear of his sudden death about a month later.

I returned to Rhodesia House with the service members of our staff, and had to fight my way into Rhodesia House where great and most friendly crowds were gathered, all of whom had now heard the news. One of them shouted "well done" as I walked into the building, whilst inside everyone was calm and collected. We had received no prior warning of this dramatic event from Salisbury and communications seemed to have ceased. There was no point in worrying Salisbury with requests for instructions. They had enough on their plate at this moment, without distractions from Rhodesia House.

Hardly had I reached my office when my P.A. brought me a message from the Commonwealth Relations Office. Mr. Bottomley wished to see me at once. It was nearly lunch time, so I decided to forgo this meal, and asked my secretary to get me an apple and a meat pie, to await my return. The cold air near the Embankment had given me an appetite and I would have preferred to go round to Gow's for a proper meal, but there appeared to be some urgency about Mr. Bottomley's request.

There were huge crowds outside 10 Downing Street. All eyes were focussed on the entrance and the car slipped unnoticed through the gate to the inner quadrangle of the old Colonial Office buildings. I was duly ushered into Mr. Bottomley's office. Sidney Brice, our Political Counsellor, and Denzil Bradley had accompanied me, but this was to be a purely private meeting and they were excluded from the interview.

Mr. Bottomley greeted me cordially. All through these difficult days my warm feelings towards him personally had not changed, and I hope he too felt the same. With some embarrassment he asked me if I supported my Government in its action in declaring

149

an illegal independence. With equal embarrassment I replied that I was a Rhodesian and all my roots were in Rhodesia. With diplomatic dexterity I evaded a direct reply. This did not imply that I disagreed with my Government's actions. But my position in London was unique. My country was not regarded by Britain as a sovereign state and I was technically a rebel, even a traitor. I was moreover a retired British regular officer of the British Army. Horrid visions of the Tower of London flashed through my mind. This subject had been a prime jest during the past few months, often made by my friends who had promised to feed me with buns through the bars. Now this joke was coming perilously near home. I contented myself with replying that my opinions on the matter were my own and should my congé be required, I was more than willing to accept.

The doors did not burst open and a file of beefeaters enter. Instead Mr. Bottomley handed me a letter. With bated breath I read it and let out a sigh of relief. I was to be treated with courtesy and compassion. For this I was and am grateful.

The letter to be published that day in the Press by the CRO ran as follows:

"My dear Skeen,

I am writing to inform you that in the absence of any statement from you declaring your opposition to the unilateral action taken by Mr. Smith, attempting to seize independence, you are no longer acceptable to the British Government as High Commissioner for Southern Rhodesia and you are requested to leave the country. The diplomatic privileges and immunities at present accorded to you will cease at 12 noon Saturday, November 13th.

Yours sincerely,
Arthur Bottomley."

I rose and thanked Mr. Bottomley for this document, we shook hands warmly and I took my leave.

On the way back to Rhodesia House I showed this document to my companions who told me that although it appeared that I had only 48 hours to leave the country, this was not the case. I could stay longer but only as a private individual. But I was anxious to get back to Rhodesia and do what I could to help my country in this difficult period. In addition I mused over the word "immunities" in the document. The loss of privileges did not worry me, but I valued my immunity for the next 48 hours, so I decided to remove myself and my family and as many of my belongings as possible out of Britain by noon on the following Saturday.

I returned to my office and my meagre lunch, and studied the telex reports which by now were pouring in from Rhodesia. The whole issue had been put most admirably by our Prime Minister in a broadcast he had made at 1.15 Rhodesian time, but it was not reported in full in the British Press, and lest it should be forgotten I give it in full below.

It was prefixed by an assurance that no one should be allowed to believe that the taking of independence marked a radical departure from the principles by which we have lived, nor should anyone be under the misconception that now the Constitution would be torn up and that the protection of the rights of all peoples, which are enshrined in that Constitution, would be abrogated and discarded.

"Now, if I may, I would like to say a few words to you. Today, now that the final stalemate in negotiations has become evident, the end of the road has been reached, it has become abundantly clear that it is the policy of the British Government to play us along with no real intention of arriving at a solution which we could possibly accept.

"Indeed, the latest verbal and confidential message delivered to me last night implied that on the main principle which is in dispute the two Governments have moved further apart.

"I promised the people of Rhodesia that I would continue to negotiate to the bitter end and that I would leave no stone unturned in my endeavours to secure an honourable and mutually acceptable settlement.

"It now falls to me to tell you that negotiations have come to an end. No one could deny that we have striven with might and main and, at times, leant over backwards to bridge the gap which divides us from the British Government.

"My Ministers and I have not arrived at this decision without the deepest heart searching. We have sat for days in ceaseless conference trying to find any possible way of achieving negotiated independence, as we undertook to the country that we would do.

"But I would be failing in my duty to all of you who live in Rhodesia if I was to permit this country to drift in the present paralysing state of uncertainty. The bitter lesson from the Federation is constantly in the forefront of my mind. In that case matters were permitted to drift and plans for action were formulated too late to prevent the destruction of this noble concept of racial harmony.

"However, Rhodesia has not rejected the possibility of racial harmony in Africa. The responsibility for the break-up of the Federation was Great Britain's alone.

"Their experiment failed and they are now trying to foist this same dogma on to Rhodesia. We are determined that the same will never be allowed to happen here.

"Neither let it be thought that this event marks a diminution in the opportunities which our African people have to advance and prosper in Rhodesia. Far from this being the case it is our intention in consultation with the chiefs, to bring them into the government and the administration as the acknowledged leaders of the African people, on a basis acceptable to them.

"It is our firm intention to abide by the Constitution, indeed we have never asked for any other than independence on the basis of the present Constitution, and only such amendments are intended as are necessary to adapt it to that of an independent country.

"With regard to the position of Members of Parliament, judges, civil servants, members of the armed forces and members of the police, provision has been made for all of them to carry on their duties and, for all are deemed to have complied with the requirements of the new Constitution, they will continue to carry on their normal work.

"All present laws will continue to operate and the courts will continue to enforce them in the usual manner.

"We are doing no more than assuming the rights which various British Ministers have, in the past, indicated are ours, and in fact this Constitution was the one which would carry us to independence.

"Let no one be persuaded that this action marks a change towards our neighbours in Africa, to whom we have ceaselessly extended the hand of friendship and to whom we have nothing but good will and the best of intentions.

"We have never sought, nor will we ever seek, to interfere or in any way attempt to influence their policy in their internal affairs.

All we ask in return is their good will in permitting us to look after what are, after all, our own private and domestic affairs.

"I wish to make it clear, as indeed I have on many occasions in the past, that we in this country have no quarrel whatsoever with the people of Great Britain, the differences of opinion which we have are entirely with successive British Governments.

"The people of Britain are the kith and kin of many Rhodesians, and the people with whom we have the closest affinity, both in our way of life and our conception of justice and civilisation.

"How can anyone suggest that we would harbour hostile sentiments against those with whom we fought shoulder to shoulder against a common enemy in two world wars?

"Our admiration and friendship for the people of Great Britain is real and enduring. Let there be no doubt that we in this country stand second to none in our loyalty to the Queen, and whatever else other countries may have done or may yet do, it is our intention that the Union Jack will continue to fly in Rhodesia and that the national anthem shall continue to be sung.

"Most of you, I know, have longed for this day, but a few on the other hand have had reservations. However, I would say to you that there can be no future for this great and splendid country of ours if we are to remain drifting in this constitutional twilight.

"To those who believe it would be in our interest to continue as we are I would point out that the British Prime Minister implied in his speech to Parliament on his return from Rhodesia that should the result of the Royal Commission go against Rhodesia the British Government reserved the right to call a conference which implied the changing of our Constitution as a result.

"It would appear that if this is the British Government's real intention we shall not be allowed to go on as we are . . . even if there had been a Royal Commission.

"There can be no solution to our racial problems while African nationalists believe that provided they stir up sufficient trouble they will be able to blackmail the British Government into bringing about a miracle on their behalf, by handing the country over to irresponsible rule.

"There can be no happiness in this country while the absurd situation continues to exist where people such as ourselves who have ruled ourselves with an impeccable record for over 40 years are

153

denied what is freely granted to other countries who have ruled themselves in some cases for no longer than a year.

"There can never be long-term prosperity which is so necessary for the nurturing of our endeavours to improve the standard of living and increase the happiness and better the lot of all our people while the present uncertainty exists.

"No businessman could ever seriously contemplate a massive long-term investment in a country in which chaos and confusion were always a future possibility.

"Whatever the short-term economic disadvantages may be, in the long term steady economic progress would never be achieved unless we are masters in our own house.

"To those of you who fear the short-term effects of economic sanctions I would say that while we in no way minimise the possible hardship and inconvenience they may bring about, none the less we are firmly convinced that in the long run, because of our natural resources and the enterprise of our people, there will be brought about a prosperous and better future for everyone.

"Week after week we have seen businessmen passing through here on their way to South Africa who say that while this state of uncertainty continues they will not even contemplate a serious possibility of investment.

"However, they also say once we have solved our constitutional difficulties and are independent, then they will be very interested in undertaking serious investigations and inquiry with a view to investment.

"That some economic retributions will be visited upon us there is no doubt. Those who seek to damage us do not have any great concern to the principles to which they endlessly pay lip-service, for if they really believed in these principles – which they ceaselessly proclaim – then they could not possibly connive at the many disasters which have been brought about by the premature withdrawal of European influence from countries in Africa and Asia who were nowhere near ready for it.

"There is no doubt that the talk of threats and sanctions is no more than appeasement to the United Nations, the Afro-Asian bloc and certain members of the Commonwealth and, undoubtedly, some action will be taken.

"But I cannot conceive of a rational world uniting in an endeavour

154

to destroy the economy of this country, knowing, as they undoubtedly do, that in many cases, the hardest hit will be the very people on whose behalf they like to believe they are invoking these sanctions.

"We, for our part, will never do anything in the nature of taking revenge on any neighbouring African state for what other countries may do to us, but it is none the less inevitable that if our economy should contract as the result of such actions taken by others then what jobs were available would have to be reserved for our own Africans, thus bringing hardship not only on our own people but on those people from adjoining territories who work here.

"If, as some have predicted, there are repercussions elsewhere in Africa, I would warn those people who contemplate taking action that it will be their actions and not ours that have precipitated these events.

"Whatever the consequences may be, and whatever difficulties may present themselves, we are a people who, in the past, have striven and prevailed in circumstances of the utmost adversity.

"The mantle of the Pioneers has fallen on our shoulders and we will, I am sure, be able to face any difficulties which may occur, fortified by the same strength and courage which distinguished our forefathers in days gone by.

"I do not believe that many of the extreme consequences which have been forecast by various would-be Cassandras, both here and abroad, will come to pass. But whatever may befall us, I have the profoundest confidence and belief in the determination of our people to stand united and to prevail in the face of any adversity.

"The safety of our homes and the freedom of our people alike depend on the conduct of each one of us at this critical time.

"In the lives of most nations there comes a moment when a stand has to be made for principle, whatever the consequences. This moment has come to Rhodesia.

"We may be a small country, but we are a determined people who have been called upon to play a role of world-wide significance. We Rhodesians have rejected the doctrinaire philosophy of appeasement and surrender. The decision which we have taken today is a refusal by Rhodesians to sell their birthright, and even if we were to surrender, does anyone believe that Rhodesia would be the last target of the Communists and the Afro-Asians?

"We have struck a blow for the preservation of justice, civilisation and Christianity. In the spirit of this belief we have this day assumed our sovereign independence. God bless you all."

The manner in which Honor heard the news was peculiar. She was busy in the kitchen of our house when Julia, who was as usual glued to the T.V. upstairs rushed down with the announcement that an important item of news about Rhodesia would come on in five minutes. She went upstairs and heard the bald announcement that "U.D.I. had been declared in Salisbury" – this was at the very moment that I was on my way to the Abbey grounds. She and Julia took a taxi to Rhodesia House, towards which one or two other wives of the staff were also making their way. She arrived there before I had returned from the ceremony I was attending. A very old friend and the best man at our wedding had also come over to ask us to lunch, but owing to my appointment I was unable to accept, so he took her and Julia out.

When they returned we set about making arrangements for our departure. We booked seats on a South African Airways plane due to leave on the following afternoon. We had declined to consider the shorter trip by VC10 through Nairobi, as we had no faith in the Kenya government's respect for protocol.

Honor departed to pack up our few belongings. It was fortunate indeed that some of them had already gone to Salisbury with me during my last journey, and even more fortunate that we had delayed in asking for their return. This time there was to be no frantic rush to Cornwall to collect our daughter from school. We had prudently kept her with us till we would be certain that the Royal Commission was an accomplished fact.

Our household goods had been sent back over a month before. This was not due to any foresight on our part, but to the fact that there had been numerous burglaries in the neighbourhood. Our furnished house already had ample knick-knacks and we had never unpacked everything we had brought over. They had therefore seemed safer in Rhodesia than in Britain. We still think this is so.

There were numerous visitors to Rhodesia House that afternoon, as can be imagined. All were anxious to help in the new situation that faced my country. No names can be mentioned for obvious reasons, for the penalty for helping "traitors" might be severe, at least in intent if not in fact. We made arrangements to keep in

156

touch, and with their help I disposed of the stocks of cigarettes and liquor in the office – not to be drunk there, but to be removed.

At least this helped to dispel some of the gloom they felt. These preoccupations were interrupted by some lighter moments. Students from London School of Economics, that hotbed of left wing intrigue, saw fit to stage a demonstration. These were the same people who had held a teach-in at which Mr. C. G. Tracey had rashly appeared. These shaggy and unkempt individuals came shouting down the Strand, and circled the building like story book savages round a cooking pot filled with choice missionary. Unfortunately for them, the police were out in force and their wilder antics were checked and thwarted by this splendid body of men, from whom we had recently obtained a large number of recruits for our BSA police. The office workers and others in the Strand buildings near our premises added to the excitement by pouring jugs of water on the heads of these demonstrators, an element with which few of their number appeared to have had much previous contact, judging by their appearance.

I think most of the Press and bystanders could not fail to be impressed that a majority of these demonstrators belonged to the coloured races who make so free with the hospitality of the long-suffering British. I rejoiced at this demonstration which was repeated twice next day for I felt it could do nothing but enlist sympathy for Rhodesia. It was also obvious that the average Englishman in the street was quite out of sympathy with their behaviour, and Alfie, who sold newspapers on a pitch outside Rhodesia House, and one of our most forthright and outspoken supporters and friends, had some pithy comments on these people which I cannot print.

It was dark outside and late when I returned to our Chelsea house. The place had been discovered and was being besieged by the Press. Desperate photographers, having asked in vain to enter the house and take pictures of "family interest", attempted to take flash-lit snapshots through the fan lights over the front door, so that the drawing-room curtains had to be hastily drawn to prevent similar attempts. In view of the circumstances I felt that a diplomat should not comment on the situation whilst under orders to leave, and so to the numerous calls on the telephone and the visitors who knocked on our door that evening I gave the same reply. Fortunately two policemen took up stance outside our house and stopped this incessant knocking.

As our kitchen was in the basement and in full view of the street, we did not dare put on the light and cook a meal. We crept into it in the dark, and dined on bread and cheese. It was quite impossible to sally out and feed in a restaurant. This was possibly quite the most unpleasant evening Honor and I had ever spent and we went to bed early and turned off the telephone.

16. The Return

The aircraft that was taking us back to Rhodesia was due to fly out of London airport in the afternoon, so we were up early next morning to complete our packing, settle a few minor tradesmen's bills in Chelsea, and clear the house up.

In the grey light of dawn I peered out of the third floor bedroom window and saw a few dejected pressmen and photographers still sitting patiently in cars round the square. Either they were early arrivals or had slept in their vehicles, hungrily waiting like Canadian wolves round some Klondike gold miner's dying fire for their prey, or perhaps a better simile might be like cats round a mousehole.

I felt intensely sorry for them, for the November weather was bitterly cold. I thought for a moment of offering the hospitality of a cup of warm coffee, but realised that this would only result in their sense of duty overcoming their gratitude, and I stifled this kindly impulse. However, I would have to face them sooner or later and give them a statement to satisfy their editors. It does not do to antagonise the Press, and it was antagonistic enough to Rhodesia as it was.

So I went downstairs while Honor completed our packing, and composed a message for them. The first paragraph, designed to mollify them, was handed out to them that afternoon by Jack Brendan, who quite rightly felt that something must be given them, if only to clear them out of Rhodesia House. The rest of the message I promised them at the airport on my departure, the time of which I would let them know.

I think this silence of mine on the subject of the declaration of independence was correct. We Rhodesians had behaved with dignity all through this period of suspense, and I intended that we should maintain it to the last. No apologia was needed, the explanations had long ago been given, and recriminations served no useful purpose. Interviews with the Press could only have led to this sort of thing, and possibly destroyed what sympathy we had in Britain.

Because it was my single and final statement, awaited with such impatience, it was printed in all the newspapers and given out on the radio. As it was cyclostyled and distributed to every journalist at the airport, and was sent to the editors of the other journals, there could be no possible misquotation or distortion of its contents. This was just what I wanted.

I give the message in full:

"Since yesterday noon I have not unnaturally withstood a siege from your colleagues, and I have not been able to give you a statement. Please acquit me of discourtesy to you or any appearance of brusque indifference to the very difficult task you have in doing your duty in informing the public. At all times I have had the utmost sympathy and understanding of the often uncomfortable and trying nature of your task, especially in this cold November weather.

"But the fact of the matter is that as a diplomat who has been given 48 hours to pack his bags I felt I was not at liberty during that period to say anything.

"Now that I have left my post I have the liberty to say something. This is what I have to say. Please prefix the above to what follows:

"Despite what you have heard last night and will hear in the future, the Rhodesian case is quite simple.

"Rhodesians have the 1961 Constitution. To reach a settlement the Rhodesian Government has leant over backwards to assist the U.K. Government. We have gone far in adjustments in the Constitution to meet them. It is incorrect to assume that Mr. Smith refused in his last telephone conversation to accept a Royal Commission on his own terms. The final offer was still so hedged with uncertainty that it nullified the whole Commission. We in Rhodesia believe in evolution and advancement on merit, and to be free to guide the people of Rhodesia towards this end; an end where merit and responsibility transcend race or colour.

"Those of you who watched their T.V. on Thursday night, will be as horrified as I was at the calibre and demeanour of the African nationalists who talked of murder by night with such obvious relish. These are the people to whom power will inevitably fall should the British Government's proposals be accepted. How would you face such a prospect?

"There are many Africans who hold seats in our Parliament and senior positions in our Civil Service. There are two such men on my

160

staff at Rhodesia House for whom I have great affection and regard and many others like them in Rhodesia. It is with them and not those such as we saw on T.V. last night that the future lies, and it is with them that we shall build our country. A country in which all races shall rise to the highest position of authority on a basis of responsibility and merit.

"It has been stated that time was needed in this dialogue between Governments. But we have been talking for three years and more. Further delay could have had no other result than what has happened in Zanzibar – Tanganyika, the Congo and soon in other parts of Africa.

"There will be no more opportunity for Rhodesia to state her case in London.

"You will be subjected to a single point of view from now on in which the Communist fellow traveller will have a major say. But please think of us in difficult circumstances trying to preserve your British way of life in a world in which those values are being eroded daily.

"As for my personal position, for seven generations my family has served the Crown faithfully and my loyalty is to the Crown alone, separate from the shifting politics of Westminster, and policies which often differ from the majority opinion of the British public.

"All we ask of the great British public is sympathy in the days ahead, assuring them of our affection and the acknowledgement of ties of blood and tradition, while asking for true understanding of the great and unselfish aim we pursue, which is –

"A Rhodesia, loyal to the Cown, and to the true and long-term happiness of all our peoples of all races. Farewell."

I hoped it would give a good impression, as it expressed the thoughts and feelings of Rhodesians on the whole issue.

I had a number of letters from America, France and England after I returned to Rhodesia, which showed that our attitude was appreciated. Some of these particularly touched me. They are given here.

From France:

"Dear Brigadier Skeen,

Many of our countrymen, like ourselves, are sad to see you leave London in the present sorry circumstances.

We admire your restraint and the dignity of your statement on leaving just as we admire the integrity of your Prime Minister.

We wish you and all fellow Rhodesians a happy outcome of your noble stand, and we will always be proud to know that we belong to the same stock."

From U.S.A.:

"My dear Brigadier Skeen,

I was very much touched in reading your statement as you left London. I have the deepest sympathy for you and for all Rhodesians.

Arthur Bryant has written an editorial in the *Illustrated London News* – perhaps you have seen it – and in a paragraph he says, 'If, instead of trying to force a small British nation to accept a situation which we should certainly not accept for ourselves – the subjection of our libertarian polity to a backwood and uneducated people – we were to assume such a responsibility for the common good for the peoples of Southern Rhodesia, both European and African, it could make the future of a democracy for all in that country a reality and lay the foundations, in that vast, wonderful land of promise, of a great and expanding multi-racial society.'

Here in Washington, David Lawrence, an able historian and writer, expresses the same views.

It is beyond me why there is not more outspoken support of the Whites of Rhodesia and their right under conditions of today to demand independence on their own terms.

I wonder if you have read the *Life of Washington* by Jared Sparks (who was a President of Harvard College)? In many speeches Washington expressed similar feelings and views as many loyal Englishmen have today in Rhodesia. If you do not have a copy of this book, I would be glad to send it to you if you would like to read it."

And from England:

"Dear Brigadier Skeen,

May I venture to thank you for your letter on leaving Britain? It was dignified, generous and charitable. Amid all the vindictiveness of this inexpressibly sad time it shone like a golden candle in a dark night – simple, warm, illuminating and inspiring. Your words of affection towards the British people are more than reciprocated. There is no doubt that 90% of us are in sympathy with you and seek to deny you nothing that we do not enjoy ourselves, and that we consider to be yours by title, and by merit, including the priceless heritage of sovereign independence. We consider you to be not sinners but sinned against, not rebels but patriots.

We know that you will uphold British values and ideals far better than we do ourselves, for this you have demonstrated amply, not only in the wars, but in the past few weeks. Please keep your lovely candle of faith in us and affection for us burning right into the future and do not let bitterness and recriminations so alien to our breed, extinguish it in the depth of this tragedy. Until you come back again, Sir, for Rhodesia is one of the family and will always remain so.

With warmest regards from your admiring and sorrowing compatriot."

But I anticipated. Having dressed, packed and breakfasted, we had to run the gauntlet of our front door and pavement.

This was no easy task. The car had arrived and gingerly opening the door, we admitted the chauffeur. He was a big man and the door had to be almost fully opened to let him in. At once half a dozen lenses were thrust through the door and the flash bulbs popped. Half the luggage was removed in this way, while we handed it carefully through the drawing-room door which was not visible to these peering cameras. On one of these trips Julia, determined to see that her suitcase was safely in the car, appeared in the doorway, and after being eagerly snapped, she gave what I thought to be a press interview with admirable aplomb. I was a bit nervous lest she should repeat some of my "off the record remarks", but apparently she was also a budding diplomat. No word of her utterances was repeated, but pictures described to be of family interest, were later published.

Honor had left an empty milk bottle in the basement kitchen window with a notice "No more milk, please" written on a sheet of High Commission notepaper, for want of other paper. This was photographed and published later in the *Illustrated London News* of all journals. Nothing seemed too trivial to be of interest. One of our suitcases bore SKEEN in large letters on it. The chauffeur, case and lettering were photographed at the boot-end of the car with its diplomatic registration number, and this also appeared in a newspaper.

There is a well-known picture of a Russian troika dashing through the snow with a pack of wolves in hot pursuit. One of the occupants has been thrown out to divert the wolves and lighten the load. We now employed this tactic, though in a more humane way. I forced my way through to the car, with cameras whirring and "no comment" on my lips, a dangerous phrase by the way, and to be avoided, for the Press can now read a wealth of insinuation into it, and we drove off with the pack in full pursuit.

Honor was left with only the police on the doorstep. She was able to go out later and pay the bills and do a little final shopping. The car returned for her in due course and removed the rest of the luggage. Franca who had arrived to clean up the place, also departed at the same time in a taxi with groceries and wines for which we had no further use. I hear there are three or four remnants of empire, with a few thousand inhabitants ripe and clamouring for independence. If this house is not too humble for their High Commissioners, I can recommend it, but I am sure that their new-found dignity will be satisfied by nothing less than Kensington Palace Road.

On arrival at Rhodesia House I found that our aircraft was still at Luanda and would not arrive in London till early next morning. It was hoped that it would be able to take off on its return trip by 9 o'clock next day. The only other flight was one to Lisbon at 11.35 a.m. on the same day, but this was cutting it a bit fine. We were determined to depart in dignity from the V.I.P. lounge with the full diplomatic privileges that did not expire till noon. We had no desire to creep out as private individuals and go through all the usual customs and immigration formalities that this entailed. But the delay imposed something far worse which was another night of siege in our house in Chelsea, now quite empty.

Here the kindness of Dr. Carel de Wet, the South African Ambassador, and his wife came to our rescue. I had walked to his office, unnoticed by the Press who were dogging our footsteps, to say my farewell. Hearing of our previous night's adventures, he suggested that Honor, Julia and I spend the Friday night at his house where we would have complete privacy. Apart from looking forward to staying with the De Wets, I felt it would be a good opportunity of discussing with him the wider issues of the Rhodesian action, and how it would affect both our countries in the long term.

All through the independence negotiations the South Africans had kept properly aloof and non-committal, unlike so many other nations who had butted in on their own initiative or through British insistence. We Rhodesians appreciated this and well understood the reasons, for we knew where the true interests and the sympathies of the South African people lay.

The British Government, I think through false intelligence and biased reporting, nurtured an extraordinary idea that the Rhodesian Civil Service and the Armed Forces and Police would not entirely support Mr. Smith and his Government in the event of an assumption of independence. There was much talk of the oath of service to the Crown, which in this sense was an oath to Mr. Wilson and his colleagues. As it was, they thought that the Rhodesian Government would topple at once through such opposition.

A peculiar document appeared in Rhodesia House which caused hilarity with some and indignation with others. It was addressed to Rhodesian civil servants in Rhodesia House, and required them to sign their allegiance to the British Government. This act of crass folly played right into our hands and I gave copies to friendly journalists who published it with remarks on its unfairness and even iniquity. It created much sympathy for us.

I know that to CRO eyes the High Commissioner had created a bad example in supporting his Government, but perhaps they hoped he was unique amongst Rhodesians in London. This was not the case. I held a meeting with the staff and we discussed the whole situation of our future. There were some bitter references to this document, and remarks about the Kenya settlers and how they had fallen for this kind of promise.

Although the two High Commissioners were being withdrawn, the respective staffs of the two High Commissions would require some time to clear up their missions and return home. Both in a sense acted as hostages for the other, and the slower withdrawal of officials and their families would obviously be a matter of later arrangement.

Rhodesia House had by now ceased to function as a mission, and its task was to wind itself up. This would be undertaken by the Deputy High Commissioner, a permanent civil servant, and it was into his able hands that I now handed over my responsibilities. There was a considerable number of long service locally recruited officials and house staff whose future was uncertain. To them would fall the task of caretakers when the bulk of the Rhodesians had departed.

It was our intention to retain as many of these as the British Government would allow, and to safeguard their jobs and pensions. Those who had been recruited temporarily might have to go to other jobs, but they would stay on till the end of the year. These were matters that would now be settled by External Affairs in Salisbury and the Commonwealth Relations Office. The arrangements were very civilised and I do not think anyone had any complaints.

Apart from Rhodesia House, a number of other Rhodesians in Government service came under its wing. These were mostly service personnel and a few railwaymen in the provinces. Arrangements were being made to repatriate them.

Funds had not been formally frozen at this stage, so I made a prudent visit to my bank where I withdrew my personal account. I was not so fortunate with scrip and other assets with my lawyers, and these are still in London.

On my way back on foot to Rhodesia House I was unfortunate enough to be spotted by photographers, who like courtiers to ancient Royalty, walked backwards in front of me along the Strand pavement and took a number of regrettable snaps, one of which appeared in a national daily captioned the "Loneliest Man in London". Unfortunately it was not true. Like Greta Carbo "I longed to be alone", but was not to be permitted this luxury. As I approached my friend Alfie at his news kiosk by Rhodesia House to present him with a gift of cigarettes and later whisky, they came at me like fleas in a long untenanted room, and I had to endure another session of "no comment" and photographs.

Honor and Julia had arrived with the last of the luggage in the office. We were joined by some old friends who had lost their all in Kenya and were enthusiastic supporters of our action. We had a picnic lunch and derived some more amusement from a second sortie of weirdies from the London School of Economics who were disporting themselves outside our windows.

After lunch Honor departed with Julia for Highveld, the De Wets' house, and I watched the two figures being swallowed up in the Press throng as they forced their way to the car. By now the police had provided not only an escort car but six motor cycle out-riders. Not wishing to embarrass the South African Ambassador by this ostentatious arrival, I requested that the outriders be dispensed with and this was done.

There were thank you letters to sign and a host of small tasks to do, interspersed by friendly callers wishing us good luck and num-berless telephone calls in the same vein. I said good-bye to as many of the staff as I could and made my preparations to leave the office.

This was not so easy as it sounds. Despite the small bone we had thrown to the Press and the promise of a bigger meal on the mor-row, the pack had increased, bursting into the reception hall and even venturing upstairs. Just at that moment the circus from the London School of Economics made its third arrival on the scene. It came into serious conflict with the police, who presumably be-coming tired of them, arrested several for obstruction and bundled them into Black Marias. This scene was too much for the press photographers. I saw them rush into the mêlée which was moving up the Strand towards the City.

I quickly grabbed my baggage and nipped out into my waiting car by the side entrance. One laggard from the pack spotted me and rushed madly for my car, and I grinned at him triumphantly. He obtained the shot he desired and it duly appeared in juxta-position with a serious Mr. Wilson, with the caption "a study of expressions".

At the Carel de Wets' I signed his book with our names and the remark: "Flight from Egypt". It may one day be an amusing and interesting exhibit.

All embassies and High Commissions in London have a residence which their governments have bought for their representatives. In the days of the Federation such a house had been bought for the Federal High Commissioner, but as I have already told, this man-sion now belonged to the Zambian High Commission. They are very good investments, for with inflation and the devaluation of currency these properties, even if only acquired a few years ago, are worth two to three times their original price. Apart from this, with the high prices of rented properties in Inner London, a very considerable economy accrues to the treasury of the mission's country. In my view house properties should be bought for all senior members of a mission's staff and not only for its senior representative.

Highveld is such a property. It stands in its own grounds and together with South Africa House off Trafalgar Square are material assets to the Republic.

Apart from the financial aspect, a house of this nature is of the greatest use to an Ambassador or High Commissioner. A great deal of entertaining can be carried out on a more intimate and less formal level than receptions given in the Embassy itself. With protocol prices for liquor, lunch and dinner parties can be given far more cheaply than in clubs and hotels, and the diplomat's special allowances given him for this purpose can be stretched much further. In addition he can accommodate the ministers and senior servants from his own country and save it considerable sums in hotel bills.

Here, for the first time, we saw how a diplomat should live and be able to carry out his functions properly. The De Wets gave us a separate suite in this lovely house, and made us feel thoroughly at home. After dinner and a look at the T.V. where we saw the result of gauntlets we had run the whole of that day, we went to bed, prepared for an early start the following morning.

We woke at 6 a.m., packed and were seen off by the Ambassador and Mrs. De Wet. The quiet and privacy of this short stay did much to restore our nerves, and we were more than grateful for the kindness of our hosts. The car was outside, flying its flag for the last time. This flag, possibly the last to be flown by a Rhodesian High Commissioner in London, is now framed as a momento in our house in Rhodesia. The police car was discreetly waiting round the corner. We drove off through the empty streets to London airport and arrived there about 7.30 a.m. The aircraft was due to take off in an hour. As I had expected the place was thronged with camera-men and journalists, and to these I gave a short interview and a chat before the T.V. cameras in the press room. They were promised my statement the moment we had taken off.

They saw this interview as follows: "A military looking man with thinning hair and gingery moustache puffed his pipe and chatted inconsequently in the VIP lounge at London airport yesterday. But in his eye was just the hint of a tear." I suppose the smoke from my pipe must have got into it.

They then took "family interest" photographs for the umpteenth time, with particular attention to Julia clutching her dolls and looking wistful. She responded magnificently, subdued her excitement at returning home again and enjoying another holiday from school, and put on the appropriate expressions that they required for their sob stories. This photograph blown up to quarter page size appeared in a Sunday paper with a circulation of millions, captioned: "Little Julia Skeen stands at London airport clutching her dolls with a trace of bewilderment on her face at this sudden upheaval in her life." I see she must join some public relations firm when she grows up.

There was a final photograph taken on the steps to the Boeing. At this stage Honor let the side down badly for in contrast to my and Julia's expressions of solemnity she was grinning broadly. She excused this lapse later by explaining that she had been caught unawares and was laughing at one photographer who had toppled over backwards in the effort of getting a shot.

The Commonwealth Relations Office had done me proud. The Assistant Chief of Protocol had come to see me off. I had seen something of both him and his brother while in London, and look forward to meeting them again. Members of Rhodesia House staff had also come to see their High Commissioner off, and a number of old friends. On the whole it was a cheerful gathering and we got a splendid send-off, and still with three hours of diplomatic immunity in hand.

The fore-cabin of the aircraft was only half full and we could spread ourselves. The relief of getting out of London was enormous, and we settled down to enjoy the trip which was to be a long one, for the South African Airways made only two stops, one at Lisbon, and one at Luanda in Angola, making a great sweep around the bulge of West Africa to avoid flying over the black states who did not like South Africa. To what petty expedients do these new states go to lighten the enormous chip they bear on their shoulders!

We arrived at Lisbon a couple of hours after leaving London, and here we saw Harry Reedman, our Diplomatic Agent, who had settled in nicely by now and was in good heart. I had half an hour with him and his staff in the airport buildings, where I filled in the most recent events in the crisis.

After all too short a halt, we were in the air again, for the long flight to Luanda. We read, slept and fed, and chatted to the cabin crew and other passengers. Being a South African aircraft we were with friends.

We reached Luanda towards midnight, having made good time. Then we were on the last hop, a short one to Salisbury. Owing to the changes in time schedules caused by the previous delay in the aircraft's arrival in London, and the speeding up of flight times, we arrived at 2.30 a.m. on an almost deserted aerodrome. My son and nephew were there to greet us, with two duty members of the airport staff, but no one else.

We borrowed an airport car for our luggage and got into our son's car and drove to their flat in a Greendale suburb. Here we erected a camp bed for Julia and settled down for the remainder of the night.

On the morrow, a Sunday and the third day of Rhodesia's independence, I would report my presence to the authorities, in case they did not know I had arrived back. 115 days had passed since Honor, Julia and I had departed on our mission to London.

It seemed like a 115 years, so much had happened. Our unheralded arrival had brought one great benefit: No reporters were at the airport and none were baying round our flat. It seemed too good to be true after the nightmare of the last evening in Chelsea.

I later discovered that there was a censorship in force. This again seemed too good to be true.

17. The Dust Settles

Sunday, 14th November, had seen Rhodesia independent for almost three days, and apart from what we had read in the British newspapers we were quite ignorant about happenings in the country.

My first anxieties were to find out how this momentous decision had been taken by our fellow Rhodesians, both European and African, and the second was to inform the authorities of the situation in England, not the least being the position of the staff at Rhodesia House.

I rang up the Secretary of the Cabinet at 8 o'clock and informed him of my arrival. It appeared that there had been some hitch over the arrangements to meet us at the airport owing to the early arrival of the aeroplane, and the car and officials had arrived after we had left. I was sorry that they had therefore got up in the middle of the night for no purpose, but otherwise it was of no moment.

My son drove me to Milton Buildings, home of the Cabinet Secretariat, and then left me to drive his mother and Julia back to the Vumba. I intended to follow them as soon as possible. I delivered various messages, had a signal sent to Rhodesia House concerning the allocation of certain funds for information purposes, and then reported to Cliff Dupont who asked me over to lunch where I could tell him in detail such news as I had, and give him my assessment of the British Government's intentions.

It is of interest to note that my signal to Rhodesia House arrived too late for action to be taken because the British had frozen our funds. I had tried hard to disburse these funds immediately after our independence had been declared, but treasury regulations, designed for times of peace, had not permitted this to be done on my sole authority. This is a point that might be noted for the future. The Ambassador or High Commissioner should have overriding authority over all regulations in times of emergency, and he could then be held answerable personally for his actions at a future date. As a result several thousand pounds which could have been put to great use by Rhodesia were lost to the British Government.

171

Being without transport, a car was allotted to me and I drove out to Cliff Dupont's house. I related the events in London over the past ten days and discussed what I thought would be the British Government's action. He in turn put me in the picture as to events in Rhodesia.

From this I learnt that an unforeseen complication had arisen. Sir Humphrey Gibbs, the Governor of Rhodesia up to the assumption of independence, had decided that he was still the legal Governor and had not resigned as had been anticipated. I was given to understand that he had informed the Government that this would be his intention. I also learnt that the Chief Justice, Sir Hugh Beadle, whom I had last seen a few days previously in my London office, was staying at Government House, presumably as an adviser on the legal position. At least that was the story given out in the Press.

Sir Humphrey Gibbs had therefore persuaded himself or had been persuaded that it was his duty to remain in Government House as a rallying point for elements who supported the Wilson Government and who were hostile to the Rhodesian Front. The intention was obviously to gather sufficient support in the Civil Service, Police and Armed Services, together with the general public, to upset the "Rebel" government of Mr. Wilson's imagination, and restore the *status quo*.

I have already referred to the fact that the British Government was receiving false information through its sources in Salisbury as to the true feelings of the Rhodesian people. This was confirmed by the writings of political commentators in British papers during the past week, and again by an article in the *Illustrated London News* which reported Sir Edgar Whitehead's views on the situation.

The sort of people, belonging to what one might call the "old establishment" who used to be in touch with the British High Commission, were the same who belonged to what can be described as "the Government House set". These people, few in number, had been going to Government House to pledge support to the ex-Governor, and presumably this movement had led the British Government to think that the bulk of the people would support this move for a return "to constitutional ways".

Another fact about which the British were misinformed, or fatally ignorant, was that they were dealing with their own kith and kin.

Threats of sanctions and punitive measures, applied in order to increase the support for Sir Humphrey Gibbs, would and did have the opposite effect.

There was only one factor that might influence a section of the people, who, while supporting the Government, were as yet unaware that an assumption of independence was necessary. This was the suggestion that we could have continued as we were under the 1961 Constitution. The dangers that lay in this train of thought, and the real and hidden purposes of the British Government had to be explained to them.

Under the 1965 Constitution, which was in effect the 1961 Constitution, only amended in so far that it took ultimate control away from the British Parliament, it was necessary to have a Head of State. It had been thought that this person should be called a Regent. I had already said that this might be an unfortunate name, and under the 1965 Constitution, although the word had been mentioned, an interim title had been evolved: The Officer Administering the Government.

The question now arose who should fill this office. I had already been informed that on relinquishing the post of High Commissioner in London, my name among others was being considered. This matter was brought up by Cliff Dupont. I explained the reasons why I considered myself unsuitable and one of these has already proved valid. Already at the time of writing no less than five African states have had upheavals in which Generals and Colonels have become Heads of State.

I felt that an impression of a military coup must be avoided at all costs. I went so far as to suggest that Cliff Dupont himself, a lawyer, would be a far more suitable person for this post. There is a mystique about the law in England, and a lawyer, like a doctor, is always above criticism.

After lunch I returned to my son's flat to make up my arrears of sleep, and then later on that evening to report to the Prime Minister at his house.

Besides the Prime Minister and Cliff Dupont, Lord Graham, the Minister of Agriculture, and Des Lardner Burke, the Minister of Law and Order, were present and we were later joined by P. K. van der Byl, the Deputy Minister of Information and one of his senior officials.

The main subject of discussion was the complication caused by Sir Humphrey Gibbs remaining in Government House. Before leaving England I had been informed by all our friends that on no account should Sir Humphrey Gibbs be in any way molested or insulted and I had replied that the Rhodesian Government had no intention whatsoever of taking any such action. We agreed on this matter. In fact, our enemies were only waiting for some action of this kind to be taken in order to counteract the favourable view the British public were taking of our declaration of loyalty to the Queen and the retention of the Union Jack and national anthem.

There was one great danger however in Sir Humphrey Gibbs's remaining in Government House. He had connections with the British High Commission which with its office facilities and means of communication, could and would form a nucleus civil service through which he could act. In my view it was essential that this High Commission, like our own in London, should be neutralised and its influence reduced to a minimum.

The most we could do, without in any way interfering with the ex-Governor's personal comfort and dignity, was to withdraw such facilities as distinguished him from a private person, though living in the Government's property. This was done, and it proved to be a wise decision. It was hoped that in time the Rhodesian public would forget him, and this is what is happening.

The whole question of Her Majesty's position in regard to the dispute between the two Governments had to be cleared up through our Information Service. I wrote down the whole story of the letter I had been instructed to deliver into her Majesty's hand, and how this had been frustrated. It demonstrated clearly that in these constitutional matters the Monarch was no more than the ruling party in Britain. Loyalty in this sense, bound up with oaths of service, was in fact loyalty only to one's own elected government. In this case the loyalty owed was to our own legally elected Government and not to one 6,000 miles away, and in whose composition we had no say. This statement was incorporated in a Press communiqué which appeared next day in the papers.

It did much to clear up the confused position arising from Sir Humphrey's unforeseen actions. At the end of the meeting I privately put my views on the appointment I had discussed that morning to the Ministers present.

The next day was to be a very long and busy one. I spent some time discussing Rhodesia House with the Minister for External Affairs, Cliff Dupont, and officials. There was to be some sort of *quid pro quo* over the two High Commissions. I urged the view that as many expatriate staff from the two missions as possible should be withdrawn. At all costs the British members of the High Commission in Salisbury should be reduced to a minimum. The larger their numbers in Salisbury, the greater would be the danger of their contacting hostile elements and acting as a civil service to the ex-Governor. The position of the locally recruited staff in Rhodesia's High Commission in London should be safeguarded as far as possible. To balance these numbers therefore, we should allow Rhodesian recruited staff in Britain's High Commission to remain. In the event we had six Rhodesian members of our staff left in London and above thirty of the locally recruited ones, and presumably something of this nature remained in Salisbury to represent British interests.

I have spoken of the alleged support for the Wilson Government through Sir Humphrey Gibbs which existed in Rhodesia and particularly Salisbury at this time.

The peculiar thing about these people was that they were by and large the wealthy members of our society. Their ties with Britain were strong, and I would say that they had one foot in each country, the right and larger foot being in England. At a pinch, in the event of an African nationalist government in Rhodesia, they would not be much inconvenienced and their opportunity of making money unimpaired. Ultimately they would retire to England, a country to which in any case they paid many and frequent visits. They were not in fact true Rhodesians, although they may have taken out citizenship and were electoral voters. They were in a minority and were largely concentrated in the wealthier and more fashionable suburbs of Salisbury. There were others scattered round Rhodesia, whose main ties were with Britain. They were as unrepresentative of Rhodesia as those expatriate British sun seekers are of the West Indies or the South of France.

If sanctions inconvenienced these people, or our independence from Britain offended them, their course of action was simple. They could depart to where their apparent loyalty lay, and where they could feel more at home. Many of these people made an ostentatious habit during the next few days of signing Sir Humphrey Gibbs's visitors' book. Some supporters of the Government did likewise, under the misapprehension that they were showing a proper loyalty to the Sovereign.

Later, on the appointment of Cliff Dupont as Officer Administering the Government, another book was opened in various cities and the flood of signatures soon showed where the loyalties of the great majority of Rhodesians lay. This absurd "battle of the books" soon died away. Presumably a small coterie still haunts the private residence, at it is now, of the ex-Governor, nostalgically talking of vanished power and glory and maybe plotting with Mr. Wilson's aid some sort of restoration, which in the most unlikely event of its occurrence would only ensure Joshua N'komo's installation in these precincts.

Monday was the fourth day of our independence. While I had been in Salisbury during the week of the British Prime Minister's visit, I had been co-opted on a Cabinet Sub-Committee on Information. I resumed my seat on this, and spoke on factors affecting public opinion in Britain.

It was realised that the people of Rhodesia had to be put in the picture, for apart from the Prime Minister's statement on our assumption of independence, nothing had been said. It was essential therefore that the Ministers got on the air and told people as much as they could about the situation and our plans for the future. Being free, I was asked to be the first to do this, and to inform the people what I had learnt in London, and how the British viewed the situation. Therefore I was despatched to the RBC studio for an interview by Harvey Ward. This was scheduled for 15 minutes, and there was no time to prepare a script.

Two points stood out on which I hoped to be questioned, and on which I was.

One was the question of loyalty to the Crown and the oath which all the Services had been required to take. This was exercising the minds and consciences of many people, and Mr. Wilson's Government was making much of this question in order to confuse the issue and split the Rhodesian nation.

The other was the question: "Why had it been necessary to assume our independence, when we had the 1961 Constitution?"

If Mr. Wilson's propaganda made any headway on these two points, then there might be a real danger of disunity in our ranks.

176

I give the transcript of this broadcast, delivered *extempore*, which accounts for its somewhat unliterary composition.

QUESTION: Brigadier Skeen, how did you see your task when you arrived in London?

ANSWER: When I arrived in London, and before I even reached London, I decided that my task was firstly to make quite plain, to British politicians, and to the public, that we in Rhodesia stood by the '61 Constitution and required our Independence as soon as possible on the basis of that Constitution and we were not, I repeat not, going to get involved in a series of meetings, conferences or negotiations apart from that basis. Now, it took a very great deal of time for this approach to penetrate, and I found that one of the reasons for this was that the High Commissioner in Salisbury had been reporting that the will of our people here was not as firm as I knew it was, and this was largely, I think, because the High Commissioner moved in circles, very narrow circles, which did not nearly reflect the views of the bulk of the people. I took steps at once by various means to correct this impression, and shortly after the Prime Minister's arrival, and after the early negotiations which as you know ended in deadlock, I think they finally realised we were in earnest and determined. So that first task was achieved. As for my second task, before I left Rhodesia I mentioned, and it was reported in the Press, that I felt our best chance of success was to interest the British public in our case and get them to put pressure on their politicians to meet us. I found, when I arrived in London, that there was a great sympathy for us, but of course it was inactive sympathy and somewhat ill-informed, so I took steps to increase this sympathy and to put across effectually the situation in Rhodesia and what we represented, how our society worked, what we were doing for the African population, how much better we ran things than the other countries which had already claimed independence, and put a case across by all the somewhat limited means, I regret to say, at my disposal. And then, when the Prime Minister arrived, he made a very favourable impression at his T.V. interviews, press meetings, and his general behaviour. He roused a tremendous amount of support and sympathy and he helped to spark the dormant sympathy we had in the country at the time. And so I could say, we had in a large measure put Rhodesia on the map, and people were aware of us, aware of our situation and our problems. We then had a very great deal of sympathy. If later you want to ask me questions on how this sympathy actually works, I will be able to answer you.

QUESTION: Well, Brigadier, to get down to what you said, what were your impressions of the chances of Rhodesia getting a negotiated independence when you first arrived in London in July?

ANSWER: Well, one always hopes, and when I arrived I hoped this might be possible. But I had long realised that the policy of the British Government was to string us along as they had been doing for so many years, and this actually was the fact. Now when the Prime Minister arrived in London he brought things to a head, and he really got down and tried to negotiate. Of course, I don't think Mr. Wilson ever had any intention of giving us our independence on the 1961 Constitution, because I think they intended just as soon as possible to hand us over to what I would describe as African nationalist rule as in the other countries, and I think this is due to the pressures of the Afro-Asians of the Commonwealth, and the United Nations. In fact I was virtually told that this was a very big factor in the British point of view. So therefore you can take it that I don't think there was any hope at all of us getting independence on the 1961 Constitution however hard we tried, however hard we leant backwards, because the simple fact is this, and I want everybody to realise this, because there are many people in my audience today who think we could "chull" along as the expression goes on the '61 Constitution for ever and ever amen, allowing it to take its course. Now this was quite out of the question. We were in for the chop in June. I will repeat that. We were in for the chop in June, because in June next year, or July possibly, there would be the next Premiers' Commonwealth Conference, and at that Conference I think you can take it that Britain is abdicating her position as the head of the Commonwealth with this new Secretariat they are forming under Mr. Arnold Smith, and she would have been able to have washed her hands of us and not be able to put this thing off as she did last year and the year before. So we would have been faced at that time with the situation of another ultimatum, either suspension of our Constitution unless we acceded to the demands of this Premiers' Conference, or we would have had demands for more Constitutional Conferences, and so on and so forth, and if we had refused and dug our toes in, the situation would not have been allowed to carry on under the 1961 Constitu-

178

tion. We would have been faced with the situation we are faced with now, which is sanctions and pressures. So please disabuse yourselves of the idea once and for all that we could ever have gone on any further with the '61 Constitution. So what has happened is the best that could have happened in the circumstances. We have, I should say, as an example of ordinary life, had to take an operation to save our lives at this moment whereas if we had delayed it, when that operation inevitably came we would probably have died under it. So we had no choice, and those who ever doubted the wisdom of what we have done, may realise now that there was no other choice.

QUESTION: Brigadier, getting back to the British public, how did you find their view of the situation?

ANSWER: Well, the British public I think now has a pretty good idea of our situation and our aims. We have done our best to let them know what it is. But you must remember that the British public is a very vast public, and there are a great number of them, especially among the working classes, who are in the greatest sympathy with us and this is probably because of their own particular problems – they are faced with immigration and so forth. They are on our side, the bus drivers, the newspaper sellers, the barrow boys, charladies, that sort of people. The intellectuals, probably not touched by these same problems, are not in sympathy with us. Then there is the great mass of the, shall I say, farmers, the people in the country; they sympathise with us, and how far that sympathy would act I don't know, because all these people are very involved in their own private affairs. And then there is a very important section of opinion, largely Conservative, of people who know Africa, of people who know the world, who know the countries outside the shores of Great Britain, and many of these people not only have witnessed but have suffered themselves what was going to be in store for us. I mean Kenya people and civil servants from all over the world, and they were not only on our side but were terribly disturbed that we were going to go the way their people went. In other words, they were terrified that we would either continue as we were doing or accede to the British Government's demands. They, quite frankly, are jubilant on what has happened, and the reason is that it has restored, to some extent, their own self-respect in a vicarious way. And finally, there is a great mass of people in England who are thoroughly sick and tired of this constant appeasement of the Afro-Asians. At one time these people, the Afro-

Asians, were regarded as the underdogs, but the British public now are beginning to think of themselves as the underdogs, being pushed around. And therefore they have got sympathy with us as fellow underdogs in a sense, because of this overwhelming demand and arrogance of persons who were only recently independent and who cannot run their own countries properly. And so I think there is a general broad sympathy for us, and one can hope that this is having a pretty good effect on the politicians; in fact I think it is conceivable that Mr. Wilson's visit out here so hurriedly was caused by the need to restore his image in England owing to this feeling.

QUESTION: Brigadier, following on this same line, what is the significance of the British sympathy?

ANSWER: At one moment I think they were getting bored until a few days ago; I think now that a lot of them respect us. In fact I should think pretty nearly the whole lot of them respect us, and I am hoping, this is all one can do, that they will sympathise with us and, now that the die is cast, that they will, by silent pressure, prevent these sanctions from having the harsh effect that might have been intended. My own personal belief, and this is just my personal belief, is that if the British public maintain their sympathy for us I don't think that the British Government will dare to impose the full force of these sanctions on us, but only impose them to the extent that they can appease the United Nations and Afro-Asians and save the situation from developing into a world quarrel, shall we say.

QUESTION: Brigadier, there is the question of the Crown. What do you think about the position of the Crown in this matter?

ANSWER: Well, to my mind there are two monarchs. The first is one's personal monarch, the undying monarchy, the Queen in person, and to us Rhodesians this is a very real loyalty. Then there is the other monarch, the constitutional monarch, the legal monarch, and of course the legal monarch in that sense is merely the monarch of the party in power in the country at that time. And so, when one talks at this moment of loyalty in a constitutional sense, one is virtually talking of loyalty to Mr. Harold Wilson and his colleagues who actually do not, I think, represent the majority of the people in England. So any of us who are worried about this sense of loyalty on the constitutional side, I stress the constitutional side, can remember that they need not worry, they are merely being loyal to Harold Wilson and if they want to be loyal to Harold Wilson and the forces that mean to destroy this country outside England and elsewhere, then go ahead, it is not the Queen they are being loyal to in the constitutional sense, but to the ruling party in England. But we feel here in Rhodesia, or at least I do, that the Queen is our own personal monarch to whom we owe our loyalty, and, in the constitutional sense our loyalty is to the Queen and to our elected Government which is the Government which rules us at the time, in other words Mr. Smith's Government, and therefore our loyalties are to the Queen in the constitutional sense, and so the effective Government, Mr. Smith's Government, the legal Government of this country, and in the personal sense to the person of the monarch.

QUESTION: Brigadier, do you feel that there is a move now in Britain to divide the people of Rhodesia in this particular hour?

ANSWER: I should say the move is a political one. I cannot say the British people are involved. I would say the politicians view the situation like this: They would like through the Governor who, as I say, appears to have a personal loyalty to the ruling party in England – I may be wrong – to create a group of people who may or may not be therefore recognised as the nominated Government of Britain in Rhodesia and round that nucleus to build up a resistance to our legal *de facto* Government. Now they can only do this by sanctions, to make it sufficiently uncomfortable for people to repudiate the present Government, and turn to them. Of course these people would then be negotiating, if they succeeded, with the British Government on the British Government's terms, and we would go exactly the same way as all the countries to the north of us, probably even worse, and those people who are acting in that way, or who would act that way against Rhodesia, of course are destroying themselves as well as Rhodesia; the utmost folly for them to rally to this British Governor, I would call it. And therefore I stress to all Rhodesians the simple fact that we must all stick together, everyone of us, and despite any hardships – they are never all that great – to carry on as usual, to stick by the Government, reject with contempt any ideas of splitting us like this on Mr. Wilson's behalf and ride out the storm ahead of us with good heart and confidence, and I am quite sure that within six months, as short a period as that, provided we remain united, the country goes ahead, and there are no disturbances of any kind and this applies of course to the African peoples as well. It is to their interest to do this and we must all act as though nothing had happened. Then these aims of the British Government to split us will be defeated. It is the greatest danger we face now, disunity amongst our ranks. Whatever your personal feelings were before, I think I have dispelled for you the idea that we could have gone along on the '61 Constitution happily and that U.D.I. was a mistake therefore. I have dispelled that idea I hope, because, as I say again, we were due for the chop in June anyhow, and under worse circumstances. So, we must stick together, and we will pull this thing off, and I think that in six months, as I have been assured by many of my friends in high positions in England, it will all be forgotten, and we will have earned the respect of the world and we will take our place again.

QUESTION: Brigadier, finally, how were you personally received as the Rhodesian High Commissioner in England?

ANSWER: We were, my wife and I, received in a most friendly fashion, in fact it was almost embarrassingly so. We were deluged with pressing invitations possibly because we were a curiosity in our peculiar situation in the world at the moment, but largely out of the goodness of heart. And a peculiar thing was that at any of the banquets and dinners we attended, when Rhodesia was mentioned in a toast it got far the loudest applause of any. Those in the diplomatic world were very friendly and sympathetic and in official circles I was received with the greatest courtesy and wherever I moved amongst the public they were most friendly, and they seemed to understand, or try to understand, our situation.

It lasted exactly 14 minutes, and was repeated by request on the following Thursday during the 15 minutes allowed for the Rhodesia to Rhodesia broadcast. I am told that it greatly helped to clarify many people's minds on our assumption of independence and the need for it, and I discovered afterwards that a large proportion of those who were still uncertain, swung round to support the Government in its action.

Everything I said in this interview was the exact truth, as I saw it in London, and I had received confirmation privately from influential people who had come to see me in Rhodesia House on all these points, especially on the British Government's intentions to bring the whole matter to a head in 1966 and ensure early African nationalist rule by abrogating by some means the 1961 Constitution. Of this latter fact there is no doubt in my mind at all, and I checked and rechecked my information on this important point by several different means.

The broadcast over I had just time to have lunch and then fly off to Bulawayo where I was due to appear on television at 6 p.m. At Bulawayo I was collected and driven out to the studios where a T.V. interview took place. The time given me on the programme was too short and I was not able to get across all I wanted.

Then I was hustled back to the airport just in time to catch a return flight to Salisbury. I got some sleep on the way, and woke up as the aircraft touched down at 8.35 p.m. There was some hitch over a car to meet me, which caused some delay, but it was eventually located and I had just time to reach the Borrowdale studio on the other side of Salisbury, eat some sandwiches raided from the closed canteen, and appear once again in front of the cameras.

This interview was the last on the night's programme, starting at 10 p.m., and lasted just over half an hour. Here I was satisfied that I had got across all I needed. I believe this interview made a big impression and I had a number of telegrams, letters and personal messages from people who were grateful that at last they understood the situation and its background.

Here again the R.T.V. received a number of requests for a repeat for the benefit of those who had missed this programme owing to the lateness of the hour. So the following Monday the Profile Programme was allotted to my old friend John Gaunt, our diplomatic representative in South Africa, back in Salisbury for a post-independence visit and myself. We privately called it a Flanigan and Allen show and announced ourselves to the Borrowdale receptionist on arrival as such. Tension in the country had abated somewhat and this was a much more light-hearted appearance, and had the added interest that the situation as it appeared in South Africa was given alongside that of London.

In between these two shows various ministers carried out the same programme of radio broadcasts and T.V. interviews at Salisbury and Bulawayo. In these cases they dealt with the situation as it affected their respective portfolios.

The people of Rhodesia were by now fully informed, and I think any incipient support for Sir Humphrey Gibbs and Mr. Wilson, if any existed apart from the circles I have mentioned, had been dissipated.

There was little more for me to do in Salisbury. High Commission affairs were now being handled by External Affairs. I visited various Departments on the Tuesday and briefed them on various matters that concerned them in London and Rhodesia House.

I was gratified to learn that like the Minister in Washington, Air Vice-Marshal Bentley, now back in Rhodesia, I would receive six months' salary on the abolition of my post. It was the first and only golden bowler that I had ever received, for I had missed the golden bowlers issued to the British Army in 1950 and 1956. But this also I was destined to forgo. A pity, for it was a nice sum, and one I could well do with after the heavy expenditures which Honor and I had made from our personal incomes during our short stay in London.

Before leaving Salisbury I was happy to receive a telephone call from Cliff Dupont to inform me that at a Cabinet meeting that afternoon he had been offered and had accepted the appointment of Officer Administering the Government.

I congratulated him on this very patriotic act at this juncture in our history, and in view of the peculiar complications caused by Sir Humphrey Gibbs's unexpected action. Cliff Dupont has done great things for Rhodesia without thought of self and with the sacrifice of his personal interests, but I think his acceptance of this post at this time was the crowning climax of his long struggle for an independent Rhodesia, and his greatest service. I, for one, look forward to him being recognised by Britain as our first Governor-General, or failing that the first President of our country.

There was nothing to keep me in Salisbury, so piling the rest of our luggage into a car provided by the Government – the last free transport to which I was entitled – I drove back home to the Vumba and arrived there for lunch on Wednesday, 17th November, almost four months to a day since I had first left it for London.

So finally ended what was possibly the fullest and certainly the busiest and most interesting four months in my own and Honor's life.

18. Aftermath

During this first week of our independence an overseas visitor must have been struck by the quiet calm that pervaded the country. The motto was "business as usual", and an air of confidence was evident all round. If there were any that were dismayed or disgruntled, they kept their opinions to themselves, and they were evidently in a very small minority.

To the African population our change in status made no difference at all. The nationalists, of course, through their paid intimidators tried to start strikes, particularly in the factories in Bulawayo, but the workers were not in tune with their thoughts and the arrest of these lawbreakers soon brought them flocking back to work.

According to the theories of the liberal papers in England, theories to which the British Government presumably subscribed through the poor advice they had received from their experts, there would be revolts and uprisings amongst the African people. Some English weeklies hopefully talked of Mau-Mau type of operations, presumably on information given them by their friends, the exiled African nationalist thugs, sitting smugly in Bloomsbury. The African chiefs had already since 11th November given their whole-hearted blessing to our independence, and the vast mass of peaceful Africans saw in this event some added security to their future and a final remission from the attentions of nationalist intimidators whch had in the past made their lives a nightmare. From now on, British interference removed, they knew where their future lay and were content. They, as is usual with the African, gravitated to the support of the strongest and the winner, and all they wanted was to continue living their lives undisturbed by politics and political upheavals.

The house of cards that Mr. Wilson had expected to crumble at the first threat of sanctions had proved to be made of hard and durable material. He was now obliged by the pressure of the Afro-Asians to make good his threats. But by imposing commercial, financial and other sanctions, he began to make mistake after mis-

"It's a hold-up! If you don't hand over Rhodesia, I'll shoot!" (From the "Sunday Express", December 5, 1965. Permission: London Express Service)

take. Considering that those who had financial connections with Britain, through pensions and dividends, were the most likely to support the ex-Governor in a bid to overthrow the Government, he stopped all pensions and dividends from England to Rhodesia.

By this act he so infuriated these people, amongst whom I number myself as a pensioner, that he drew them together more solidly behind the Government. The action moreover was ineffective for the Rhodesian Government countered at once by assuming responsibility for these pensions and dividends. He also got into disrepute with many of his electorate who considered pensions as sacrosanct. He might also have sown doubts in the minds of millions of his own state pensioners in Britain that their own pensions might at some time be jeopardised for political reasons.

In order to correct this impression the Lord Chancellor then announced that the British Government was prepared to continue paying pensions, but omitted to say that these would be only payable into blocked Rhodesian accounts in British banks, and so were useless to the pensioner living in Rhodesia. I myself shortly afterwards received a cheque for my pension, which was endorsed as only valid payable into a blocked Rhodesian account in England.

This was typical of the double talk and deceit which had characterised British dealings with Rhodesia over the past years. It was now illustrated in concrete form, and as a result the Rhodesian nation was paradoxically gaining a coherence through those very sanctions that had been designed to do the opposite. What Mr. Wilson was doing was like taking a handful of damp earth, likely to disintegrate if handled carefully, and squeezing it into a granite rock.

Meanwhile a vacancy had occurred in Parliament through the resignation of his seat for the Arundel constituency by Cliff Dupont. Nomination day had been fixed for the 14th December and polling day for the 6th January 1966. Various people had suggested that I put my name forward for nomination for this seat, but I was reluctant to do this, as my home was in Umtali. However I was given to understand that this proposal had come from members of the Arundel constituency themselves, and later I was approached by a senior member of the Constituency Committee, who I had been informed was a prospective candidate and was prepared and anxious to withdraw his name in my favour.

It appeared to me that this was a time in Rhodesia's history when it was one's duty and privilege to assist the Government in any way, and so I allowed my name to be put on the list of approved candidates, but stipulated that the choice must be that of the constituency, with all the usual procedures of interview and nomination that were now the rule of the Rhodesian Front Party. I myself whilst a Divisional Chairman – before I had gone to London – had upheld the view that the Party constitution should insist that only the constituency branches through their council had the right to choose a candidate.

The Arundel constituency after due deliberations through these procedures selected me as its candidate, a great honour considering that I did not live in the constituency.

Honor and I both knew this constituency through working in its committee room during the famous election in which Sir Roy Welensky was defeated by Cliff Dupont, and were acquainted with many of the party workers in Arundel.

This nomination meant that if elected, we would have to leave our home in Umtali and move up to Salisbury where we already had a flat. This was not such an upheaval as it might seem, because we had virtually put our property on a care and maintenance basis when we left for London, not expecting to see it again for two years. At the moment we were really camping there, with many of our belongings packed and stored.

Many people thought that this election would be contested by some prominent member of the old establishment in order to test support for the fictitious "legal" government under the ex-Governor. The opposition party, the United People's Party, had decided that the election held under the 1965 Constitution was "illegal" and declined to take part. The minuscule Reform Party decided not to contest elections until Rhodesia had established herself as a country no longer under an international cloud. This was a wise and patriotic decision.

We Rhodesians could well dispense with internal party disputes until we had overcome sanctions and were able to indulge in this luxury. Indeed, it was to be hoped that the full give and take of party politics so necessary to a democracy would establish itself in due course, but now, while we were virtually in a state of war, was not the time.

As nomination day drew near, there was no sign of an independent candidate coming forth. The day before the election a mysterious individual announced he would contest the election. He refused to divulge his name, which appeared a very odd way of winning a seat in Parliament. Four minutes before nominations closed he appeared before the Returning Officer with a nomination form containing nine names, one less than the minimum required. In these four minutes he gazed wildly up and down the street, looking for some Arundel voter to complete his form, but failing to find one he departed unnominated. One wonders if this unknown individual was a practical joker, or slightly unhinged by the events of the past month. No one will know, for he has never been traced.

So this election was uncontested, and I became a member of Parliament for Arundel on the 14th December. I attended my first caucus two days later, and was warmly welcomed by my new colleagues, most of whom I had known and worked with on party matters for years.

There are hazards in becoming a member of Parliament on the continent of Africa, but they are no more in Rhodesia than at Westminster. The worst that can happen to one is the displeasure of one's constituents, who in the Rhodesian system of democracy have a far greater control over their representative than in England.

But in other parts of Africa, where the unqualified franchise is extended to all and sundry, frequent and unfortunate things may

188

happen to the aspiring politician. I am told on very good authority that the French Assembly Building in Paris, to which not only metropolitan members but those from the overseas territories of the French Union are sent, contains a memorial plaque to a member from some African state which reads: "Sacred to the memory of Monsieur . . . Eaten by his constituents." It would be instructive to attend a constituency selection committee meeting and discover the qualifications required for a candidate. Presumably a well-fed, plump and tender applicant would have a good lead over other competitors. There they must prefer in all senses a tender politician and abhor a tough one.

I hoped that in this new capacity I would be able to forward the interests of my constituents who had placed such faith in me as to choose me for their representative, and also place such knowledge as I possessed of affairs in and out of Rhodesia at the disposal of the Assembly and the Government. As we cannot draw two salaries from Government funds it was thus that I lost my golden bowler, a sum nearly four times as great as six months' Parliamentary salary.

By now the British Government was in serious difficulties with the numerous African members of the Commonwealth. Poor Mr. Bottomley and his Minister of State had to start on their travels again. Zambia egged on by the members of the Organisation of African Unity demanded British troops on the south bank of the Zambezi. Ultimatums were given to the British to crush the Rhodesians by mid-December.

I hope by now the British had realised what I had been telling them in London, that it was high time they stood up to these recalcitrant and spoilt coloured children of theirs. Maybe they had, for to my surprise I heard on the news that Mr. Bottomley had stated that "Britain would not be pushed around by them". There seemed to be resistance by the British Government to the idea that British troops should guard the Kariba dam. The Royal Scots, earmarked for this task, happily for them, never arrived. But the Air Force did, and this concession to Dr. Kaunda's demands was ungraciously accepted as an insult owing to the age and type of the aircraft provided.

It was noticeable of course that these aircraft, occupying the airfields of Zambia, not only provided protection from a highly improbable Rhodesian attack, but also from occupation by other powers, such as Egypt or Russia. Britain, if only to a feeble degree, had resisted the unreasonable demands of the African states and the result was an immediate hedging on the threat to break off diplomatic relations. When the ultimatum expired, only two Commonwealth states namely Ghana and Tanzania, the most subject to Communist influence, carried out their threats. Mrs. Barbara Castle however assured her latest protégé that aid would still be forthcoming. To this gesture the Tanzanians quickly replied, by throwing a spanner into the air-lift operation designed to assist her colleague and neighbour and indirectly help her own Communist inspired designs. Air Force personnel working in Tanzania on the airlift were ordered to leave and, pending their replacement by civilians, remove the Queen's uniform and put on mufti.

Having gratuitously insulted the R.A.F., the President of Tanzania turned his attention to the Royal Navy. It was reported that a frigate transporting oil was told to haul down the white ensign and replace it with the red ensign of the merchant navy. If this was true one can imagine the feelings of the officers and the ratings of this warship. Neither Napoleon nor the Kaiser and Hitler succeeded in doing this to the Royal Navy, but a Communist inspired dictator from the African bush had brought it off single-handed.

The British nation has for generations revered its navy, which since long before Trafalgar and Nelson had acquired a place in their hearts that the Army had never succeeded in obtaining to the same degree. One wonders what they thought about this action, and if anything will ever make them turn in exasperation on these seedy upstarts who endlessly insult Britain one day and whine for alms the next.

An oil embargo was next imposed on Rhodesia. The chief sufferer was of course Zambia, whose oil was refined and transported through Rhodesia. With all the goodwill in the world Rhodesia could not provide Zambia with oil if she was denied the opportunity to supply it. Sterling balances were frozen and seized by the British who claimed Rhodesian financial assets wherever they might happen to be placed. Unable to obtain payment for the coal which she supplied Zambia, the Rhodesians applied realistic royalty on the coal she was transporting to the north. In effect it merely put the price of copper up by £5 a ton – a negligible sum when compared with the £600 a ton odd that copper was fetching at that time.

A fantastic scheme was evolved to transport petrol to Zambia by air. The cost to the British taxpayer was tremendous. Dr. Kaunda then demanded that Britain should bear the added cost of her coal. The British taxpayer was being asked to bear a prodigious sum to support the lunatic policies of his Government towards the African states. Appeasement on this scale had even outdone Munich.

A serious situation was arising in Zambia which would threaten the stability of that country. The Rhodesians had never borne any ill-will towards Zambia, and regretted the unnecessary troubles that were afflicting her neighbour. In order to help and alleviate this distress, the Rhodesian Government offered to provide, without any conditions, oil for Zambia from her refinery and transport it north if the oil was sent to Beira for that purpose. Moreover she offered to withdraw the additional coal royalties. What could have been more reasonable and fair, and this would save the British taxpayer enormous sums of money which were being wasted on the air-lift.

Dr. Kaunda refused this offer thus illustrating for all to see that the welfare of his country was less important than the ideology of the OAU and the Communists. He seemed determined to wreck his own country, if thereby he could embroil Britain and the world in a bloody struggle along the banks of the Zambezi. One hopes that the British public will be allowed to know these facts, and that they are indirectly financing the aims of world-wide Communism.

Towards the end of 1965 Rhodesia, then in her sixth week of independence, was calm and confident, and adjusting herself to the effect of sanctions. That these would become more severe was a fact of which everyone was aware. Preparations were going ahead to meet these with ingenuity and resolution. Hardships were expected, particularly through unemployment, especially in those sectors of commerce that depended on imports. These were problems to be met and overcome.

The people of Rhodesia were aware that in their efforts to survive as an independent nation they had assumed a role of world-wide importance. To them had fallen the lot of drawing attention to the unwarranted degree of control that a group of semi-bankrupt and dictatorially-ruled black states, all inexperienced in government and statesmanship, had obtained in world affairs; that, if this state of affairs were to be allowed to continue, the end would be one of chaos and disaster to Western civilisation, and the only gainers would be the Communist world.

Rhodesia had stood up to this and called a halt. The whole fury of the liberals and fellow travellers, witting or unwitting tools of the Communists, was turned upon them not for what they had done, which was to sever themselves from British control, but for the danger their action would have on Communist designs for world conquest.

This heroic role would strengthen Rhodesian determination to win through, for their action was not only on their own behalf but on behalf of Christianity and the Western civilisation it had created.

This growing knowledge would become a spiritual weapon which would defeat the forces that were arrayed against them, and strengthen them to resist even the most intolerable pressures. Thus when victory is achieved, Rhodesia will take her place among the nations of the world, with a prestige far greater than her size and position warrant, and her inhabitants will take a first place amongst the peoples of the world with the proud boast on their lips:

"I am a Rhodesian."

2 January 1966
Umtali, Rhodesia

Postscript

The foregoing narrative was finished on 2nd January 1966, at which time Rhodesia had been independent for only seven weeks. The reader will have realised that the real stumbling block to a recognition of Rhodesia's independence on her 1961 Constitution, even with the additional liberal amendments and concessions offered by the Rhodesian negotiators, was the desire of the British Government to appease the African states at all costs. Before these states had acquired any say in Commonwealth and world affairs, the issue had been simple.

Before 1953, the year in which the Federation was formed, we had been offered our independence on no less than three occasions without strings or conditions.

Now, on behalf of these states, Britain has imposed severe sanctions on the only stable Commonwealth country in Africa, and regardless of the lessons learnt in other parts of Africa appears bent on dragging Rhodesia down to the same level.

Since 11th November no less than five African states have experienced revolutions in which military dictatorships have emerged. One of these upheavals has occurred in Nigeria, which for a long time had been held up by liberal propagandists as the bright example of African democracy. Others will soon follow her example.

With Nelsonian blindness the churches and progressive opinion have ignored the brutalities of such regimes as Zanzibar and Burundi, and the shocking murders in Nigeria, without for a single moment hesitating to attack the one country in which such events do not occur – Rhodesia.

The irony of this was revealed at the Lagos Commonwealth Conference, convoked on the initiative of the Nigerian Prime Minister, at which he and his fellow African statesmen called on Britain for increased sanctions and ultimate force being used to bring down the stable *de facto* government of Rhodesia. Within a week his own government had toppled in chaos and he himself was assassinated.

Vast sums are being spent by the British taxpayer to implement

". . . and when you've starved out Smith, we demand sanctions against you if you don't tear up your Immigration Bill!" (From the "Daily Express", December 20, 1965. Permission: London Express Service)

sanctions against Rhodesia and to support Zambia in the suicidal policy she is pursuing towards her neighbour. Valuable trade is being lost to the British, and commodities essential to her economy such as tobacco and copper will be increased in price.

Apart from logic and justice, the question arises whether Britain can afford to let her own interests be jeopardised by dictation from outside forces of such a nature?

Outside the Republic of South Africa, Rhodesia is by far the most peaceful and well-governed country in Africa. Since her declaration of independence she has experienced no internal disturbances. Both her African and European people are united behind the Government. Sanctions have only served to stiffen their resolution, whilst events elsewhere in Africa have made all races in the country more determined than ever to follow the path of evolution rather than that of revolution.

The main sufferer will be Britain whose economy at this time cannot carry the cost of this futile exercise, which is solely aimed at added chaos in Africa by terminating stable and progressive government in Rhodesia.

194

A more sterile policy than that of the Wilson government could hardly be imagined.

Is it not time for the British public to take control of the situation and remove it from the hands of their political leaders before they too suffer the consequences of an appeasement even greater than Munich? – an appeasement to Communist designs through the stalking-horse of African nationalism.

What therefore is the solution? This lies in the acceptance of Rhodesian independence on her 1965 Constitution – which is in effect the 1961 Constitution amended only in so far that it gives *de facto* and *de jure* independence of Whitehall – and thereafter to leave it to the Rhodesians to justify their good faith and intentions in developing a society in which justice is done to all.

Sanctions, which harm everyone and serve only to stiffen Rhodesian resolution, should be called off before British business concerns lose all that they have built up in Rhodesia, and their place is taken by other interests.

All that is required of the British people is to take a long, hard, cold look at their new Commonwealth, and then to prune away the dead wood and clear the weeds that are choking that organisation, thus calling a halt to the process of disintegration that is taking place in front of their eyes and involving them in the ruin.

Then a strong and united Rhodesia can be expected to resume the ties and loyalties to Britain that have been so grossly betrayed and abused by successive British Governments over the wasted years.

RHODESIA: THE FACTS

Is Rhodesia Progressive?

Rhodesia has been self-governing for forty-two years. It was annexed to the British Crown in 1923 after the electorate had been given the choice between responsible self-government and incorporation in the Union of South Africa. By a substantial majority they voted for self-government. Since then the progress that has been achieved has been the result of the energy, foresight and hard work of the Rhodesian people themselves, and Africans have contributed largely to this development, of which all races in Rhodesia are justly proud.

When the Rhodesian Government was formed just over four decades ago, it took over the administration of a pioneer country in its initial stages of development. It might well have been expected that a century would elapse before real progress and modernity were achieved. Now, forty-two years later, here are the facts of Rhodesian advance in all fields of its public life.

In 1890 the African population numbered about four hundred thousand. Today, by virtue of the end of tribal war, and the prevention and cure of disease, the African population exceeds 3½ million. Additionally, about a half million Africans from other countries choose to live and work in Rhodesia, presumably because conditions are very much better than in their own countries.

The white population has increased steadily by constant immigration and has now reached a figure of nearly a quarter of a million. The majority are people of British stock who have made Rhodesia their home and country in response to repeated and solemn assurances from successive British Governments that their future in Rhodesia was guaranteed and assured.

Political advancement has been rapid. The franchise is based solely on merit. Every individual, regardless of race, has equal rights to the vote, providing he or she has the necessary qualifications. All seats in Parliament are likewise open to any adult of any race who has the required qualifications.

Rhodesia is one of the few countries in Africa where a genuinely non-racial democracy is peacefully emerging before our eyes. All this has been achieved in the few years – as we measure history – that Rhodesia has governed herself.

Salisbury, which hardly existed sixty years ago, is now a modern town of 320,000 inhabitants. Bulawayo has 220,000. In the towns and in the country a relationship of mutual respect and trust exists between African and white Rhodesians. The distinction is now becoming outdated. All races in Rhodesia now regard themselves purely as Rhodesians, as loyal and active partners in the development of this truly wonderful country, about three times the size of England with a population density of approximately twenty-five people to the square mile and with one of the best climates in the world, 'a country situated on a great plateau that makes its air vigorous, health-giving and unique.

To sustain a constantly rising standard of living for all Rhodesians, it has been necessary constantly to increase exports. This has been achieved by energy, imagination and hard work. In the decade 1954–1964 many exports trebled, others doubled or greatly increased. Thus the tobacco export increased from twenty million to thirty-five million pounds, meat products from two million to over four million, clothing from two and a half million to four and a half million, and other industries, including mining, increased very substantially. In return, Rhodesia is a rapidly expanding market for imported goods – her best customer and supplier is Britain.

Progress is spectacular. In the south-east, in the Lowveld, the production four years ago was about 12,000 tons of sugar and a little beef. The figures last year were 160,000 tons of sugar and over 100,000 tons of citrus. Development is only beginning. The immediate target is a hundred million pounds' worth of exportable products produced by a million and a half Rhodesians.

The salaries and wages of all Rhodesians have increased at a remarkable rate and are now among the best in Africa. A fitter can earn ten shillings an hour. The cost of food is not higher than in Europe and income tax is negligible. This is the free enterprise modern society of today and tomorrow in action. All this has been achieved by the unity of all Rhodesians.

New industries and foreign investment are encouraged by a progressive government policy and this has resulted in rapid expansion of the tobacco crop and the crops in maize, groundnuts and cotton.

Livestock, very important to Rhodesia, constantly increases in number and quality. Mining has been rapidly advanced by the adoption of modern techniques. The output of gold, asbestos, chrome, coal, copper, tin and other minerals shows the results of their dynamic policies. Rhodesia has many excellent customers for its products; for instance, the United States imports nearly half its metallurgical chrome ore requirements from Rhodesia.

Rhodesia, with clean, modern factories mushrooming, is manufacturing a large range of products from cotton to tyres and has become the second largest manufacturing nation in Africa, with the Kariba Hydro-Electric scheme the main supplier of power. Industrial relations are negotiated through twenty-one industrial councils and fifty industrial boards.

Housing for all Rhodesians, regardless of race, has been a priority with Rhodesian Governments. The Health Service, with a doctor for every 4,500 inhabitants and three hospital beds for each thousand persons, is one of the best in Africa.

Phenomenal efforts have been made by the Government in the field of education, for education is the spearhead of Rhodesian progress in both the political and industrial fields.

In 1953 approximately 263,000 children were attending school. In 1965 this had jumped to nearly 700,000. Government expenditure on education has grown to over twelve million pounds, with 20,000 teachers working in 3,600 schools.

This is the new, modern-minded nation we now call Rhodesia. Its record during the last forty years far outstrips that of most European countries. And this has been achieved without any form of dictatorship and with the basic freedoms upheld, without fear or favour, by the Rhodesian courts.

The question asked was: Is Rhodesia progressive? And the answer must be that seldom in the long and brave history of human endeavour has so much been achieved for so many so well and in so short a time.

How is Rhodesia Governed?

We now come to the question: How is Rhodesia governed? And the answer is: By a constitutional form of democracy such as one would expect Rhodesians to have adopted.

There are sixty-five members of parliament and the government party has a cabinet of twelve members with such portfolios as the Office of Prime Minister, the Ministries of Justice, Law and Order, Local Government, Agriculture and Natural Resources, Internal Affairs and Social Welfare, Labour, Commerce and Industry, Roads, Education and Mines, Immigration, and Lands and Water Development.

There is a completely independent judiciary with a chief justice and six puisne judges. The law is administered to all races with complete impartiality. This is recognised by all Rhodesians, though it is never mentioned in propaganda directed against the Rhodesian Government by parties or persons often without any first-hand knowledge of the country.

The basis of Rhodesia's democratic system is the secret ballot. The qualification for a vote is based on merit alone, not race. There are two voters' rolls with a higher qualification for the A roll. For a lower qualification there is the B roll. The A roll voters elect members for fifty constituencies. The B roll electors return members for fifteen electoral districts which also cover the whole country. Africans have captured nearly all the B roll seats and form the official opposition at the present time. They are all actively engaged in their parliamentary duties. They are not languishing in gaol as are the opposition in a number of African states that have been granted "instant" one-man-one-vote democracy.

The following are the qualifications for the "A" Roll:

(a) Income of £792 or ownership of property of value of £1,650 or

(b) Income of £528 or ownership of property of value of £1,100 and completion of a course of primary education or

(c) Income of £330 or ownership of property of value of £550 and four years' secondary education or

(d) Appointment to the office of Chief or Headman.

The following are the qualifications for the "B" Roll:

(a) Income of £264 or ownership of property of the value of £495 or

(b) Income of £132 or ownership of property of the value of £275 and two years' secondary education or

(c) Over 30 years of age and income of £132 or ownership of property of value of £275 and primary education or

(d) Over 30 years of age and income of £198 or ownership of property of value of £385 or

(e) Kraal heads with a following of 20 or more heads of families or

(f) Ministers of religion.

Provision is made for a person paying for property by instalments to qualify for the "B" roll. A married woman is deemed to have the same means qualifications as her husband if she does not qualify in her own right. (This applies to one wife only; a necessary provision as polygamy is still practised by many Africans.) She has, of course, also to fulfil the other appropriate qualifications herself.

There is no legal impediment to a Rhodesian of any race becoming Prime Minister, Member of Parliament, Judge of the High Court, Head of a Government Department or practising in any profession. Attainment of these positions is purely a question of merit and qualifications.

The present constitution provides for ever-increasing African participation in Parliament as more and more achieve the necessary qualification for the vote by virtue of education, earning power and property ownership. Eventual majority rule is assured.

The main classes of Africans on or eligible for the A roll are employed in the Civil Service or Railways, or are holders of trading licences, operators of transport services, senior schoolmasters, purchase area farmers and professional men.

The rate of African enfranchisement increases year by year and, if it were not for intimidation by a few "nationalist" politicians, there is no doubt that orderly and sufficiently rapid progress towards a completely integrated political society would be achieved. The enormous acceleration in educational facilities for all races, provided by the Government, assures that the pace of African participation in Government will be increased year by year, but, in so far as the Government of Rhodesia becomes African, it will still be responsible, trained to regard fellow Rhodesians as countrymen first, regardless of race. This, surely, is the kind of advance which Africa sorely needs.

It avoids alike the dangers of an ignorant population at the mercy of get-rich-quick politicians, and the temptation for an irresponsible leader to take over the Armed Forces and Police and rule as a virtual dictator, enforcing his own ego and his own interest by a propaganda campaign of adulation and perjury.

Apart from the franchise there is another aspect of Rhodesian Government, equally important, with roots deep in African history: the organisation of the tribes under their chiefs. This organisation has been attacked as if it were an invention of the Rhodesian Government to deny democracy to the Rhodesian people. In fact, the tribal structure is completely indigenous, a system suited to the African ethos, to the culture, customs and beliefs of the tribes. Destroy it, and a vacuum would be created into which greedy men would quickly step. Retain it in the interest of Rhodesia, and a strong traditional core of law and order, of justice and equity, of family and tribal bonds is preserved that can play and is playing an important role in the whole forward movement of the nation. The family, the village, the tribe, the chief: these things are dear to the African. The Government has no right to smash this structure and does not intend to do so.

Some understanding of the role played by the chiefs of Rhodesia is essential to any understanding of the country and certainly a necessity before passing any kind of judgment on the Rhodesia of today and tomorrow.

Nearly half Rhodesia is tribal trust land, land reserved exclusively for the tribes whose traditional ruler in domestic affairs is their chief. Seventy-five years ago the chiefs were the lords of life and death, the absolute rulers of their tribes. Their modern role is very different but it is still based on the veneration of the tribe for its chief, and in the 1961 Constitution the essential role of the chiefs was recognised by Britain. A tribesman was defined as "a member of a community under the control or leadership of a chief". Legislation passed at the time channelled this authority into its modern outlet. An act was passed establishing the Council of Chiefs and charging the chiefs with the duty of "making representations to the Minister in regard to the needs and wishes of the tribesmen in the tribal area".

By using this residue of the prerogative that remained in the hands of the chiefs and by establishing a direct link between the chiefs and the Cabinet, the Government effectively enfranchised the entire tribal population which could not possibly have participated in a modern ballot election.

The system, perhaps because it is an African system and not an imported Western political concept, works well. The wishes of the tribesmen reach the Government speedily and accurately at any time. The tribesmen do not have to wait for an election to make their wishes known. They feel that through their chief they have direct access to the authority that can get things done. This system of government through chiefs has been one of the major successes of modern Rhodesian Government techniques. It is never mentioned except in disparagement by the critics of the present Government, but it deserves serious study and attention. It is an experiment in grafting traditional authority on modern executive government and the chiefs have shown themselves forthright and able in carrying out their duties and responsibilities.

It is not enough to know that the opinions and wishes of the tribes are made known to the Government through the Council of Chiefs. We must know, at least in outline, how the system works in practice before we pass any kind of judgment on it.

The criteria should be: Is it acceptable to the people? Does it on the whole procure their happiness and interests? Is it reasonably speedy and not subject to corruption?

The whole tribal concept revolves around the chief. His word is law and obeyed unquestioningly. But he is no dictator. A whole complex of customs restrains and guides him as, in fact, custom directs a constitutional monarch. He acts through his representatives, being unable to investigate every matter personally. Next to the chief comes the headman, like the chief himself usually hereditary, then the kraal head and then the family head. The family may be a very large unit comprising relations of both wife and husband.

African tribal Rhodesians understand this system and how to work it. It has, in fact, in a short space of time changed warring tribes into peaceful neighbours. It has secured immediate representation of tribal views to the Government, who have proved that they can cut through red tape to act on the representations made to them.

Many chiefs are educated in the Western sense. Others use educated members of the tribe to act as advisers when the question under decision seems to indicate that this is necessary. But the daily concerns of a chief are disputes over land, water, boundaries, housing, marriage, or the ownership or possession of cattle or crops.

The chief is never off duty. He cannot close his office door. Any tribal member has a right of direct access to the chief. Although the procedure is to direct matters through the chain of headmen this right of direct access is never denied. The voter in the West cannot as a rule see the Minister, but the tribesman with a grievance will go direct to his chief and be heard.

The Rhodesian tribesman has no regard for modern Western political techniques. He sees that often they corrupt both the politicians and the "electorate". His own system, modernised as it is, affords him the kind of direct representation often resulting in swift action that he knows, understands and appreciates.

This whole system of government through chiefs in the tribal areas depends on the traditional position and authority of the chiefs themselves. Experience has shown that the chiefs have adapted themselves to their present role with skill and assiduity. As of old, they come to a village to celebrate a wedding, to mourn with a family which has lost its head, to settle on the spot a dispute that has perhaps become heated. Wherever the chief goes authority goes with him for his powers are based not on intimidation or corruption but on respect.

The break-up of this system, in order to substitute for it a secret ballot in a one-man-one-vote Western democratic technique, would wreck the orderly lives of the tribes. All those who are interested in the peaceful evolution of this great country should try to understand this. The role of the chiefs is an essential part of the Rhodesian scene.

We posed the question: How is Rhodesia governed? The brief answer is that outside the tribal areas it is governed by a Parliament on the British pattern, elected by voters qualified by merit alone, which leads to increasing African participation in government in a multilateral society. In the tribal areas the elaborate but effective system we have described, culminating in the Council of Chiefs, is the instrument of government.

Both forms of Government, side by side, have proved themselves to be good for they have produced and sustained one of the most stable and progressive nations in Africa.

What are the Facts of the Negotiations between the Governments of Rhodesia and Britain?

These negotiations have been subjected to so much misrepresentation that it is essential to get the facts clear.

There is no room here to trace the history of the relationship between the two Governments from the beginning. It is sufficient to say that the British Government always appeared to regard the grant of independence as a part of the overall policy whereby the Empire has been transformed into the Commonwealth.

But in the meetings between Mr. Smith and his Ministers and Mr. Bottomley and the British Prime Minister at the beginning of October 1965 it became clear that the Rhodesian delegation had been invited to London not to negotiate a settlement but to receive an ultimatum.

The ultimatum was specific. The attitude of Mr. Wilson's Government was: Either you accept our five points or we will not grant you independence. This was a remarkable way of inviting Rhodesian goodwill and co-operation.

Let us take in order the five points on which the British Government insisted and the reasoned Rhodesian reply to each point.

Point 1: Unimpeded progress to majority rule.

The British Government assumed that the Rhodesian Government opposed this. They do not. What they oppose is hastening the rate of progress which was deliberately adopted to suit Rhodesia. The British Government seemed to assume that the Rhodesian Government, once in the saddle, would cast aside their undertakings in this respect. To put it mildly, anyone following the long history of this matter will not find duplicity on the Rhodesian side of the boundary.

Point II: Guarantees were required that there would not be retrogressive amendments of the constitution to retard African advancement. The Rhodesian Government accepted this. In any case a two-thirds majority is required for any such amendment under the 1961

Constitution. In addition the Rhodesian Government offered a senate composed entirely of chiefs.

Point III: There would have to be immediate improvement in the political representation of Africans. The Rhodesian Government offered a virtual enfranchisement of the entire population on the B roll.

Point IV: Racial discrimination must end. The British Government were concerned to alter or amend the Land Apportionment Act. This Act is designed as much to protect Africans as Europeans. The Rhodesian Government agreed there should be continued progress towards ending racial discrimination and pointed out that it was embarking on more and more multi-racial projects as in the University of Rhodesia and the United Teachers' Training College at Bulawayo. They can be trusted to continue their progressive policies.

Point V: The British Government would need to be satisfied that any basis of independence was acceptable to the people of Rhodesia as a whole. This would entail departure from a carefully constructed machinery of government designed to promote peaceful Rhodesian progress. A referendum on such a proposal would be counter to all local conceptions of authority and order, and might well lead to chaos. It reflects, once more, the fact that the British Government are attempting to impose Western political methods on a country in which they are not acceptable.

There is one final and additional point we may add to these demands made by the British Government on the Government of Rhodesia. It is that during the London talks the British Government made no concession of any kind. All the constructive new proposals came from the Rhodesian Government. It is perfectly well known that the attitude of the British Government reflects the pressures brought to bear on it, largely by African nations who have been unable to bring to their people the commercial prosperity or the peace and freedom enjoyed in Rhodesia.

We have asked and answered three questions. We have found that Rhodesia is a progressive, dynamic young country. We have found that its political system is based on conceptions that the Rhodesian people understand and which are calculated to assure not only increased African participation in government, but the peaceful and

205

steady growth of a new nation proud of its heritage and its achievements and bold and confident as to its future.

We have found that in the most recent negotiations between the Governments of Rhodesia and Britain the Rhodesian Government has been reasonable and constructive and we have indicated that there should be the possibility of settling the issue of Rhodesian independence, given goodwill and understanding on both sides.

Friends of Rhodesia and friends of Britain will pray that as time passes the Rhodesian people and their Government, their aspirations, intentions and motives, may be better understood so that all Rhodesians may look forward to a future of spiritual freedom and material prosperity, playing an increasing part in world affairs and showing by their example that an African nation can be an example to others in the difficulties and challenges of a rapidly changing world.

A STATEMENT ISSUED BY THE RHODESIAN PRIME MINISTER

The Rhodesian Government, during this week's discussions, have done their very best to span the gulf between them and the British Government. The latter for their part have offered no concessions. The talks were conducted in a friendly atmosphere, and if there is one thing that has to be said it is that Mr. Wilson and his colleagues have been open and frank. It is all the more regrettable, therefore, that they have not seen their way to granting independence to Rhodesia in keeping with moral obligations which exist from past assurances.

The basic principles which have assumed such importance were put to us in February this year as "the principles on which the British Government would need to be satisfied before they were able to contemplate the grant of independence". There is no promise in this sentence, even if we did manage to satisfy them, that they would go beyond the "contemplation" stage. This basically explains the whole of the Rhodesian case against the British Government: No specific offers, nothing that one may accept as firm or as a basis for negotiation.

No wonder then that any Rhodesian Government would be ill-advised to give anything away without being able to rely on something being guaranteed to them in return.

Now to deal with the five principles:

(1) The principle and intention of unimpeded progress to majority rule, already enshrined in the 1961 Constitution, would have to be maintained and guaranteed.

The British Government have assumed that we are unable to accept this principle. On the contrary, the Rhodesian Government have requested independence on the basis of the 1961 Constitution and are prepared to work that Constitution.

What we are not prepared to do, is to increase the rate of progress to majority rule in view of all the evidence that is before us today about the inadvisability of rushing such important matters.

We maintain that this constitution in theory and in practice, satisfies the first principle completely. The 1961 Constitution, it must be remembered, was one accepted by the British Parliament itself, and was the direct result of negotiations between the British Government of the time, the Rhodesian Government and all racial groups and parties in the country. It is not a question of the pace of advancement so much as the responsibility of those being advanced and of the end result which should concern us.

(2) There would also have to be guarantees against retrogressive amendment of the constitution.

The Rhodesian Government have accepted this. The existing constitution provides that normal constitutional changes can be made by a simple two-thirds majority; that right already exists, and it is a retrogressive step to ask the Rhodesian Government to accept further restrictions on that right.

(3) There would have to be an immediate improvement in the political status of the African population.

The Rhodesian Government have accepted this in principle and have offered a senate which would be composed 100% of Africans. In addition the Rhodesian Government are prepared to extend the B roll to virtual adult suffrage and this would give an estimated one million of male adult Africans the vote.

(4) There would have to be progress towards ending racial discrimination.

The attitude of the British Government was that the Rhodesian Government were not prepared to take specific steps towards ending racial discrimination, and that we would never amend or repeal the Land Apportionment Act. This is quite inaccurate. The Rhodesian Government's attitude is that times and circumstances will require modifications and amendments of the Act. In fact, the Government are already considering the setting aside of non-racial areas for both business and residential purposes in town and country.

This Act is the fundamental Land Act of Rhodesia, and it is quite unrealistic to suggest that it could be abolished overnight. Moreover, it was conceived and it exists more for the benefit and protection of the African than for the European.

The Rhodesian Government had not interfered with existing multi-racial institutions, notably the University of Rhodesia. The latest development in Bulawayo, with Government blessing and assistance, is the coming establishment of the United Teachers' Training College which will be multi-racial.

(5) The British Government would need to be satisfied that any basis proposed for independence was acceptable to the people of Rhodesia as a whole.

This requirement is completely at variance with the other four principles, or they with it. Were the two Governments to come together on the first four principles, what would be the point of their exposing their negotiated agreement to the whims of an electorate composed mainly of persons who are not familiar with constitutional difficulties and so risk a rejection of what two responsible Governments, with all the wisdom and experience at their disposal, have agreed upon as good for the country?

The Rhodesian Government, therefore, consider that the requirement is quite meaningless or else merely a device to ensure that no understanding reached between the Governments can with certainty be implemented.

In answer to accusations made in the Press, I wish to make it clear that the emergency regulations and provisions for restriction have nothing to do with racial affairs. The people who are affected, which includes all races, are restricted for security reasons, and the British Government should know well that such measures are necessary when agitators are at work.

There is complete freedom of the Press in Rhodesia and always has been. One newspaper, the *Daily News*, owned by the Thomson group, was suppressed for security reasons, and this action was successfully defended in the High Court.

A constitutional conference has been mentioned as a possible solution. We have already been through this process in 1961, and successively. The conference, at which one of my present Ministers was present, was presided over by Mr. Duncan Sandys, who was then Secretary of State, and after the usual difficulties which any conference has to contend with, did produce recommendations for a constitution which ultimately formed the basis of the constitution which we have now. Why should we have to go through the process again to achieve the same results?

There is talk that a unilateral declaration of independence would be an act of rebellion. I deny the truth of the statement because Rhodesians will do nothing that will amount to a withdrawal of allegiance in the slightest to the Queen. I wish to make this crystal clear.

Zambia will not be affected in the slightest by any declaration of independence, and we wish to do nothing to render their position even slightly embarrassing. But on the other hand, of course, if people decide for their own reasons and purposes to take reprisals against us we are sufficiently capable of defending ourselves.

The Government in Rhodesia is the last one to attempt to put the clock back. One has only to consider that we are the people who live in the country and that we will do nothing which could be interpreted as imposing anything on the majority of the people when they refuse to accept it. We are part of the country, and we have to live with the decisions that we make.

Nor is it a question of Britain's legal authority being withdrawn from the country. Britain never had any legal authority: Everything that has been done in the country has been done by the country's own Government and without any prompting or direction from Great Britain.

I am, of course, glad to read that there is no suggestion of Britain's being prevailed upon to employ the use of military force. I think this would be against all British tradition. And it would also be against our own tradition. As I have said, we will not use force, and it is quite mischievous for anyone to make such a suggestion.

I am greatly obliged for the understanding and sympathy shown to us by large numbers of people in this country, and I would like to say that, whatever decisions we may have to take in the interests of our country, it will be our constant endeavour to encourage and maintain the friendliest of relations with this country and with all who have sent us expressions of goodwill.

INDEPENDENT RHODESIA

"We have struck a blow for the preservation of justice, civilisation, and Christianity, and in the spirit of this belief we have this day assumed our sovereign independence. God bless you all."

With these solemn words Prime Minister Ian Douglas Smith of Rhodesia ended a historic broadcast on 11th November 1965. The nation – and indeed, the whole world – now knew that Rhodesia no longer recognised any outside suzerainty; that a little country was prepared, if necessary, to defend its rightful heritage to its utmost ability.

The Prime Minister's historic broadcast marked the end of a twilight of uncertainty, doubt, and at times, deep frustration. While Rhodesians steeled themselves to face up to whatever retribution other people might seek to visit upon them, they did so with a great surge of hope, determination – and relief.

All the equivocation, deceit and procrastination were now over. It was like coming out of a dark cave into the clean, free sunlight. They would – and if necessary they will – pay any price.

It was Prime Minister Smith who read the Declaration of Independence. It was Prime Minister Harold Wilson and his colleagues who rendered this inevitable. They left Rhodesia no other choice.

The story really begins in 1923 – more than 40 years ago – when Rhodesia became a self-governing Colony. From that date there was established an unblemished record of progress, stability, justice and orderly government. Standards already second to none on the continent of Africa were raised for all Rhodesians. Medical services, schools, railways, roads, churches, fine cities, housing, factories, technical and agricultural colleges – a University – all the things that go to make the modern progressive state; the proud legacy of 42 years of self-rule. Rhodesia has its faults and has made mistakes. But on balance it is proud of its achievements.

When the Pioneers first arrived in the latter part of the last century, thrusting through malarial bush in ox waggons, they found a savage, untamed wilderness. Sickness, tribal war and slavery – along with in-

211

credibly primitive ignorance – were the lot of the comparative handful of tribesmen they encountered. The estimated African population of that time was about 300,000 at most. Because of the hospitals, doctors and nursing staff introduced by those first white Rhodesians, and the march of civilisation, the African population today has grown to nearly 4,000,000, of which 2,000,000 are children – tribute in itself to the country's medical advance.

A state was established that became the envy of other countries in Africa. None could match Rhodesia's achievements in social services, economic expansion and constant, orderly government.

Throughout this whole period its citizens remained dedicated to the British way of life. They based everything on the principles of fair play, tolerance and opportunity for all, and they remained unswervingly loyal to Britain; their deep affection for the Crown remained unsurpassed.

In 1953 the now defunct Federation of Rhodesia and Nyasaland was established. Of the three territories involved, Rhodesia was the only one, by virtue of its selfruling status, to put the matter squarely to the people in a referendum. The answer was "Yes" and thenceforth Rhodesia put all her efforts into making a success of Federation. Economically tremendous strides were made.

The story is well known that in 1963 the British Government rejected its own creation and without the concurrence of either the Rhodesian Government or the overall Federal Government dissolved the Federation. Meanwhile, in 1961, the Rhodesian people accepted, by referendum, a new constitution which conferred independence "within the Federal framework".

The 1961 Constitution was the result of round table talks between all parties and all races, presided over by Britain's then Commonwealth Secretary, Mr. Duncan Sandys. African nationalists accepted it to a man . . . and within days repudiated it to a man. It is emphasised that, whatever may now be said, the 1961 Constitution was sold to Rhodesia as conferring independence subject to Federal ties.

When Britain unilaterally dissolved the Federation, it became apparent that in her eyes the independence Rhodesia had been granted "within the Federal framework" had largely evaporated – but at the same time all the concessions and agreements Rhodesia had made to achieve this non-existent independence were still binding. In short, it had been misled into making extraordinarily generous concessions – for nothing.

While Rhodesia continued scrupulously to observe the 1961 Constitution in the belief that it was the basis for sovereign independence, the British Government was clearly determined to use the new situation as a means of swiftly promoting so-called majority rule.

It took two years of intensive negotiation and finally something close to an ultimatum to wring this out of the British Government. The 1961 concessions were not enough. The 1961 Constitution was no longer considered a fair basis for independence.

The fundamental difference between the Rhodesian and British Governments was this. Rhodesians believe that the reins of government should be held in responsible hands. The colour of those hands is immaterial. The majority of those capable of exercising a vote, and thus being responsible for government, are Europeans by virtue of their culture and heritage. In time a greater proportion of the population will become eligible to vote and therefore exercise an increasing and, it is hoped, responsible influence. The British Government on the other hand believe in what they euphemistically term "majority rule", by which they mean black rule, which is blatant racialism. The fact that in several previous exercises of this kind the one-man-one-vote principle in Africa has led to one election, one party, one dictator, is apparently of no consequence.

When the London talks broke down in October 1965, the Prime Minister, Mr. Ian Smith, told a press conference: "The British Government has categorically stated that it no longer believes that the 1961 Constitution is an appropriate basis for independence. This is contrary to everything we have been led to believe in the past."

This disclosure, flashed back from London to Rhodesia was taken as a clear indication by most Rhodesians that the British Government was planning to doublecross Mr. Smith, just as it had Sir Roy Welensky, the Federal Prime Minister.

During the talks Mr. Smith had offered the British Government his full acceptance of the principles of unimpeded progress towards majority rule as enshrined in the 1961 Constitution. He offered a means of providing the frequently referred to "blocking third" against amendment of the entrenched clauses in the Constitution with an Upper House comprised entirely of Africans. As the first representative of a country which has honoured every guarantee and commitment it had ever entered into, he was prepared to offer guarantees ensuring that there would be no tampering with the constitution.

But as Mr. Smith himself said at his press conference: "Every time we moved towards them (the British) they moved further away from us." It is clear that the only concessions offered came from the Rhodesian Prime Minister.

But if Mr. Smith failed to make headway with the British Government he certainly succeeded with the British people. Expressions of sympathy and goodwill poured into Rhodesia House from all over the United Kingdom.

Back in Salisbury Mr. Smith received a further appeal from Mr. Wilson; Rhodesia's Prime Minister responded with the offer of a solemn treaty guaranteeing the inviolability of the constitution. Then came Mr. Wilson's dramatic announcement that he would fly to Rhodesia.

Rhodesians began to ask themselves: "Is he in earnest this time, at last? Surely he can't still by stalling . . . or can he?" He could! Mr. Wilson and his Commonwealth Relations Secretary, Mr. Arthur Bottomley, arrived with an impressive corps of 50 British civil servants.

Hopefully Rhodesians began to wonder if this enormous retinue meant that in addition to top level talks, there would be liaison at all levels in the process of working out the complicated details of independence.

Mr. Wilson embarked on talks with individuals and organisations. Of those whom he chose or agreed to see, the majority had never received a single vote from the people of Rhodesia and were in no way representative of public opinion.

While the British Prime Minister gave only one hour of his time to the Council of Chiefs (the acknowledged leaders of 80 per cent of the African population) he gave nearly a full day to rival nationalist delegations led by men who had either never fought an election or who had never had a vote of any sort cast in their favour.

Hope surged again in Rhodesia when it was announced that proposals for the establishment of a Royal Commission were to be considered by the two governments. The Rhodesian Government was prepared to abide by the findings of such a Royal Commission with the proviso that the Commission's terms of reference should be to find out whether or not independence, on the existing constitution appropriately amended to accord with the views of the Rhodesian Government, was acceptable to the majority of the people in Rhodesia.

It is probable that with goodwill on both sides – and this was certainly forthcoming from the Rhodesian side – the Commission could have evolved its own *modus operandi* which would have been acceptable to all parties. But on his return to London Mr. Wilson had clearly done some rethinking . . .

In his statement to the House of Commons, he hedged the proposal with so many conditions that it became hopeless. For example, he laid down how it should operate instead of leaving it to the Commission to make its own proposals in an interim report. He insisted that the Commission should make known throughout Rhodesia the British Government's opposition to the views of the Rhodesian Government, thus seeking to turn an intended impartial body into a propaganda vehicle.

He stated that unless the Commission's report was unanimous it would be unacceptable – and on top of all that he "reserved the British Government's position at all stages". In other words, had the Commission finally come forward with a unanimous report in favour of the Rhodesian Government, the British Government could still have rejected it.

Rhodesians felt that had Mr. Wilson really been sincere about the Royal Commission proposal, he would himself have stayed in Rhodesia to reach agreement on its terms of reference. Leaving Mr. Bottomley behind for 24 hours, ostensibly for this purpose, was no more than a token gesture.

They now believe – and reluctantly so did the Rhodesian Government before it was driven to take the final step – that Mr. Wilson's visit with his coterie of civil servants and the later arrival of the British Attorney-General, Sir Elwyn Jones, was a gigantic charade intended to convince the British electorate that "I did everything humanly possible."

Two further events occurred before the Declaration of Independence. On the night of 10 November 1965 Britain's High Commissioner in Salisbury delivered a verbal message to the Rhodesian Government. He was invited to put the message in writing. This he refused to do.

Finally, there was a telephone call from Mr. Harold Wilson in

London to Mr. Ian Smith in Salisbury at 9 a.m. on 11 November 1965. This conversation was tape-recorded in London without the knowledge of the Rhodesian Prime Minister, and a transcript was later published from Mr. Wilson's office at 10 Downing Street.

The substance of the conversation was to the effect that the British Prime Minister considered reconciliation was still possible (but in terms of the conditions he had laid down concerning the Royal Commission). The Rhodesian Prime Minister could not see how reconciliation was possible in such circumstances.

Finally, Mr. Wilson offered to send a senior Minister to Rhodesia. As no less a person than the British Prime Minister and his Commonwealth Relations Secretary had been in Rhodesia a few days earlier, was it to be wondered at that Mr. Smith rejected this offer?

It surely could only be regarded as a further delaying tactic to throw Rhodesia off its guard and to promote further uncertainty and procrastination until the so-called "Rhodesian problem" could be handed over to the Commonwealth Conference in 1966. Were Rhodesia to wait for that event its fate would be sealed irrevocably. With a majority of Afro-Asian members, the outcome would have been inevitable.

So it was that at 1.15 p.m. on 11th November 1965 Prime Minister Ian Douglas Smith introduced Rhodesia's Declaration of Independence in a nation-wide broadcast with the words: "Whereas in the course of human affairs history has shown that it may become necessary for a people to resolve the political affiliations which have connected them with another people and to assume amongst other nations the separate and equal status to which they are entitled . . . "

Since then sanctions have been mounted against Rhodesia. A little cynically Rhodesians have noted the official line of the British Parliamentary Opposition that it would not oppose sanctions "so long as these are not punitive" – as if sanctions could be anything but punitive.

They have noted the measures taken by Mr. Wilson's Government – many of them incredibly petty and spiteful, and others destined not to undermine Rhodesia's economy as was obviously intended, but world confidence in Britain's fiscal integrity.

For example, one of the most paltry and reprehensible measures inspired by Mr. Wilson was to block payment to about 2,000 British pensioners living in Rhodesia. These pensioners, many of them disabled ex-Servicemen, had served Britain well. While there was no legal obligation on the Rhodesian Government to look after these people, on the grounds of compassion and humanity it immediately created a fund so as to honour Britain's responsibilities. Pressure in Britain compelled that country's Government not to renounce its obligations to these people; the fund created in Rhodesia was put into "cold storage" – for use in case Mr. Wilson's Government introduced further vindictive measures against these unfortunates. And sure enough this happened! Having driven Rhodesia from the sterling area Britain will now only pay these pensions in sterling – a currency which is worthless to her pensioners in Rhodesia. However, the Rhodesian Government successfully anticipated this latest example of Britain's chicanery and will now operate its emergency pension fund.

As for Britain's integrity, the world's financial houses will know what to think of a government which seizes reserves in an effort to resolve a political dispute.

We do not deny that sanctions may create unemployment – a somewhat curious purpose for any government which claims to base its doctrines on the welfare of the workers! The deliberate creation of economic distress which will hit those who can least afford to be hit (in our case, mostly immigrant African workers from neighbouring states) is both cruel and futile. The Rhodesian Government has its own plans for the alleviation of any distress that may be caused by Mr. Wilson's "cripple Rhodesia" strategy.

Let us consider the wider implications of sanctions. The cost to the British taxpayer is already astronomical. Countless millions will have to be found to finance Mr. Wilson's designs.

It is a personal campaign, of course; Mr. Wilson knows that if – we say *when* – Rhodesia wins through, he may find himself in the political wilderness. To save himself, he is committing massive amounts of British taxpayers' money to his campaign. As a corollary he is actively working for the cause of world Communism.

Countries like Tanzania, Ghana and others which have had countless millions in aid from British and American taxpayers, are now virtually Communist satellites. These are the countries whose bidding Mr. Wilson is rushing to do – while Russia and China laugh on the sidelines.

217

Cash grants totalling nearly £19,000,000 have recently been made to Zambia; a further £12,000,000 will be required to operate an air-lift of dubious efficiency because of inadequate airports, Africa's torrential rains and distances that make the Berlin air-lift look like child's play!

By filching Rhodesia's capital reserves in London, Mr. Wilson has been obliged to assume responsibility for that country's public debts which in one way or another are guaranteed by the British Government. These total £108,000,000.

Even at this early stage in the exchanges it is costing British tax-payers more than £150,000,000 – and this takes no account of Rho-desia's trade with Britain which last year injected £35,000,000 into Britain's economy. The cost to Britain of having evicted Rhodesia from the sterling area is inestimable.

All this, the best part of £200,000,000 is only the start!

More sanctions may follow, but they will neither wreck Rhodesia's economy nor bring down its Government. They will certainly not deflect Rhodesia's people from the course they have chosen for the preservation of Christian values – and indeed, the British way of life – in this part of Africa.

All the dire predictions so sedulously promoted in the world's Press of violence and mayhem inside Rhodesia in the event of a UDI have been proved utterly untrue. They have just not material-ised. Rhodesia has not "gone up in flames". Indeed, African sup-port for Government action transcends the highest expectations.

Rhodesia's Armed Forces, Police and Civil Service have loyally continued to carry out their duties. Commerce and industry are facing up squarely and determinedly to the sanctions designed to smash Rhodesia's economy.

We know that they will have effect, that they will create austerity and even hardship. We are not dismayed by this knowledge; it is not much more than 20 years ago that most of us were facing such diffi-culties although not alone.

While Mr. Harold Wilson and his colleagues continue to try to destroy the peace of Rhodesia; while countries which have appro-priated millions of pounds in aid from British taxpayers have the impudence to talk about "expelling Britain from the Common-wealth" unless British soldiers are sent to fight British people; while massacres, public hangings and violence elsewhere in Africa ostensi-

218

bly pass unnoticed by the world at large, Rhodesia continues as an oasis of calm and stability.

Its affection for the British Crown and people remains undiminished. Rhodesia still flies the Union Jack. Its national anthem is: "God Save the Queen".

Sovereign, independent Rhodesia faces the future with calm confidence. It is the earnest desire of all its people that the breach which has opened between the mother country and Rhodesia will heal. Rhodesians believe it will – but not at the price of the destruction of all Rhodesia has built up.